TWICE UPON A SALISBURY STAGE

'Plaza Suite', January 1971: Michael Stroud and Nancie Herrod
(photographer Peter Brown)

TWICE UPON A SALISBURY STAGE

*The story of Salisbury Playhouse
and its two theatres*

1945 – 2000

ARTHUR MILLIE
Playhouse Archivist

THE HOBNOB PRESS

First published in the United Kingdom in 2022

by The Hobnob Press,
8 Lock Warehouse,
Severn Road, Gloucester GL1 2GA
www.hobnobpress.co.uk

British Library Cataloguing in Publication Data
A catalogue record for this book is available from the British Library

ISBN   978-1-914407-19-2

Typeset in Minion Pro 12/15 pt.
Typesetting and origination by John Chandler

Front Cover: Joanna McCullum in 'The Importance of Being Earnest' (photographer: Keith Pattison), and Michael Mears in 'The Recruiting Officer' (photographer: Keith Pattison).

Back Cover (clockwise from top left): Hattie Ladbury and Sam Marks in 'The Winslow Boy' (photographer Robert Workman); Daniel Crowder, David Hounslow, Sally Scott, Cate Hamer and Suzy Aitchison in 'Way Upstream' (photographer: Robert Workman); Jonathan Newth, Duncan Wisbey and Paul Slack in 'The Spire' (photographer: Keith Pattison); Richard Frost, Brian Honeyball, Freddie Lees, Penny Jones and Christine Absolom in 'Charley's Aunt' (photographer Peter Brown).

CONTENTS

Act Three: The New Playhouse

FOREWORD

Stephanie Cole

I am honoured to provide an introduction to your book – the story of the Salisbury theatre and the men and women who worked there from the great Reggie Salberg who was a wonderful man with Oliver Gordon as director and also a great farceur.

So many actors and backstage staff cut their teeth at Salisbury. They were years of hard work and laughter and learning. I am ever grateful for my time there.

This book is dedicated to all those people who have been involved with the Playhouse. Those who have worked there, those who have performed there and those who have watched there.

But it is particularly dedicated to four people, without whom there would not be the Playhouse that we know and love today:

Alan Corkill, Robert Hawkings, Alan Richardson and above all 'the Godfather of the Playhouse' - Reggie Salberg.

ACKNOWLEDGEMENTS

I could not have written this book without the help, encouragement and support of so many people.

I must start by giving a special thanks to my colleague, Peter Brown for all his help with the photographs and for his expert advice. Most of the photographs in the book are his.

Peter became interested in photography whilst still at school and eventually went on to study photography at Salisbury College. In 1965 he was appointed the Playhouse's official photographer, a position he held for 30 years. He also became well known for his photographs of Salisbury Cathedral.

As well as photographing many famous actors such as Timothy West, Stephanie Cole, Christopher Biggins and Ewan McGregor he has also photographed many other personalities including Jessie Matthews, Davy Jones, Dickie Henderson, John Craven, Charlton Heston, The Beatles and the Queen Mother!

I have been very fortunate in meeting and interviewing the following Playhouse people:

Betty Anderson	Peter Bryant	Patricia Brake
Christopher Biggins	George Baker	Stephanie Cole
Christopher Benjamin	Alan Corkill	Elspeth Cochrane
Jack Chissick	Jonathan Cecil	Margaret Denyer
Helen Dorward	Frank Ellis	Lionel Guyett
Nellie Horlock	Chris Harris	Stephen Howell
Michael Lunts	Roger Leach	Nicholas Lumley
Knight Mantell	Ian Mullins	Tim Meats
Joan Pullen (For Francis)	Jane Quy	Alex and Peter Romanes
Alan Richardson	Prunella Scales	Derek Smee
Veronica Stewart	David Simeon	Michael Stroud

Reggie Salberg	Sorrell De Tony	Josephine Tewson
Tim Treslove	Robert Whelan	Brenda Wade
Sonia Woolley	Timothy West	Barbara Wilson

and have received correspondence from:

Robert Aldous	Beryl Bainbridge	Derek Benfield
Frank Barrie	James Cairncross	Keith Drinkel
Christine Edmunds	Robin Ellis	Malcolm Farquar
Annie Hume	Richard Kane	Bob Miles
Kevin Moore	Donald Pelmear	David Ryall

as well as many letters from theatregoers.

Thanks to Leslie Black, Alan Clarke, Neil Leacy, Keith Pattison, John Walmsley and Robert Workman for providing photographs, and to all the other photographers for giving me their permission to use their photographs.

Thanks to John Chandler and Hobnob Press for making an idea become a reality. To John Hall for proof reading the book and to Alan Corkill for checking two important chapters. To Frogg Moody and Peter Hunter for many coffee chats and advice. To my fellow archivist Jane for her support. To other colleagues and theatregoers for their advice and support.

Above all though, my love and thanks to Angela, Graham and Russell (a better writer than I could ever be) and to Debbie and to Aunt Jean. They all gave me the encouragement and the support I needed and they told me that it could be possible.

My thanks to all the authors and publishers from whose books I have quoted. Please let me know if I have unintentionally missed anyone, and I will set matters straight in future printings.

'The Greasepaint War'	John Craven Hughes
'The Heart of the City'	John Bavin
'My Life Story'	Joe Louis
'Fighting For a Laugh'	Richard Fawkes
'Dear Me'	Peter Ustinov
'Diary'	Denis Constanduros
'Off Stage'	Charles Landstone
'Operation Greasepaint'	Eric Keown

'Just William'   Kenneth Williams
'Hello!'   Leslie Phillips
'The Way to Wexford'   George Baker
'Exit Through the Fireplace'   Kate Dunn
'Just Biggins'   Christopher Biggins
'A Passionate Life'   Stephanie Cole
'Mr. Home pronounced Hume'   William Douglas Home
'My Love Affair with a Theatre'   Derek Salberg
'Bringing Down the Curtain'   Olivia Turnbull

'I regards the theatre as the greatest of all art forms, the most immediate way in which a human being can share with another, the sense of what it is to be a human being.'

OSCAR WILDE

INTRODUCTION
PROGRAMME NOTES

In his introduction to *Endless Street*, John Chandler wrote:

> Let us make a few things clear from the outset and so avoid
> misunderstandings later on. This is not a comprehensive history of
> Salisbury, nor is it an authoritative history of Salisbury – Rather it
> is a personal exploration of some of the themes which I have found
> interesting and important whilst studying the history of Salisbury and
> which I am bold enough to hope will likewise interest my readers.

This explanation also sums up my attitude towards this story.

This is my interpretation of the story of Salisbury Playhouse.
Other people will have different ideas and will come from different
backgrounds but I can only write from the knowledge I have gained
from working as Playhouse Archivist, from the study I have made of
the Playhouse history and from my own point of view.

I apologise now to those readers who are going to be upset by
what I have said or what I haven't said; about the people I should have
mentioned and the stories and facts that I should have included. I
can only hope though, that to the majority of readers this story will
evoke happy memories of being involved in some way with Salisbury
Playhouse.

With my colleague Jane Ware, I have been Archivist at the
Playhouse since 1996 when we took over from Alan Richardson who
originally set up the Archives under David Horlock. It is thanks to
Alan that the Playhouse now has a very comprehensive collection of
memorabilia from all the productions that have taken place in both
the Playhouse buildings from 1943 to the present day.

Our aim though, has always been to bring the past alive to theatregoers. Programmes and photographs look neat and tidy in their boxes but they are not seen and the Playhouse story needs to be told and to be shared We have always believed in writing articles, putting on displays and giving talks about the Playhouse in order to bring the past alive.

Our belief has always been that "our past creates our future" and it is true to say that without the struggles and the trauma the hopes and the dreams of the past, there would not be a Playhouse standing today. They are the seeds from which our Playhouse has been able to grow and to flourish.

This story has been in my mind for a long time and over a considerable period I have interviewed many people and received many letters and information from people associated with the Playhouse. I am very grateful to all of them and also to those who considered it important to compile scrapbooks of the early years and of other important decades. The programme notes, the books, the minutes, the documents have all been part of a huge jigsaw that I was able at last, thanks to lockdown to unravel. If nothing else, those constant lockdowns have given me the time, space and the opportunity to make sense of all of this information.

I believe that the Playhouse has an amazing story. From a tiny Methodist chapel to a large flourishing theatre that is now the envy of many a city, these buildings have been full of amazing characters. The story of the two buildings is an essential part of the story but it is these characters that have built the Playhouse and it is these people that I hope will bring the story to life.

In his book John Bavin called the Playhouse 'The Heart of the City'. I believe it always has been and always will be and I sincerely hope that I have done justice to this very special place.

I hope also dear readers that this story will bring you much pleasure and that as you read the chapters and look at the photographs, you will want to exclaim out loud, 'I can remember that!'

Please take your seats as the curtain is about to rise and the story is about to begin.......

PROLOGUE
BUILDING A DRAMATIC NEW FUTURE

On a busy April morning in 2007, a Salisbury solicitor could be seen walking along the top corridor of the Playhouse complete with hard hat, fluorescent yellow jacket and a sledgehammer, accompanied by a selection of patrons, friends and members of the youth theatre Stage 65.

Then, in a scene reminiscent of the meeting of the construction workers in the middle of the Channel Tunnel, Andrew Wiltshire, a partner at Wilson's solicitors, officially broke through the wall separating the Playhouse and the new extension.

It had been announced by the Board of the theatre that in November 2004 they would be embarking on a project to build an onsite rehearsal room and community and education space at an originally estimated cost of £1.2 million of which the Playhouse would have to raise £700,000. VAT refunds would bring in £400,000 and the Arts Council had pledged £100,000.

Another project, another appeal for money, hadn't those with long, Playhouse memories heard all this before?

Yes, but those with long memories will remember how much the people of Salisbury love their local theatre and how, as in the past, if money is needed, then somehow it would be forthcoming.

The appeal was officially launched at a private function in January 2005. Over 150 guests, a selection of Salisbury's wealthy and influential, plus a sprinkling of those who had helped to develop the Playhouse's solid reputation, were invited to a presentation by Joanna Read, the present Artistic Director and Helen Birchenough, the Chairman of the Development Committee. They were also treated to a glimpse behind the scenes at a technical rehearsal of the current production: Noel Coward's "Relative Values."

That event alone raised £30,000 but as Joanna Read said: "We don't just want people's money - we want the link. It's a holistic thing - what can we give to people and they to our work?"

The Playhouse has always been an important part of the community and once again the Playhouse could show how much it cared for it by creating this new community and education space where many people of all ages could feel part of the Playhouse family.

More money began to appear. Some in the shape of large pledges from big foundations such as Garfield Weston and the Rayne Foundation and the theatre was delighted to receive £45,000 from the local firm of Wilson's the solicitors who were equally delighted to be part of the project. "What makes the Playhouse so interesting for us, is that alongside high quality and challenging programming, they have a strong commitment to the local community and to create opportunities for young people and from a business perspective, the Playhouse is able to offer us a genuine partnership."

However, the donations were varied: from local celebrities such as Sting who chipped in with £20,000 as well as the hard earned money raised by the Friends of the Theatre which echoed Reggie Salberg's wish, when money was being raised for the building of the new Playhouse, that he wanted it to be "built by a thousand people" and he was concerned that "the small men" would be able to play their part."

Because of the strong links with the community one can see the reason for the community and education space but why the need for a rehearsal room?

Imagine you have been cast in a Playhouse production, where are you expected to rehearse? You cannot use the stage because of the present production and there is certainly no room in the crowded backstage area. So you go for a fifteen minute walk up the Devizes road, in all weathers, to a rather run down, damp, cold building called Moose Hall which the Playhouse has been renting for some time. It is not very large and could not accommodate a full mark up of the main stage leaving you to rehearse in a space smaller than you would be performing on stage.

If you were in a large cast you would be struggling even more. Props and other items would have to be transported from the theatre and your eleven o'clock coffee break would not be in the comfort of the theatre restaurant. You would eventually appear at the Playhouse when it was time for technical and dress rehearsals. Only then would you feel part of the Playhouse.

At the official opening of the extension Joanna Read said: 'The rehearsal space is the engine room for the Playhouse. It is the heart of all our work. Not to have that heart at the centre of the building seems crazy. Our most important work has been happening off site in a damp, run down hall where no one could see it or even engage in it. The new rehearsal room brings all our creative work together and gives it transparency and an accessibility that is essential for good arts practise and good work. Actors love the Playhouse and we have been lucky to attract some of the best actors of today to work here. Now we can recognise their dedication with a modern, well-lit and ventilated rehearsal space. Acting is a very vulnerable task, emotionally, actors are required to be very open and direct; it's easier to do this if you are working in a relaxed and appropriate environment, one that is comfortable and supports what you do. Happy people always do their job better and we can see the benefit on stage.'

Fundraising and one-off unique events such as "An Evening with Matthew Kelly" and "The Battle of the Sexes" with Timothy West and Prunella Scales continued to flourish and in June 2006, with more than £1.25 million already in the kitty, a special ground breaking ceremony took place at the site of the extension.

Support had come from more than 1,000 donors and in 2005 the appeal was enhanced by £165,000 which was raised through a 12 week phone campaign championed by Prunella Scales and involving more than 3,000 of the Playhouse's most loyal supporters.

Appropriately, breaking the ground was Helen Birchenough and Lady Benson, president of the campaign accompanied by other dignitaries and invited guests and as a nice touch, two children from Pembroke Park School - the future watching the future begin.

Work then began in earnest. Peter Hunter laid aside his role as the Playhouse's Chief Electrician to act as Project Manager and the construction firm, Drew Smith Ltd, announced that the building should be completed within eleven months. They promised to work closely with the theatre staff and would make sure that there would not be any unscheduled "noises off" to spoil any performance!

The final icing on the cake was a donation of £190,000 from Tescos to enable the fund to reach its target.

With much proud ceremony the extension was officially opened on 5th July by that hard working telephonist but above all much loved actress, Prunella Scales. Prunella joined the Salisbury Company in 1952 and with her husband, Timothy West has always been an important member of the Playhouse family. In her speech she said: "I learned my job from Salisbury audiences."

Jack Wills, Chairman of the Board said: "We are regarded by our peers as a beacon of light in the diminishing and dimming world of regional producing theatre. We felt it vital to make that light burn even brighter."

The new extension was crowded with people from all decades of the Playhouse story. All must have been very proud to have been part of that story and they must have looked at the new extension with great pleasure in the knowledge that the Playhouse is very much alive and vibrant and that there will be many more exciting chapters to the Playhouse story. The light will indeed continue to shine.

I am sure that Prunella's mind must have skipped back to those early days in the original theatre in Fisherton Street when she played the oldest shoe child in "Babes in the Wood". I am equally sure that there were many ghosts of the past present. None more so than Reggie Salberg who must have smiled with a very broad smile of satisfaction that all those early struggles in the old building were worthwhile.

Perhaps there were also some Methodists looking down and thinking about that old building in Chapel Place because that is where the Playhouse story really starts.

ACT ONE

The Early Years

1

IN THE BEGINNING THERE WAS A CHAPEL

O N THE MORNING of Saturday 29th May 1869, Mr. S.P. Yates of the Wilton Carpet Factory woke up early, panicking slightly as he had agreed to carry out a very important task that his colleague Mr. Charles Jupe of Mere was unable to fulfil due to a 'domestic affliction.'

The Primitive Methodists had struggled in the city and had held meetings in various places around the city including Greencroft and a room above a stable occupied by mules in the old George Yard. At present they occupied a small building at the back of Fisherton Street. Now however they were to make a new start and half the sum to construct a new building in Fisherton Street, £1,700 had been raised and the laying of the foundation stone, by Mr. Yates was to take place that afternoon.

The ceremony duly took place with great pomp and piety much to the satisfaction of the gathered clergy and Mr. Witt of Fisherton, who was the contractor and designer of the building.

In a cavity of the stone was placed a copy of the *Salisbury and Winchester*

Methodist Chapel, c.1869
(Photographer Unknown)

Journal together with a paper containing the names of the mayor of the city and the contractor.

Prayers were offered after the hymns. Mr. Yates said: 'The object sought by the erection of the chapel was the worship of the "Divine Being" and the good resulting in the construction would only be known in eternity.'

Whilst the Reverend Pearson: 'had no doubts that the spot on which they stood would in future be the scene of many conversions and the erection of this humble chapel would be the means of increasing the number redeemed in Heaven.' He heartily wished the Society might bring the Chapel to a speedy and successful completion.

The Reverend Short added that he was pleased that: 'they were all agreed in their endeavours to free immortal souls from the thraldom of Satan and he had no doubt the labours of their minister would be blest of God.'

At the conclusion of the ceremony, a large amount of money was placed on the foundation stone including £10 from the afflicted Mr. Jupe.

Mr. Witt set about his task diligently and the chapel was ready to open with a special service on Thursday 18th November when Mr. Varley from London was invited to speak.

The chapel was built in the Italian style. Inside was a fine moulded panel gallery with stained elevated seats. In all it would be able to seat 400 worshippers.

At the back was a schoolroom and on the side of this were a classroom and a vestry, 'with a place for boiling water for tea meetings.' The two adjoining houses, one of which was for the use of the minister, were built to match the chapel.

Services continued there for 40 years, but over this time, the building suffered extensive damage, mainly caused by flooding, and it was costly to keep it in good repair. In particular, the worshippers complained that the side entrance was practically impassable owing to there being no footpath, nor the possibility of finding funds to secure one. So once again the trustees had to think again and move to a more stable environment, this time in Dews Road.

The last service there was held on Sunday 25th October 1915 and the trustees agreed to dispose of the premises to Mr. Albany

Albany Ward (Image from John Chandler)

Ward, a pioneer of the cinema in Salisbury and also the Managing Director of the New Theatre in Castle Street.

A prominent figure in the local entertainment field he was often involved in rumours and it was said that in 1915 he fell very ill and decided to send the Bishop a cheque for £1,000 to redeem himself. However, after a few days he soon felt better and promptly cancelled the cheque!

The Methodists agreed to sell the premises to him on the understanding that he was going to convert the building into a garage. Considering his background, this was very naïve of them because it wasn't very long before he spent the princely sum of £7,000 converting it into 'The Picture House'.

The trustees were very angry that their House of God was going to become a place of entertainment but having neglected to obtain written assurances from Mr. Ward they were unable to do anything.

The chapel was duly converted into a cinema which included several alterations to the front of the building and it is possible that this is when the foundation stone so diligently laid by Mr. Yates just to the left of the doorway was destroyed.

Mr. Ward commented that 'the pleasing feature of the work is that it is practically the outcome of local talent.' There was a local architect, Michael Harding as well as local artists and builders. Salisbury's prominent department store, 'Style and Gerrish' did the upholstery.

The Methodist Chapel had gone but that muddy, wet side entrance lives on in the name of 'Chapel Place.'

No more worship of the 'Divine Being', now more a worship of all things Hollywood.

Fisherton Street showing Picture House, 1928 (Photographer Unknown)

On Monday 11th December 1916 'The Picture House' opened with a showing of 'The King with his armies on the Somme' and the cartoon: 'The Tanks'. In the midst of boom time for motion pictures, Salisbury had acquired another cinema.

At the Picture House tea was served at all matinee performances and the receipts from that first day's performance were given to the Mayor's Fund for the Salisbury Infirmary.

Donald Head remembers:

On Saturday mornings there was a special children's programme, almost invariably cowboy films. I remember Tom Mix particularly well. It was 6d to go in but that was quite a bit of money in those days and one had to prevail on one's parents for 'money for the pictures' but it was not always forthcoming. In view of the 'cowboys and Indians' flavour of the programme, the audience contained few girls. There was a lot of cheering and stamping of feet. The carpets could never have been vacuumed because the stamping raised clouds of dust which swirled in the beams from the projector and got up one's nose. Whenever I smell dust my memory goes back to The Picture House!

Films continued there throughout the 1920s. Many of them were silent and were accompanied by a piano to lend dramatic effect to such offerings as 'The Perils of Pauline' and 'The Adventures of Pearl White.' But then on December 23rd 1929, the local *Journal* advertised; 'The Perfect Alibi' starring Chester Morris and Mae Bush. However, this was no ordinary film show as the advertisement included the tag lines: 'The 100% Dialogue Film Sensation with Singing and Dancing! See! Hear! and Marvel!' Yes, the talkies had arrived in Salisbury!

The projection box was at the back of the stalls and the projectionist was often assisted, during his school holidays by a young Francis Pullen who was later to become a very active member of the board of directors at the Playhouse as well as being the Chairman of the Theatregoers' Club.

The Thirties were the heyday of early cinema in Salisbury with the 'Gaumont Palace' in New Canal and then the 'Regal' in Endless Street competing for the movie lovers' ninepences and two shillings.

Gradually though, the facilities at 'The Picture House' were falling behind the other grander cinemas and on 18th September 1937 the old 'Picture House' closed its doors. Many local people regretted the passing of the old cinema, as it was a favourite on account of its small size and its cheerful, homely atmosphere.

So the old 'Picture House' had to close but long live 'The New Picture House' which opened next a few yards away!

This was billed as Salisbury's latest luxury cinema and it duly opened on Monday 27th September with the epic film: 'King Solomon's Mines' starring Paul Robeson. The opening ceremony was carried out by the Countess of Radnor with the band of the 12th Royal Lancers in attendance. Surely though the greater attraction was the film star Nova Pilbeam who appeared accompanied by six young starlets!

A link for the cinemagoers who still pined for their old 'Picture House' was that the popular manager, Mr. G.A. Howes was quickly appointed manager of 'The New Picture House'!

The old 'Picture House' building was put up for sale but it seemed that nobody was interested in purchasing it and it stood empty for some time. So what saved it? Surprisingly the onset of war in Europe. The military were looking for buildings that could be requisitioned and it became a drill hall for No. 1. Company 43rd (Wessex) Division

Signals Rgt and also an army recruitment centre. Stan Crouch of Redlynch remembers it well: 'I remember clearly sleeping there for a few nights. Some of us had to sleep in the balcony which was cleared of seats. The balcony was sloping so although we started the night in neat rows, by morning we were always in a heap down at the front!'

However, after a while the unit moved to Mere and once again the building stood empty, although for a brief while during 'Wings For Victory' week it became a cinema again and film shows were given by a mobile unit of the National Savings Committee.

The old building desperately needed rescuing and in 1943 a saviour appeared in the shape of Basil Dean who had created ENSA (Entertainment and National Service Association) with Leslie Henson. He was on the look out for premises which could be transformed into a Garrison Theatre similar to other established Garrison Theatres in the military area of Salisbury Plain.

So from a chapel to a cinema and now the building was to become a theatre.

2
EVERY NIGHT SOMETHING AWFUL

S OMEONE ONCE SAID that war was five percent fun, five percent fear and ninety percent boredom. It's during this time of inactivity that the need is greatest for some sort of diversion. ENSA was created in 1938 to fill this need. It was the largest theatrical management ever seen, producing everything from shows, concert parties, new plays and revivals of old favourites. This huge logistical operation was co-ordinated from London's Drury Lane sending artists to all parts of the world including in 1943, to Salisbury.

In his book *The Greasepaint War* John Craven Hughes recalled: 'In company with the butcher, the baker and the candlestick maker, actors and singers and musicians went forth to the Second World War. Some wore His Majesty's uniform; others marched under the banner of ENSA. The entertainment army grew from the smallest beginnings until all non-combatant members of the theatrical, variety and musical professions became involved in its affairs in one way or another.'

There were many entertainers to whom ENSA was a lifeline as it provided them with a fixed salary of £10 per week for artistes and £4 per week for members of the chorus. Some were therefore earning more from ENSA than they ever did as performers pre war.

All had to wear the ENSA uniform as Basil Dean was worried that if they were captured they could be construed as being spies. The only artist never to wear a uniform was Tommy Trinder who, when it was put to him said: 'If I ever get captured then I deserve to be shot!'

The role call of artists who appeared in ENSA productions is to read the story of entertainment of that era. It included such luminaries as Arthur Askey, Frankie Howerd, Jessie Matthews, Ivor Novello,

Laurence Olivier, Margaret Rutherford and Richard Tauber; who in many cases were often asked to appear in some of the remotest, most uncomfortable and sometimes downright dangerous battle areas.

On D Day, George Formby was in the first wave ashore and gave an impromptu performance within three hours of landing to the men of the US 6th Airborne Division.

ENSA had a very wide area to cover both at home and overseas and sometimes the entertainment was spread rather too thinly so the popular translation of the acronym was 'Every Night Something Awful' or 'Even the NAAFI stands aghast'!

The troops though were never too critical , and men who were bored or stressed were prepared to watch anything and they went to see plays, ballet and concerts, perhaps for the first time and discovered that they actually enjoyed what they were watching.

For the first time, the military authorities accepted the place of entertainment in service life and the colonel who thought the only relief his men needed was a game of football and a cold shower was soon in the minority.

It is reported that one army doctor commented: 'The only thing that can relax a body as taut as these bodies is a tub of hot water or a good belly laugh and we can't get the hot water!'

The derelict building in Fisherton Street did not stay empty for too long as the Royal Engineers moved in and in four weeks they thoroughly cleaned it and redecorated the interior which included new pastel-shaded curtains for the stage. They also increased the stage space by removing two walls. A new lighting system was installed and the old projection box beneath the balcony became the theatre's 'Box'. Behind the stage four dressing rooms were constructed to accommodate 20 people. The rooms behind the balcony, from which refreshments were served when the building was a cinema, became the offices. Finally they provided seating accommodation for about 500 theatregoers. It was then ready to open as the Garrison Theatre, Southern Command.

The theatre profession also took a hand in preparing for the opening night and in his book *The Heart of the City* John Bavin recalls:

The actress Constance Cummings was invited to see it being set up. Upon arrival she was taken into a dark auditorium but at one end there was a pool of light. It came from a bare electric light bulb held in the hand of the producer Murray McDonald. In the other hand he held a paintbrush with which he was painting some white lines on the auditorium walls. Beside him stood another figure, paintbrush in hand, 'topping' his white lines with strokes of gold. It was Edith Evans.

The opening of the Garrison Theatre (Imperial War Museum, given by Neil Leacy)
(left) Opening speech by Lt. Gen. Sir H.C. Loyd.
(right) Lt. Gen. Sir H.C. Loyd with Brig. W.A.M. Stawell talking to John Clements
and Constance Cummings

The Gala Opening show on 11th October 1943 was '*You Asked For It*' starring Constance Cummings, John Clements and Fay Compton. This was followed by the first play: Emlyn Williams' '*Night Must Fall*'. He directed the play and also took one of the leading parts. This was closely followed by '*Blithe Spirit*' and Noel Coward himself came down from London to produce it.

The pattern of work was that shows were rehearsed for a week, during which time the theatre was closed, followed generally by a run from Tuesday to Saturday with special shows such as recitals and concerts to be held on Sundays.

Always aware of the close proximity of the Army stationed on Salisbury Plain there would be such notices as 'In the event of an alert, a notice will be displayed but the performance will continue.' and 'Imminent danger will be advised from the stage.'

Southern Command Entertainments
—————— Branch ——————

presents

The

Garrison Theatre

Salisbury

ON

SUNDAY, 10th OCTOBER, 1943

1st PERFORMANCE TO BE OPENED BY
AIR COMMODORE I. J. SITCH

2nd PERFORMANCE TO BE OPENED BY
LIEUT.-GEN. SIR CHARLES LOYD,
K.C.B., D.S.O., M.C.

Garrison Theatre

Monday, 18th October

at 5 o'clock & 8 o'clock

Personal Appearance of

EMLYN WILLIAMS

IN HIS FAMOUS PLAY

"Night Must Fall"

with

ELLIOT MASON   GLADYS HENSON

BETTY ANN DAVIES KYNASTON REEVES

EDWARD PETLEY   DOROTHY BAIRD

DOROTHY TURNER & FRANK FREEMAN

(left) You Asked For It programme cover (First show), October 1943
(right) Night Must Fall programme cover (First play), October 1943

Admission was usually restricted 'For Services Only' but occasionally servicemen were allowed to invite civilian friends; and even more occasionally the shows were open 'For the Civilians of Salisbury.'

Admission was kept low, 6d for officers and 3d for other ranks. However, there was often some confusion as to who exactly was a 'serviceman'. The Home Guard was allowed in, but only in uniform and for a while, Merchant Seamen were not. One wrote to the local paper: 'Surely those heroes who sail through submarine and mine infested waters with the Royal Navy should be included.' – Eventually they were.

Betty Anderson, who became a leading light in the Theatregoers' Club, belonged to the Timber Corps, a branch of the Land Army and was stationed at Zeals. She remembers hitchhiking to Salisbury because she wanted to see the Ballet Rambert. She marched up to the box office and belligerently said: 'Can I come in and see this in my own right or do I have to pick up a soldier to take me in?' Fortunately the Commanding Officer was in the Box Office who replied: 'Come in by all means, never let it be said that I put a young lady on the streets!'

Another Commanding Officer however, was not so pleasant. In March 1944 Joe Louis, the reigning world heavyweight boxing champion was on a tour of army bases in England where he staged 96 boxing exhibitions in front of over two million soldiers. Unfortunately in his autobiography 'My Life Story' he disclosed: 'In Salisbury, England, in March 1944, I tried to buy a ticket at a civilian theatre. The woman said she was sorry, but the American commanding officer in that area said she was not to let negroes in, only white soldiers. The story got to Lieutenant General John C.H. Lee, who was General Eisenhower's deputy. There was an investigation, and the commanding officer who made the rule was promptly shipped back to the States.' If the people in the theatre had known what a distinguished man they had with them that day, he would surely have been invited on to the stage and certainly not refused entrance.

ATS girls billeted at the Theological College in the Close were frequent visitors to the Garrison Theatre.

Joan Chambers: 'Saw Glynis Johns getting off a bus at the railway station' and she also managed to get Laurence Olivier and Vivien Leigh's autographs in her army pay book.

Vera Smith recalls:

> Life after work was fun. Cultural life flourished – the Garrison Theatre staged plays often with a West End Cast. I will always remember Edith Evans in '*Night Must Fall*' and her spine chilling cry of 'Murderers!

And Margaret Westlake remembers appearing in '*Khaki, Navy and Blue*' with George Formby at the Gaumont Palace and singing: 'Happy and gay on two bob a day!'

Be careful where you sit though, as the serviceman 'Lofty' recalls:

> Arriving early for a performance at the Garrison Theatre one dark, winter evening Doris and I, wrapped up in our overcoats were

sitting on one of the seats provided on the concrete promenade that controlled the flow of one of the rivers that pass through the town. Doris, whose sense of direction was not her strongest point, suddenly realised that time was getting on and suggested that we went in. Before I could stop her she got up from the seat and walked straight out and over the edge of the promenade into the river that flowed below! No fears – this brave soldier made a gallant rescue!

As well as ENSA there were performances by local associations such as the Salisbury Symphony Orchestra and other service organisations such as The Central Pool of Artists and Stars in Battledress. In 'Fighting For a Laugh' Richard Fawkes notes: 'Although Stars in Battledress productions had casts and directors who could have commanded large fees in the West End, they like their variety cousins, went where they were needed and that meant rarely playing in a theatre. The cause of much of the resentment building up between Stars in Battledress and ENSA came from the fact that ENSA productions always played better locations and the performers were paid well whilst Army units received only Army pay.

In just two and a half years many famous names appeared at the Salisbury Garrison Theatre. Some already famous and some at the beginning of their illustrious careers.

As well as those already mentioned, amongst the thin, small wartime programmes you could read such names as Flora Robson, Googie Withers, Peggy Cummmins, Irene Handl, Ursula Jeans, Bryan Forbes, Raymond Huntley, Clifford Evans, Joan Sims, Kenneth Connor, Roger Livesey, James Mason, Peter Ustinov and Eric Portman. It reads like a role call from those old black and white movie days at the Odeon cinemas!

Kenneth Connor remembers acting in *'Flare Path'*:

It went down particularly well with the RAF boys. They liked the writing, which was full of RAF slang of the time, they liked the story and the love triangle, and they liked the cocky little gunner I played, always coming in at the wrong moment. It often got very emotional.

I got very stewed in a Mess one night and got talking to a real air gunner, somebody who had just come back from hell in time to see the show. When he told me he thought I was the best air gunner he'd ever come across, I couldn't stand it. I went to the air commodore who was there at the time and demanded an immediate transfer from the Army to go off on a flight with these lads.

Fortunately his fellow actors managed to stop him by hanging him up behind a door until the unit was ready to drive off!

Sometimes actors had to juggle many jobs and when James Mason appeared in 'Gaslight' he was also very busy rehearsing for his next film. In 'Heart of the City', Thomas Noble, a local taxi driver recalls how he would pick up James Mason on his own, drive him to the theatre and pick him up an hour later. 'The evening run puzzled Mr. Noble because there was no performance during rehearsal week and he was delivering his client to, and collecting him from, a closed theatre, which would be in darkness. One evening however, James Mason was not on the steps in his usual position, waiting to be picked up at the end of the hour. Mr. Noble waited about ten minutes and then he decided to go to the stage door. He found it was unlocked and as he walked in, he heard some horrible screeching coming from the direction of the stage. He saw James Mason with a violin and bow, and although he was drawing the bow across the violin strings there was no melody coming forth, just a noise. James Mason turned and saw him and exclaimed: ' I can't play this you know.' Mr. Noble replied: 'No I didn't think so!' James Mason then explained that he would shortly be in a film called 'The Magic Bow' in which he was to act the part of a first class violin player, and he had to get the fingering right on the instrument but that Yehudi Menuhin would actually be supplying the sound.' Sadly after all his efforts, he did not get to play the part after all. It went to that other matinee idol, Stewart Granger!

Many shows had the added attraction of live music being played before the show started and during the intervals. How wonderful for the soldiers. No scratchy gramophone sounds to have to put up with but to be able to relax to live music. Would audiences today be quiet enough to appreciate the same state of affairs?

This music was often played by 'The Southern Command Sextet' under the astute leadership of M. Stietzel.

This is an example of one such programme:

Overture: The Desert Song – selection by Romberg.
Vienna Blood Waltz by Strauss.
Ballet Suite by Popy.
During the first interval: La Boheme – selection by Puccini.
During the Second Interval: Thais by Massenet.
and The Sleeping Beauty Waltz by Tchaikowsky.

The group was a motley collection of members drawn from the Berlin Philharmonic Orchestra and the Vienna Philharmonic Orchestra. To while away the time during the performances they would often play chess – a hotly contested championship between the two countries.

In his book *Dear Me* Peter Ustinov wrote about his time directing Edith Evans as Mrs. Malaprop in '*The Rivals*':

One drawback of these Garrison Theatres was that there was no method of concealing the orchestra. Its members sat on the same level as the audience. It was merely the actors who were elevated. I noticed on the first night that the orchestra made use of a miniature chessboard in order to while away the time during the histrionics and often musicians would creep forward like troops in a dugout to make some snide move. ....I hoped and prayed that Edith Evans would not notice what was going on, but on the fourth night, during a brilliant tirade, she stopped dead. One eye alighted on the tiny chessboard just as an Austrian violin player had spotted a crack in the enemy defence and was creeping forward to deliver the coup de grace.

She faltered, fumbled and then with superb dramatic instinct she looked at me and said in a tone of pained surprise 'What did you say?'

She complained to the orchestra and told them not to play chess and to concentrate on the play. That night Peter Ustinov could not understand why there seemed to be no laughs coming from the audience.

When I had a free moment I rushed to the back of the auditorium in order to unravel the mystery. I did not have far to seek. The musicians

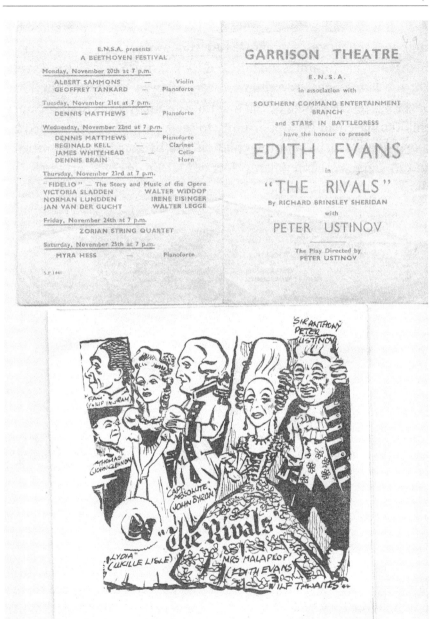

E.N.S.A. presents
A BEETHOVEN FESTIVAL

Monday, November 20th at 7 p.m.
ALBERT SAMMONS — Violin
GEOFFREY TANKARD — Pianoforte

Tuesday, November 21st at 7 p.m.
DENNIS MATTHEWS — Pianoforte

Wednesday, November 22nd at 7 p.m.
DENNIS MATTHEWS — Pianoforte
REGINALD KELL — Clarinet
JAMES WHITEHEAD — Cello
DENNIS BRAIN — Horn

Thursday, November 23rd at 7 p.m.
" FIDELIO " — The Story and Music of the Opera
VICTORIA SLADDEN   WALTER WIDDOP
NORMAN LUMDDEN   IRENE EISINGER
JAN VAN DER GUCHT   WALTER LEGGE

Friday, November 24th at 7 p.m.
ZORIAN STRING QUARTET

Saturday, November 25th at 7 p.m.
MYRA HESS — Pianoforte

GARRISON THEATRE

E.N.S.A.

in association with

SOUTHERN COMMAND ENTERTAINMENT
BRANCH

and STARS IN BATTLEDRESS

have the honour to present

EDITH EVANS

in

" THE RIVALS "

By RICHARD BRINSLEY SHERIDAN

with

PETER USTINOV

The Play Directed by
PETER USTINOV

The Rivals, Garrison Theatre programme, with Wilf Thwaite cartoon, November 1944

had now reversed their positions and sat facing the audience, their heads just visible above the rails of the orchestra. Lit from beneath, like mournful skittles waiting for the usual knocks of fate, they had dampened the spirits of all of the onlookers!

It wasn't all serious drama though. Ralph Reader presented his famous Gang Shows; there were variety shows such as '*Springtime for Henry*' and pantomimes including '*Dick Whittington*' and '*Cinderella*'. For the latter, Salisbury children were allowed to attend. The local paper wrote: 'This must be the first time for many years that Salisbury children have had the opportunity to see a pantomime presented by professional artistes and the children will be grateful to the artistes and to Capt. W. Honeyman (Murray McDonald) who arranges the shows at the theatre.

Dick Whittington cartoon by Wilf Thwaites, December 1944

There were also several shows which were specifically put on to raise money such as 'For the Salisbury Effort' and 'Where there's a Wilts there's a way' to try to raise £400,000 for Salute the Soldier Week.

Gradually the war dragged to a close and the last performance at the Garrison Theatre was '*School for Husbands*' and on V.E Day 8th May 1945 the Garrison Theatre 'welcomed any citizens of Salisbury.'

ENSA had done an excellent job. It knew however, that it was time to move on and so they relinquished the lease on the building. The little building in Fisherton Street was to become empty once again with only the ghostly memories of the songs and laughter of hundreds of servicemen to keep it company. Fortunately though it didn't stay empty for too long, Salisbury had had a taste of live theatre and now it had an appetite for much more in the future.

3
'A TOWN WITHOUT A THEATRE IS A TOWN WITHOUT A HEART'
Beatrix Lehmann

DRAMATIC ACTIVITIES AT STONEHENGE and visits from strolling players during Elizabethan times. You could go back many centuries to discover exactly when Salisbury's literary story begins. However, one of the earliest known performances of a play was of 'The Tragedy of Venice Preserved' in January 1765 at the Sun Inn by Fisherton Bridge. As drama became more popular and audiences increased, plays were performed in larger premises such as 'The Vine' in the Cheese Market and then on 14th November 1777 the purpose built 'New Theatre' opened in New Street with a production of Richard Brinsley Sheridan's 'The Rivals'.

A critic of the time wrote: 'There was a genteel and crowded audience who expressed the highest satisfaction at the elegance of the building and the excellence of the performing, who in justice to the company....are by far superior to any we have had before.'

This theatre lasted for almost a hundred years and played a prominent part in the life of Salisbury, its company often touring to such places as Winchester, Southampton and Devizes. In this new building, boxes cost 3 shillings, the pit 2 shillings and the gallery 1 shilling. The programme consisted always of a play followed by a farce, and after the play it was possible to get in for half price. The building was eventually demolished to make way for the School of Science and Art.

The Assembly Rooms at the corner of the High Street and New Canal were also used for entertainment and the Hamilton Hall in the School of Art was also used by visiting theatrical companies.

In September 1889 the County Hall on the corner of Endless Street and Chipper Lane was built. Its stage was considerably larger than any seen before in Salisbury and was capable of accommodating 175 performers with an audience capacity of over a thousand.

There was great excitement in 1935 when a new theatre in Fisherton Street was announced. In December, the *Southern Daily Echo* wrote:-

Salisbury's new £40,000 variety theatre – the Phoenix will open next August. It is to be built on the site now owned by the Magnet Domestic Stores and will have a seating capacity of 1,000. There will be no gallery but every seat in the stalls, circle and pit will be bookable. The Phoenix will be wired for talkies. Spacious vestibules, lounges and cafes will be a feature of the building, which will have a

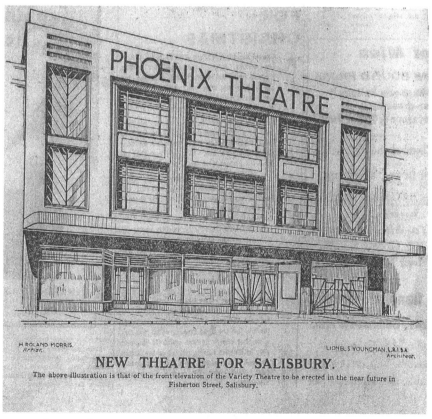

Phoenix Theatre, December 1935 (From publicity in Salisbury Journal)

large car park at the rear with an entrance from Fisherton Street and an exit into a road at the rear. No colour scheme has yet been decided but the interior like the frontage will be ultra modern.

The architect was Lionel Youngman and in the sketches by H. Roland Morris the design was beautifully art deco.

To pay for this new venture, the plan was to form a company created by public subscription. Each share to cost £1. The local paper wrote: 'Seventy five thousand copies of the prospectus each accompanied by an application form, a plan of the theatre and the site and a return envelope have been posted to persons in Salisbury and the south west of England.' Sadly though, whether it was the economic climate of the time, the preference for the cinema or just general apathy, this particular phoenix never had the chance to rise not even for the first time and the plan was eventually dropped.

However, there has always been the nucleus of theatre lovers that have wanted their own theatre in Salisbury. Local theatregoers had experienced live theatre during the war, albeit with certain restrictions, but now in 1945 the Garrison Theatre had been de-requisitioned and ENSA had moved on, but there was an empty building.

Henry Shute, the manager of the Ballet Rambert suggested to the Deputy Drama Director of the Arts Council, Charles Landstone, that the Arts Council should take over the building as the home of a resident Arts Council company which could continue to do in peacetime what had been done successfully during the war – but this time to bring good drama to civilians.

Charles Landstone supported the suggestion as did Cyril Wood the Arts Council's Regional Officer. The Arts Council had already been formulating a plan to attempt to bring live theatre to areas of the country that did not have it and the Arts Council agreed that Salisbury could be the starting point for such a scheme.

The plan was for Salisbury to have a resident repertory company to produce a new play each month, which would be performed for one week in the theatre and then taken on tour to such towns as Southampton, Basingstoke, Newbury, Winchester, Devizes, Weymouth and Yeovil. At the same time rehearsals will be taking place for the next month's production. The theatre would be called the Arts Theatre. The recently formed Salisbury and District Society of Arts, which had its headquarters in the Moonraker's Cafe in the High Street was to have its headquarters there and during the weeks of the tour it was to have the use of the theatre for recitals, concerts and amateur plays.

It was stressed that this was very much an experiment. The Arts Council was to hold the purse strings. If it was a success then the scheme could be set up in other areas as it was eventually in Coventry, Halifax and Swansea. The last two collapsed very quickly but the Coventry experiment continued to function under the Arts Council until the Belgrade Theatre was built in 1955 when it then had its own boards of directors.

The spotlight was shining brightly on Salisbury. Cyril Wood said: 'The eyes of London are very much on this experiment in Salisbury and I hope you will not let me down. I have mentioned to London that I believe Salisbury will justify the faith being placed in it.'

ENSA had left a building with a stage and an orchestra pit, There was a switchboard which provided basic lighting and there was a working telephone in the old cinema's box office. The Arts Council purchased new stage fittings and the wooden seats were replaced by plush tip-up seats which had been acquired from the Kidderminster Opera House. There was now seating for just over 400. Backstage there was a workshop and transport for the scenery when touring.

The building was ready to take on its new role. The local theatregoers were delighted to have their own theatre and not have to be restricted by military regulations. A rather pointed notice was seen in the city that read: 'It is unofficially stated that members of H.M. Forces will be admitted to the new Arts Theatre if accompanied by a civilian.'

Henry Shute was asked to take direct responsibility for the theatre's management and Barbara Burnham who lived in Coombe Bissett, was invited to become the company's resident producer.

On being appointed she declared: 'We do not want Salisbury Arts Theatre merely to imitate London or other provincial theatres. We hope to strike out on our own line, do new plays and plays that are off the beaten track.'

This aim proved to be difficult as tried and trusted plays soon became the norm as it was important to keep the money rolling in to keep the Arts Council happy.

The local author Denis Constanduros wrote in his diary:

The chief event for me in the last few weeks has been the opening of the Salisbury Arts theatre under the direction of Barbara Burnham. I spent two happy days beforehand trying to help paint scenery and generally joining in the preparations. There is something infectious about the enthusiasm and gaiety of stage people and I felt completely caught up in it.

THE ARTS THEATRE

FISHERTON STREET   SALISBURY   Tel. 2104

Lessees: THE ARTS COUNCIL OF GREAT BRITAIN.

Resident Manager · HENRY SHUTE.

THE ARTS COUNCIL OF GREAT BRITAIN

present

The Salisbury Arts Theatre Company

in

THE DAY OF GLORY

By · H. E. BATES

First Performance on any Stage   :   Directed by BARBARA BURNHAM

Guest Artist · · **RONALD MILLAR**

Wednesday, October 31st : at 6.30

FOR TEN DAYS

MATINEES : Wednesday, Nov. 7th and Saturday 10th   :   at 2.30

Next Production : **WHEN WE ARE MARRIED** By J. B. Priestley

November 26th : For One Week.

ALL SEATS BOOKABLE :   5/-   3/6   2/6   1/6

BOX OFFICE : Daily from 10 to 7.30.

N.B. – The Theatre is open to all at every performance.

The Day of Glory, October 1945 (advert in Salisbury Journal)

So after a reception held at the White Hart Hotel where local dignitaries and distinguished guests from London were invited, the Arts Theatre officially opened on 31st October 1945 with H.E. Bates new play: *'Day of Glory.'*

Frank Gillard provided a commentary for the BBC. on the proceedings. An opening ceremony was performed by the actress Beatrix Lehmann who said in her speech:

A town without a theatre is a town without a heart. It is a young adventure. It will be watched with the greatest care and sympathy. We have a building. We have a company. We have an audience. Care for each other, love each other, watch each other critically and helpfully and may you work together for a long time and prosper in your work for many years to come.

What is not often quoted is the speech made by Sir Kenneth Clark, the Chairman of the Arts Council who said:

I hope that this theatre goes on and will have lots of vivid and exciting new works....I hope great controversial works will be put on here, that you will attack each other, divide into rival camps, throw oranges about and wave your umbrellas about and fight in the auditorium!

One wonders what the distinguished guests thought about those instructions!

Like any new venture the first few months were a success. However, as members of the Society of Arts were given preference for tickets this caused some confusion and ill feeling. Many people were joining the Society purely to obtain priority tickets and membership shot up to over 2,000. One irate theatregoer wrote to the local paper:

Priority booking at the Arts must go. It is wrong in principle and disastrous in practice. If the members of the Salisbury and District Society of Arts (of whom I am one) will not pay their half crowns a year unless they get this unfair and impracticable advantage, let them cease to do so. But surely it is unlikely that many of them would, being as they are members of a Society of 'persons interested in the Arts' and pledged to the 'promotion of the Arts.' Does this though include the right to get into a theatre before your neighbour?

As this priority scheme was written in the Society's constitution the problem had to wait until the next AGM when under mounting criticism it was dropped.

The cost of membership to the Society was also increased from 2/6 per annum to 3/6 and membership stabilised. Another teething problem though, was the scheme of having to book tickets by post rather than directly at the Box Office. Any tickets that were then left were put on general sale, which one had to queue for at the Box Office. This was also eventually addressed.

That first season from October 31st to July 31st gave the Salisbury theatregoers a rich variety of entertainments.

There were five plays presented by the resident company including two which were the first productions on any stage: H.E. Bates' 'Day of Glory' and 'Garden Fete' by the local author, Denis Constanduros.

Most were produced by Barbara Burnham and the actors included: Jenny Lovelace, Angela Wyndham Lewis, Tristram Butt, Catherine Lacey, Duncan Lamont, Maxine Audley and Ronald Millar.

Seven plays were produced by visiting companies in association with the Arts Council and The Central Pool of Artists, which was still in existence despite the war ending, produced four plays including Kenneth Horne's 'Yes and No.'

There were a whole variety of amateur productions put on by such groups as The Centre Players from the Salisbury Recreational Centre; and The Boscombe Down Dramatic Club.

There were music recitals and ballet performances both professional and amateur as well as lecture recitals. Children also trod the boards as part of local groups that included The Salisbury School of Dancing and the Gwen Pinniger School of Dancing.

No one could accuse the Arts Theatre of not giving the public what they wanted.

At the end of the first season Henry Shute wrote in the end of year review:

We offer our sincere thanks to all of you who have so consistently given us your support and encouragement and we trust that we may be assured of the same regularity of patronage and warmth of appreciation in the coming season. As long as you demand first class plays and concerts put on at your theatre by the Arts Council of Great Britain we will guarantee to satisfy your demands. It all depends on YOU and YOUR FRIENDS.

The other part of this dramatic experiment was the touring policy. During this first season, as well as performing in Salisbury the company visited 18 towns. Apart from the larger towns such as Southampton and Winchester, they also visited smaller venues at such places as Blandford, Castle Cary, Frome, Hartley Wintney, Lymington, Melksham and Yeovil. Many of the venues were not ideal and in some areas it was difficult to build up an audience.

The company touring Two Gentlemen of Verona, March 1946. Tristram Butt, George Cormack, Duncan Lamont, Robert Cawdron, Maxine Audley. The photograph was taken along the A36. The company was on its way to the Avenue Hall Southampton. (Photographer Unknown : given by Les Cooper. His father Bert is the driver in the photograph.)

A letter in the *Newbury Weekly News* expressed this view:

> We think it would have been a wiser policy to have started this repertory venture with something lighter in the way of a comedy which would have attracted the man in the street. First get him there and let him appreciate that this company is made up of able actors and actresses and he will be likely to come again. Then you can start to educate him to higher things. But for a venture to lead off with the strong meat of Ibsen and then go on to Shakespeare...

And in the local Devizes paper it commented: 'Devizes audiences have been starved of this good fare for some years ('*The Two Gentlemen of Verona*') and it will take a little time to cultivate the appetite.'

The majority of theatregoers in the outlying areas though, were only too grateful to enjoy the productions of a visiting company.

In the Dorchester local paper, at the end of the first season, the theatre critic wrote: 'So we say 'Au Revoir' to the Salisbury Arts Theatre for whose monthly visits Durnovarians (Dorchester people!) are extremely grateful. Their plays have been not only entertaining but also educative and I have little doubt that they have assisted in the great drama revival now taking place in Dorset.'

In his end of the year review Henry Shute wrote:

> To all of you whom we visit on tour we extend our very grateful thanks and our assurance that we shall continue to maintain, or even raise the standards we have already set. The warmth of your welcome has left nothing to be desired, but often we wish we could visit you more frequently, that we had better facilities for presenting our productions and that you had more comfortable seats than are at present available.
>
> Increasing support for our productions may provide a solution. If there is sufficient demand we may extend our activities, and go from what might be an unsuitable hall to a cinema or theatre having the advantage of more comfortable seats, better visibility for the audience and more facilities backstage.

Unfortunately after the first flush of excitement and enthusiasm, which usually happens with any new experiment, it soon became clear that the Arts Theatre was having problems. It finished its first season in July 1946 with a deficit of £200+.

In spite of the high standard of performances plays were often performed to houses that were far from full and the tour engagements were also giving cause for concern.

Many excuses were made – the competition from the cinema, the early starting times, the difficulty of booking tickets and even the choice of plays, but perhaps it was simply that the people of Wessex were not yet ready to embrace this form of entertainment. It was a unique and exciting experiment and it must not be allowed to die. The words of Beatrix Lehmann at the Opening Ceremony had to be echoed and not forgotten: 'Care for each other, love each other, watch each other critically and helpfully and may you work together for a long time and prosper in your work for many years to come.'

The future was not secure but fortunately there remained a strong vision amongst a hard core of determined people to make this unique and exciting experiment work and eventually to grow.

4
IF IT'S THURSDAY IT MUST BE CHIPPENHAM

O N THE SURFACE, the first year of the Arts Council's 'Salisbury Experiment' was a great success. Salisbury had a new theatre and the company was taking theatre to the outlying districts. As Charles Landstone of the Arts Council put it: 'Time and effort was laid down for the first time the principle that the best the Arts has to offer is not the sole perquisite of big cities; the many in smaller centres have an equal right to its enjoyment.'

During the next few years the company continued to work very hard and achieved high standards much of the time, which was particularly commendable considering the added stress of constant touring. Their life was split between rehearsing and acting in Salisbury and spending hours in a coach travelling miles throughout the countryside. Their days were long and arduous.

However, during the next two years, they and a variety of other groups continued to give the Salisbury theatregoers a range of entertainment including two unusual Christmas offerings In December 1946 the show was 'Great Expectations' an adaptation by Alec Guinness and in 1947 they performed 'Swiss Family Robinson' One critic wrote: 'There is everything that grown ups and youngsters can enjoy' Whilst another wrote: 'The singing is not good; it is however better than the dancing. Most of the routines should be improved or eliminated.' There were many successes but profits were still tumbling.

At their AGM in May 1948, the Society of Arts announced that the average attendance had risen from 54% to 74% at the end of the season and that a production of 'Jane Eyre' had broken box office records. To counteract their losses though, they also announced

Romeo and Juliet, November 1947. Romeo: Jonathan Meddings; Nurse: Hazel Hughes; Friar: Tristram Butt. (Photographer unknown)

that the management of the Arts Theatre was to offer 5/- seats for 8 pence farthing to members of youth organisations to try to encourage a younger audience.

Also a system of season tickets would be introduced. If you paid for 10 tickets you would receive one free one. Patrons would gain free admission to the Society of Arts activities. The general public would also be able to purchase two tickets for the price of one for Monday nights to encourage more people to attend on that evening.

The actors were also performing in a building that was not originally built as a theatre and problems were often caused by the unreliable structure.

In February 1947 just before a performance of 'Les Sylphides' by the Ballet Rambert, a steady drip of water was heard. Memories of a previous occasion when a little rain had got in prevented any undue anxiety but as the ballet proceeded the drips became a steady flow of water and before long the orchestra pit was drenched. Marjorie Read one of the pianists, soon felt the full force of the deluge as the rest of the water completely fell on her. Fortunately neither the audience nor the dancers were affected. The damage was caused by the bursting of a supply pipe leading from the mains to the tank above the stage, which fed the hot water system.

As it was impossible to continue the performance an announcement was made that money would be refunded or patrons could attend another performance. Sadly though, this unfortunate and rather amusing mishap eventually led to a tragedy.

Getting ready for the next performance, Ivor John Cox, an electrician employed by the Ballet Rambert was working in the orchestra pit was which was still damp after the deluge the day before. There was a cut in a cable 12-foot from the plug end, which had just bared the rubber insulation and partially exposed the conductor wire. This cable carried a current of 230 volts, which was the normal lighting for the area. Using a pair of un-insulated pliers, he touched this cable and this, combined with the dampness of the surrounding area gave him an enormous shock. Henry Shute rushed him to the Infirmary where Mr. Cox sadly never recovered. The coroner recorded the verdict of death by misadventure.

An excellent description of life behind the stage is given in Eric Keown's article for Punch in 1949 entitled 'Operation Greasepaint':

The designer, Henry Graveney was found whistling an incantation in his witch's hideout over steaming brews of paint about to be slapped on the sets for the panto. In his carpenter's shop, the collapsible jeep which will make many children's evening, hospitably made our morning by collapsing all over the master carpenter, Stanley Astin. In the wardrobe Edward Mason and Anne Blackmore were thoughtfully concocting all manner of exotic costumes. The workshops are cramped and uncomfortable, but the fact that they have been condemned seems only to add to the pleasure of a team that is young and enthusiastic. It is hard to imagine a more practical training ground. The walls of Michael Wide's office carried encouraging attendance graphs and there is a large operations map of Wessex that would not have disgraced a bomber station.'

Bob Miles from Christchurch has many memories of working at the theatre in the early days: -

I was 15 years old at the time and attended the early performances and learnt that volunteer ushers were needed. Eileen Mackillop, the theatre secretary asked me to take a message backstage from the theatre manager Henry Shute and I remained backstage until I went into the Army three years later.

He also helped with the stage lighting:

This was controlled at a board on its own raised platform by the side of the stage access being via a ladder. There were three sections, a two-foot, a four-foot and an eight-foot run. There were slides, which went down for low lighting and up for full lights. Very difficult to operate with only one person and sometimes you had to stand on one foot and use the other foot in conjunction with two hands to provide what was required. I worked there on the hottest day of 1947 and if it had not been for the gallons of orange squash which were passed up to me I would have died of dehydration!

He particularly remembers a time in Alton when the fuse-box was blown off the wall backstage, during a performance and the stage went black. Lord Montgomery who lived near the hall always attended performances. Like most of the audience, he carried a torch in his pocket (street lights were not so numerous then) so rushed up to the stage shouting: 'Let's help them out!' A case as Bob said, of many hands making lights work!

Just as the electrician restored normality, the cast was sitting around a dining table, the leading lady was standing up to give a toast. 'Everything is alright', she said. Looking up at the 'practical' light which hung from the ceiling, she added 'we hope!' It got the biggest laugh and applause of the evening! Fortunately the play was a comedy!

Towards the end of the third season Barbara Burnham announced that she would be leaving the Arts Theatre. This season had been the company's most successful so far. Her decision to leave had been taken in full consultation with the Arts Council. In her three seasons she had been responsible for 28 plays in 24 different theatres and halls and the company had performed to 200,000 people in five counties.

On announcing her departure she wrote:

> From all sides we hear that the theatre has filled a need in our district and we can now say that the theatre is established, still better that it is a growing and living institution.
>
> A large part of our success was undoubtedly due to the permanent company who established themselves most favourably with our audiences at all places, To the writer who knows how pleasant her task was made by their loyalty, hard work and co-operation, their deserved popularity was gratifying. A theatre however, must change and grow and as we know that our theatre is now on a firm foundation, we can expect much from its future.

At her farewell party Llewlyn Rees, Drama Director of the Arts Council said: 'It is due to her more than anyone else that the Salisbury theatre has been put on the map and has reached the success it has already.' Unfortunately she was unable to attend her farewell party as she had been called away because of the death of her mother.

In a letter sent some time ago to Alan Richardson, the Playhouse's original archivist, Nevil Dickin who worked with Barbara Burnham as Set Designer wrote: 'Had she not been around during the crucial years after the War I doubt if the Playhouse would exist today. It was entirely due to her efforts in badgering the Arts Council to take over the wartime Garrison Theatre that the continuity of the theatre was preserved.' (it must also be said that Henry Shute did a lot of badgering!).

The Salisbury theatregoers however, did not need to pine too long over her departure because her successor was more than an ample replacement. He was already a very influential theatrical person and he soon moved the Arts Theatre into a period of considerable change and exciting progress – Mr. Peter Potter.

He was born on the Isle of Wight but was brought up in Lymington. He made his first stage appearance as a pixie in 'The Sport of Kings' at the Parish Hall in Lymington at rhe age of 6. He studied at Eton and Trinity College. He was destined by his parents to follow a career as a barrister but he successfully settled that problem by failing the exams. His love was the theatre and he was due to start at the Old

Peter Potter, 1949 (From old programme, photographer unknown)

Vic Theatre Drama School on September 4th 1939 but instead found himself in the Army. He served as a lieutenant in the Grenadier Guards for four years but whilst in North Africa his motor cycle had an argument with a six ton US army lorry severely damaging his right leg. After he was invalided out he worked for six months in the production department of the Ealing Studios as personal assistant to Cavalcanti, working on such famous films as 'Dead of Night' and 'Pink String and Sealing Wax.'

In the theatre he started as assistant stage manager in a production of 'A Doll's House' and from there he went to the West Riding Theatre as stage director and later as producer. He was for a year producer of the Guildford Rep Company.

In his first note to theatregoers he wrote about Barbara Burnham:

> By her enthusiasm and skill as a producer she has built the Salisbury Arts Theatre into a growing concern and I feel it a great honour to have been asked by the Arts Council to take over from her'. He concluded by saying: ' I would like to stress once more that it is only by having your continued support and indeed by building on an even larger regular audience that we can maintain the standard of performances. Our ideal will be to make each production an improvement on the last.

Soon Henry Shute also felt it was time to move on and Michael Wide succeeded him as manager of the Arts Theatre. Born in Nottingham he played in various touring companies before the War. He then enlisted in the Royal Artillery and was promoted to the position of Intelligence Officer and subsequently was appointed Staff Captain

Michael Wide, 1948 (from old brochure, photographer unknown)

in charge of entertainment of the troops in the Mediterranean. When demobbed he worked with the Arts Council as assistant regional director for the southern region. His wife had worked for ENSA and at the time of his appointment she was working in California. They both came with considerable experience and soon Peter Potter and Michael Wide became a formidable partnership. They were both indeed excellent appointments.

A short while later, making it a successful trio, Denis Carey came from Bristol to become assistant producer.

In his first season Peter Potter continued the policy of there being a touring repertory company but slowly some venues, like Devizes and Eastleigh, had to be dropped as they were proving to be too expensive and the strain was beginning to show on the members of the company. However, despite the problems, they continued to produce a variety of many excellent productions including giving Salisbury its first pantomime with an all-professional cast – '*Cinderella*'. ' All seats bookable: – 1/6 to 5/-.' Peter Potter obviously enjoyed pantomimes because one Christmas there were three pantomimes – '*Aladdin*' by the Arts Theatre Company, followed by the R.A.F. Association's presentation of ' *Babes in the Wood*' and finishing off with '*Jack and the Beanstalk*' by the theatre's second company. It must have been a stage manager's nightmare!

At another Christmas there were two entertaining productions: – '*Treasure Island*' followed by '*Dick Whittington*'. In '*Treasure Island*' an important member of the cast was Polly the parrot from Petersfield. Apparently it needed a certain amount of persuading before bursting into its lines but it was very fond of whistling!

After a year in post Peter Potter realised that it was time to create a new system and he devised a new scheme to ease the burden on the company and also to continue the Arts Theatre's outreach policy.

The company was increased to fourteen. The plan was to split the company into two smaller companies and to produce two plays every three weeks in Salisbury as against one play per month.

The plays were to run for a week in Salisbury and then go on a fortnight's tour. Salisbury would then have plays for two weeks out of every three instead of one in every four. They worked on a three-week cycle with one week between the plays being put on, during which time the theatre was occupied by visiting companies.

Peter Potter called his company his 'all star cast' and Donald Eccles, a leading actor in the company described him thus:' He has gathered around him a company which believes in the imaginative theatre enough to want to work on good plays even under difficult conditions'. To actors today it is difficult for them to imagine how strenuous the life of an actor in a touring repertory company must have been.

In February 1949 during his first season Peter Potter wrote in the programme notes for Thomas Job's '*Uncle Harry*' a description of life on the road:

In our touring repertory company for three weeks in every four, we play away from home. This entails a coach journey in the afternoon of anything from 20 to 50 miles and a return trip to Salisbury late the same night. Rarely does the company get back before midnight. During the three-week period, the play is played in nine different halls or theatres each with its own special problems for the actors and stage staff to tackle.

The plays have to be presented on stages of widely varying sizes and it is here that the actor's and producer's problems merge. Sets have to be devised by the designer to fit all stages, thus each set must be designed and constructed to act like a concertina, capable of being contracted or expanded in any direction.

On no two stages is the set exactly the same, so in each new hall, the actor must adapt his performance to the prevailing conditions.

It would be possible of course, to design a set for the smallest stage and play it everywhere, but that would mean, in the larger halls, we were ignoring the facilities offered to us.

Lighting is another problem. As far as possible we try to keep the lighting of the plays the same for the whole tour, but naturally there are slight variations from hall to hall, according to what facilities there are for hanging our lights and to what limits there are to the current that can be used.

I would not like you to think that the smaller halls see an inferior show – they don't. Smaller stages and less adequate facilities are not taken as excuses for shoddy presentation and our aim all the time is to improve our standard everywhere.

Sometimes though the set does not always fit and in November 1950 at Petersfield after the company had taken their bow, down came the final curtain plus one side of the scenery, threatening to land on half of the actors. Fortunately the men in the cast were very quick and were able to catch it before it came crashing right down. Whilst the others were holding up the offending scenery, James Cairncross unhitched the curtain and let it roll across to cover the chaos behind to a round of applause and cheering from the audience.

Malcolm Farquar a director remembers:

We went to a very small village called Huish Episkopi and we played 'Present Laughter' in somebody's sitting room. with a sort of minstrel's gallery. We played to about fifty people sitting on chintz sofas and chairs, After the performance we were served coffee and extremely large bath buns.

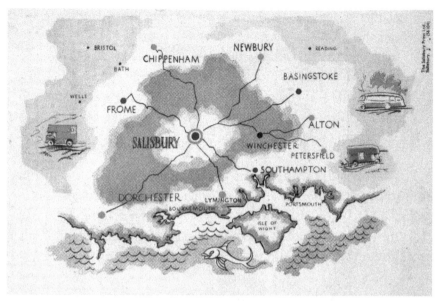

Map of where the company travelled to in the 1940s

Eric Keown in his article 'Operation Greasepaint' described the setting up of the play '*A Pair of Spectacles*' by Sydney Grundy in the parish hall of Lymington:

The crew I describe is the advance party of the Salisbury Arts Theatre, fitting up a betasselled Victorian set in preparation for the arrival of the players in their motor coach at six. We have driven down this morning through the gleaming valley of the Avon, in a lorry from which the legs of assistant stage managers and occasional sofas protrude indiscriminately; we have feasted in Lymington's enviable community centre; and now that the more obstinate bits of the school children's rice pudding have been prized from the floor, our kind hosts are settling down manfully to their expert job of assembly'.....

Three of the advanced guard are erecting the set, bolting, banging, hammering and heaving. The electrician is fixing his spots to a long bar that will be hauled up into the roof on block tackle. The prop-man is still busily unshipping a multitude of objects, from the magic spectacles to the cuckoo clock......

All this heavy and exacting work is being done in the friendliest spirit but with the utmost precision and without the waste of a second.' On a bit more at the top, Harry!' cries Peter Hicks the A.S.M, checking the alignment of the mantelpiece from the floor of the hall. 'What's that joist like? That's not bad at all.'

Including the adjustments of the spots it takes over four hours before Mr. Hicks and his mates are happy. All the furniture has had to be dusted and the carpet swept as if the Lady Mayoress were coming to tea. Then the coach arrives from Salisbury bringing Peter Potter, the director of productions and the cast.

He concludes with: 'Going back in the coach is like returning from some triumphant match. The songs for the panto nearly hit the roof.'

In his 1949 article 'A Day in the Theatre' Michael Wide also wrote about the journey home:

In the homeward bound coach some of the company are dozing, some learning lines for next week. The stage manager is working out how to get the whole of the next play into one lorry-load and the touring manager is totting up figures of the night's business. The producer moves about the coach and chats with one artist and another.

Then someone starts to sing and the rest join in; old and new songs from their own shows and songs from the hit parade. It's a tired but happy band who finally are dropped off from the coach one by one round Salisbury, 'goodnights' echoing through the dark air. The landladies, bless 'em have hot suppers waiting. Then it's to bed and 'Oh dear, that rotten alarm clock!

The 'rotten alarm clock' figured in his opening paragraph:

It's nine o' clock on a winter's morning and members of the company who didn't get to bed till the early hours are listening regretfully to the clanging of alarm clocks.

It'll need fast work to wash, dress, eat, get down to the theatre, collect mail and be at rehearsal by ten-thirty prompt; but there's no escape. Another 15-hour working day has begun.

And for some that would include that coach journey!

The company would be travelling in all weathers and on one occasion in deepest winter, taking the dangerous bend at Potterne, a lorry bringing props back from Chippenham skidded on thick ice and it crashed into the side of a house on the offside of the road. The actors were following in their coach behind and fortunately one of them had studied medicine before taking up acting so was able to check that all personnel were only shaken and none of them were injured. They eventually had tea in a neighbour's house who just happened to be a keen theatregoer, before returning to Salisbury by 2.15 am. (And that rotten alarm clock!) No, the play at the time was not Priestley's 'Dangerous Corner'!

Support continued to be good in the provinces. Mary Buxey from Newbury remembers: 'Certainly their visits for me were pure magic.' and Marie Sharp commented: 'The productions were always of a good standard. I particularly remember 'The Promise' which was very moving.'

John Leech spoke of his affection for 'Mary Rose'. 'We thought it was excellent but then we were only just married and all the trees were green!' He also remembers a time in Devizes when the play was 'Tonight At 8.30' and half the audience turned up then instead of the starting time of 6.30!

Support from the Army was also still prominent: William Roberts remembers:

Posted to Knook Camp after basic National Service training in 1949 I was uncomfortable with the hard drinking troops of the 1st battalion who had recently returned from service in Mogadishu, East Africa,

On Saturdays I would usually buy a block of Nestles Blended and go to the Arts Theatre as a haven of respectability, a refuge from the harsh realities of Infantry demonstrations in and around Imber..... The stage dialogue was a welcome counterpoint to the language heard at Knook Camp and I revelled in the contrast.

Peter Potter's first production, was Priestley play: – 'An Inspector Calls' in September 1948 and it was greeted with a full house and critical acclaim. With Denis Carey they soon raised the standard of the Arts Theatre company and created a series of excellent productions amongst many of which were 'The Winslow Boy'; 'The Rivals'; 'The Guinea Pig' 'The Taming of the Shrew' of which the Observer wrote: ' It is long since I have seen it done better than by the Salisbury Arts Theatre players with Denis Carey' and 'Murder in the Cathedral' of which The Stage wrote: ' This was a triumphantly effective production.' However they did produce 'Macbeth' with one rather bare singular set which did not go down too well with the Salisbury theatregoers, used as they were to a bit more interest and colour in their sets!

Potter and Carey also gathered together an excellent company that included Donald Eccles, Dorothy Reynolds, James Cairncross, Peter Bryant, Hugh Mathias, Margot Van Der Burgh, Sheila Sweet, Malcolm Farquhar, Joan White, Yvonne Coulette and David Dodimead again to name but a few from the illustrious company. The rest of the theatrical world was beginning to sit up and take notice of what was going on in this Wiltshire city.

Peter Potter commented: 'I have no hesitation in saying that they are easily the best I have yet had the privilege of working with.'

Peter Bryant was delighted when Peter Potter saw him in a production at RADA and offered him a job at Salisbury as 'ASM and small parts.' Peter would speak of the tremendous spirit there was at Salisbury when he worked there. Having survived the War, where he took part in many Combined Operations overseas, the warmth of the camaraderie was the perfect antidote to the uncertainty of his War years.

From working backstage and playing those 'small parts' he soon became one of the company's leading men. He would often speak of the importance to actors of having a period working back stage, something that present day actors do not have the opportunity to experience.

There were many close friends and he once said that there was one expression often used in those days, the origin of which he never did find out: : Actors would say: 'Once the curtain came down, we were at it like knives!' – however, I think we understand!

Peter, who went on with Sheila Sweet, to appear in one of the first BBC serials 'The Grove Family', remembers his days in Salisbury with great affection. He recalled: 'Newton Blick, when not wanted for rehearsal in the afternoon was inclined to make a bee-line for Charles

Peed's pub, 'The King's Arms' across the road.

This came to be known by us all when opportunity presented itself, as 'having a Blickquid lunch!'

Aubrey Morris, who played Donalbain, in 'Macbeth' suddenly found himself making an entrance in a scene that had nothing to do with him, but with great presence of mind he rather loudly declared to no one in particular 'To Ireland I, my Liege, and with all dispatch' and made a hasty exit – a Blickliquid lunch? We shall never know!'

One of the most popular and versatile actors was James Cairncross. He actually trained as a medical student but gave it all up to become an actor. In one Salisbury season he played a doctor in four productions and in another he played a character pretending to be a doctor. At the time he remarked: 'I think I have now discharged my obligation to the medical profession!'

In 2002, he wrote:

Looking back now in retirement, and in the eighty seventh year of my rackety old life, I can say hand on heart, that the Salisbury days were among the happiest and most fulfilling of my life. We hear a lot these days, from people who can have no personal knowledge of the immediate post-war years, about what a state of misery we lived in, what with rationing and shortages. One has the impression that happiness had to wait for the advent, God help us of the Beatles! I can assure you that in Salisbury, at least, we had a wonderful time.

The assurance of a season of work gave the actors a fine sense of security. The fact that one was a member of a permanent company engendered a spirit that made for good work. And of course the public got to know us on and off the stage; so that one felt one was contributing something unique and valuable to the community.

In his early days James Cairncross suffered from stage fright. A colleague told him that Evelyn Laye had solved the problem. What she would do was to go into the wings long before her cue and she would stand in a corner saying over and over- 'I am Evelyn Laye. I am Evelyn Laye. I am Evelyn Laye.' Then she would sweep onto the stage and make her entrance. Having heard this, James Cairncross was seen standing in a corner of the wings saying over and over – 'I am Evelyn

Laye. I am Evelyn Laye. I am Evelyn Laye'!

Fortunately this wasn't to last for too long and he soon became a very talented and much loved actor on the Salisbury stage.

Inevitably when looking back at the 40s and 50s there are 'signs of the times'. One of which was the question of smoking. In 2004 smoking was banned at the Playhouse but there was great excitement at the Arts Theatre in December 1949 when smoking was at last allowed in the auditorium. The following announcement appeared in the press: –

The management takes great pleasure in announcing that the city council has now agreed to permit smoking.

a) In the interest of non-smokers however, patrons will be asked to keep their smoking to a minimum and not smoke pipes.

b) Ashtrays are being installed, the ventilating system is being improved and it is hoped that from Monday, smoking will be permitted at most professional performances.

In a programme note Michael Wide wrote:

A lady complained to me the other day that a gentleman sitting next to her puffed his pipe incessantly. The tobacco was so powerful that the lady coughed all night. As a pipe smoker myself, frequently lost in the aroma of my favourite weed, may I remind my fellows that clouds of smoke can be irritating to those in nearby seats.

Pipes were very much an important accessory for many actors and their programme photograph would often show them holding a pipe. In a 1951 programme it said of the actor John Myers: 'He is fond of dogs and pipes and has an amazing collection of the latter'!

Food rationing was also a problem: In the play 'Laburnum Grove' four bananas had to be eaten at each performance. The company had been told by the Ministry of Food that bananas were only for expectant mothers and for those over 70. As they did not qualify for either they asked the public if anyone had any fruit to spare, would they be so good as to leave it at the Box Office.

A few years later, in a slightly different vein, in the play 'Fallen

Angels' a dozen oysters had to be consumed.

The play's budget would not allow this, so shells had to be found which could be filled with some kind of eatable concoction. One of the members of the Board, Guy Vizard promptly took himself off to Bournemouth and consumed 18 oysters and on returning to Salisbury proudly presented the director with the shells!

And there was huge rejoicing when in 1950 permission to have a licensed bar was granted which added to the patrons' choice of refreshments.

On a more unpleasant note whilst staying at Crane Lodge, Peter Potter's wife Elspeth Cochrane found that there was a black dancer in the ballet that was to be performed at the theatre the following week. She took him in as a lodger 'as no one else in Salisbury would take him in.'

However, some things never change: In 1948 a letter appeared in the local paper complaining of 'theatregoers who leave their manners behind. Pushing past those who have arrived on time; ignoring the interval bell and arriving late back into the auditorium. Talking all the time and eating ice cream being more important than watching the play!'

Life was difficult for the Arts Theatre Company but their enormous hard work and talent were beginning to shine through and success and an excellent reputation were deservedly theirs. In 1950 Sir Philip Morris, Vice Chancellor of the University of Bristol praised the company: 'Perhaps many in the city will realise this winter that there is first class talent here and will lend their support.'

However, dark financial clouds were beginning to cover the theatre and in the summer of 1951 the Arts Council dropped a bombshell.

5
'WE WILL PROVIDE A RAFT TO KEEP YOU AFLOAT'
The Arts Council

DESPITE MOUNTING DIFFICULTIES the 'Salisbury Experiment' continued to flourish and to give Wessex theatregoers a rich variety of theatrical experiences. However, the Arts Council continued to pull the strings and doubts were beginning to creep in concerning the viability of such a unique and expensive project. Fortunately the Arts Theatre had a strong and vocal champion in Charles Landstone, the Deputy Drama Director of the Arts Council.

He supported the project from the start and always gave it his considerable support. In his book 'Off Stage' he wrote:

Peter and Denis were a fine pair. In those years at Salisbury we saw some of the most important work the Arts Council has so far accomplished in drama. It was without equivocation, the only item in the Drama policy fulfilling the dual aim laid down by the Charter 'to increase the accessibility of the fine arts to the public throughout Our Realm, and to improve the standard of execution of the fine arts. It was a great and noble experiment.'

It was bringing drama to four thousand people a week and in a rarefied, secluded atmosphere it was building up the art of acting in a manner bound to be beneficial in the future.' He predicted that one day, 'stargazers' will find the skies in the West End, Broadway and Hollywood, thick with these clusters from Salisbury.'

Praise indeed. Though not everyone at the Arts Council saw it as a viable proposition. When they took over the lease of the building in 1945 the vision was to establish a cultural centre for the whole of Wessex, but because of the size of the population and the size of the theatre, the Arts Theatre was never anticipated as possibly fulfilling this dream. To many it was regarded as an interim measure until a larger theatre and a larger city such as Southampton became available. For years the company played regular visits with great success at the only available theatre in Southampton, a church hall about a mile outside the centre. Early in 1951, the Grand Theatre was re-opened with a repertory company so all hope of transferring the Salisbury Company to Southampton was abandoned.

The financial losses in Salisbury were beginning to make many members of the Council start to have second thoughts about the 'Salisbury Experiment' and also to many, Wessex was too much of a backwater for their tastes.

Applications to start a repertory company were continually being received by the Arts Council from other parts of the country, especially from the North and the Midlands. It was said by a member of the Council: ' The Council only has a limited amount of money to be spent each year and we are being shot at because we are spending too much in Salisbury. Charles Landstone estimated it amounted to £12,000 a year.

Charles Landstone complained that only two members of the Council, Sir Ernest Pooley and Sir Bronson Albery had ever been near the company since the opening night. In 1951 he invited Sir Bronson Albery to visit the Arts Theatre with him 'not only to see a play performed by the company but also to mingle with the artists and staff, to sense the atmosphere of enthusiasm and excitement of creation amongst these young people. I knew that the standard was unchallengeable by any company in the provinces and when the curtain went up on Noel Coward's *'Tonight at 8.30'*, I was prepared for the best. I was not prepared however, to hear within two minutes a whisper from Sir Bronson: 'This is magnificent. But it's much too good for Salisbury.'

Charles Landstone knew at that point that the die was cast and that he was beginning to fight a losing battle to keep the Arts Council interested.

The inevitable blow came in the summer of 1951 when the

The Dark is Light Enough, March 1955. From L to R: Ronald Allen, Francis Hall, Helen Jessop, Gerald Flood, Martyn Huntley, Giles Phibbs, Ronald Harwood, Margaret Rawlings, John Graham. (Photographer unknown)

Arts Council announced that it was to withdraw funding for the Arts Theatre. In September they wrote: 'We cannot with a clear conscience carry the thing on, but if local initiative can find a means to keep the theatre going we will provide a raft to keep you afloat.'

If such a group could be formed, then the Arts Council would be prepared to sublet the theatre and its additional premises at a cost to the trust and to allow the trust their entire assets, transport, scenery, costumes and other equipment for a peppercorn rent. Also they would give an initial grant of £2,000 as working capital.

To show their support for a local initiative, the City Council agreed to guarantee £500 against any losses.

This was crunch time for the Arts Theatre. Fortunately a group of enthusiastic and influential businessmen took up the challenge and under the leadership of Sir Reginald Kennedy Cox a non-profit distributing company was formed. The following were to become directors of this trust;- Messrs F. Pullen; J. Benson; E. Grant; J. Wort; W. Vizard and F. Moore. ,

Michael Wide was to continue as general manager as well as becoming a director. The trust's aims were:- 'To maintain the regional nature of the theatre and the high standard of production already set by performances in Salisbury and at the best of the theatre's touring dates and by allowing two weeks rehearsal for each production.'

Their first problems were how to make stringent economies and then what to do about the touring scheme.

The latter was to cut out some of the uneconomic venues such as Alton and Eastleigh. For the first time the resident company would play continuously at the theatre; the two companies would play one week at the theatre and one week on tour and there would not be an outside production brought in every third week as in the past. The exception would be for the city's amateur societies' presentations.

The most pressing problem though, was how to bring in extra finances to cut down the company's mounting losses. Expenditure was cut down to the bone. In the first year under the new company the cost of running the theatre was reduced to under £7,000 compared to the figure of £13,000 which was the approximate yearly cost when the Arts Council was responsible for the theatre.

Despite continual theatrical successes and continued financial support from the Arts Council and the City Council, more theatregoers were still needed as some productions were not drawing in the necessary support. Just before Christmas 1952, the theatre put on two plays that had been requested by the theatregoers – Shaw's 'The Applecart' and Barrie's 'What Every Woman Knows'. Both were financial disasters and the company was playing to half empty auditoriums. Michael Wide commented: 'Business was dire. We have reached the last ditch. We can go no further. It is now up to Salisbury.'

It gradually became obvious that the theatre's belt needed to be even tighter and a new scheme had to be introduced. So in January 1953 it was announced that the financial crisis meant an end to the touring policy. The last play on tour would be 'Worm's Eye View' and the final curtain would come down in Frome on January 28th.

Thus bringing to an end an experiment that was once called 'unique in all the world.' It had been a brave attempt to play continuously in 12 different towns (Basingstoke, Chippenham, Newbury, Winchester, Southampton, Weymouth, Dorchester, Petersfield, Lymington, Frome, Castle Cary and Melksham) in an area of 5,000 square miles with a scattered population of 400,000. The transport bill had reached the £3,000 mark so this would be a huge saving.

Those helping to support these visiting towns were naturally very upset considering that many had made financial contributions to the Arts Theatre company and were upset at the short notice of the end of the touring scheme. However, as Michael Wide said: 'It is now up to Salisbury.' This was echoed by Sir Reginald Kennedy Cox, who, in a letter to the local paper wrote:-

> In the future we propose to concentrate entirely upon Salisbury and each week we will present in our theatre here a different new play. This policy will place a great strain both upon producer and artist, but they are prepared to undertake this in the hope that their actions will be rewarded, by not only renewed, but increased support from those people who want a live theatre in Salisbury to continue. This does, and will, entail a real effort upon the part of our supporters. It is not sufficient to come oneself, but it needs also that you should tell all your friends about the plays and, if need be, worry them continuously until they at any rate, try our fare.

As always the pantomime had been a success but matters came to a head soon afterwards and the future of the Arts Theatre was in doubt.

The company had gone into weekly rep which meant a smaller grant from the Arts Council whose maximum was £3,000 a year. The directors continued to cut down on expenses. They gave up their office in Fisherton Street and had moved into the Green Room in the theatre. The telephone had been cut and there was only an extension from the Box Office. Instead of hiring furniture it was being borrowed from private houses and all transport costs had gone. The situation was this:-the theatre if filled, could hold 500 a night, and expenses were between £340 and £350 a week. If they could take £350 they could pay their way but at present this was far from happening. Reginald Kennedy Cox said:- 'What we want from you is just seven percent more at the Box Office.' He continued:-

> We have sufficient money in the bank until March 31st. What happens after that will depend on what is done now in these two vital months of February and March. Our money will finish at the end of March.

As Chairman of the Board I would have to recommend that it would not be honest to continue after March 31st.

If one more person in every 132 in Salisbury will come every week we are safe. I believe you will be able to find that extra person.

So it was up to the people of Salisbury to save the Arts Theatre by becoming regular theatregoers, but perhaps they could help in other ways as well.

Back in the autumn of 1949 it was proposed to launch a Theatregoers' Club for the theatregoers to be able to take a more active part in the theatre's activities. At the inaugural meeting in October, it was stated that the Objects of the Club were:- '1) To stimulate and foster interest in the live theatre and 2) To hold regular monthly meetings of members; these meetings to include:- a) Talks by well known theatrical personalities b) Discussions and c) Social Evenings.

It was also stated:- Premises:- 1) The new Buffet at the Arts Theatre will be open to Club Members on weekdays for morning coffee and afternoon tea. 2) The theatre will be available for monthly club meetings on Sunday mornings.

Over a hundred people signed enrolment forms and by the end of its first season membership had increased to over three hundred. Frances Pullen was elected Chairman. (Remember him? He used to help the projectionist when the building was a cinema!) Annual subscriptions would be no more than 5/- and for members under 20, students and members of HM. forces it would be 2/6.

At the meeting Peter Potter said:

Francis Pullen (Photographer Peter Brown)

In the first place I think the main thing about the club is that it must be representative of a complete cross section of Salisbury people of all ages, all professions and all trades. I think it must not just become a club for people who are only intellectually interested in the theatre but for people who take a passionate interest in the theatre. He looked forward to getting together and exchanging ideas, at the moment, I am afraid, only over a cup of coffee! [The licensed Bar was to come later!]

Before this first meeting, in the *Salisbury Times*, a columnist wrote:

I appeal to theatre lovers to attend this meeting and not leave it to the faithful few. After all it is our theatre and front and back seat purchasers have the right to have a say. The projected club has great possibilities and if it creates educated audiences it will be worth while. Perhaps too, the members of such a club speaking with one voice may lead to the removal of the no smoking ban!

(This was a passionate fight by smokers, and they had their way quite soon!)

The club proved to be a great success and lovers of the theatre were delighted to feel that they were an important part of the Arts Theatre. Initially it was formed to create a forum for theatregoers to expand their interest and knowledge of the theatre. However small, they could soon boast organising a Christmas party with a cabaret; a Fancy Dress Ball, a night of Charades performed by groups of club members and some interesting round-table discussions by visiting theatrical personalities. It was reported that Frances Day, a popular actress and singer at the time, was due to have come but she sprained her ankle at rehearsal so she sent her bulldog and Rolls Royce instead! She answered questions on the phone and agreed to appear in person the following year!

Financial problems though continued to spiral. It became obvious that more financial support was going to be needed.

As the deadline date of March 31st approached the Theatregoer's Club announced their six point plan to help solve the crisis.

1. The formation of a baby sitting scheme for patrons.

2. Members to become unofficial agents to book seats for patrons who cannot get to the theatre in time to collect their tickets.

3. Members should buy more expensive seats during this critical time.

4. When going to the theatre, members should endeavour to encourage someone not normally a theatregoer to accompany them.

5. To boost sale of books of vouchers which are obtainable at the Box Office and provide ten tickets for the price of nine.

6. Members should give their names to the management so that they might be asked for the loan of props, clothes and furniture as the theatre would no longer be hiring such items.

At a meeting of the Theatregoers Club the producer, Frank Hauser made this appeal for an incredible range of objects:- chairs and tables, sideboards, carpets and rugs, curtains and pelmet rails, standard and table lamps, and knives and forks. They wanted ladies clothes, cardigans, scarves, dresses, fur coats and they wanted men's evening clothes, coats, sports jackets and trousers, and even vests and pants! He assured the audience that the borrowed items would not go on tour but would stay safely in the theatre.

At a further meeting it was also suggested that theatregoers with cars who live in outlying districts should be prepared to collect fellow theatregoers on their way to see a performance.

Money of course was the most pressing problem so a scheme was launched which appealed to theatregoers to promise 10/- units annually as an endowment fund . This was originally suggested by Dr. Happold, Headmaster of Bishop Wordsworth School, who was a staunch supporter of the Arts Theatre. It was widely welcomed and 100 people immediately signed up.

The Chairman, Francis Pullen urged theatregoers to sign up for this scheme quickly so the committee would know how much extra money they could rely upon in the immediate future and also as a pointer to the City Council as it had considered withdrawing any financial guarantee. He wanted to show them that:- 'The public of Salisbury really want the theatre as much as they want a public library, a swimming bath, tennis courts or a park. This is part of the cultural life of Salisbury and the citizens of Salisbury want it.'

Unfortunately the council did not take very long to decide and a heavy blow fell quite soon. The city council's financial committee voted not to continue with a guarantee of £1,100 for the theatre for the coming financial year.

Michael Wide's reaction was:- 'It is a great shock. We were just turning the corner and it has come at a very bad time for us. It is just like a cold clammy hand being put across everything.'

France Pullen commented: 'My reaction at the moment is that the efforts for the appeal have got to be redoubled. I don't think we should sit down under it.'

The future of the Arts Theatre was now hanging on a very thin thread.

Such actions though by the city council proved to be fighting talk to many members of the public and Mr. Williams, a *Journal* reader, suggested the creation of a 'Fighting Fund' to raise the £1,100 which was no longer guaranteed by the city council. So now more money was being promised.

Fortunately also, the response to the endowment scheme continued to increase and in March there were 435 patrons with promises of £293.9s It was hoped that the half way mark towards the £1,000 target could be reached very soon. Attendances were also rising as theatregoers began to realise their important role in trying to save their theatre.

The Arts Council realising the grave situation decided to award the theatre with the highest possible grant for weekly rep of £1,000.

Then came a production of '*Little Women*' which was an inspired choice as it proved to be the biggest money spinner in the theatre's history. It made a profit of over £80 and there were many 'House Full' notices outside the theatre. There had been a few losses but since changing to weekly rep there was now a net profit of £85.

All this encouraged the directors to announce that the Arts Theatre would remain open for certain until the end of the present season and that plans were going ahead for the next season.

Reginald Kennedy Cox commented: 'Now is the Winter of our discontent made glorious by the sum of the Theatregoer's Club.' and he congratulated the club on its successful efforts to save live theatre in Salisbury.

Praise was also given to the acting company. Truda Panet, the secretary of the Theatregoer's Club said of them:-

All of them accepted cuts in their far from large salaries when such measures were proved to be unavoidable if our theatre was to stay open. All of them accepted too the enormous added work implied by weekly instead of fortnightly rep. Without their co-operation and unflagging loyalty there could not have been an Arts Theatre for us to help to save.

Reginald Kennedy Cox always enjoyed a celebration. He introduced two special occasions to the company. A party on stage to celebrate Shakespeare's birthday on April 23rd for which he donated the champagne and cakes so the cast could 'Toast the Immortal Bard.' and a party on stage after the first night which was known as 'The Duchess Charles.' The origin of the name has been lost in theatrical legend but thanks to Kennedy Cox, the company was never short of champagne!

The directors and the theatregoers knew that they now had to build on this good fortune. Pamphlets encouraging more people to attend the theatre and to make financial promises were distributed to every house in the city and district. It attempted to drum support by saying:-

There's a pleasure in theatregoing which no other form of entertainment can give and don't be put off by the name 'Arts Theatre', it's not a Mecca for highbrows. On the contrary, the theatre is a home of gaiety and entertainment for everybody. After all there's an art in everything – from dribbling a football to cooking a dinner.

Every week night, week in and week out, we offer a good show. Perhaps a play – funny or sad, exciting or comical – and in their proper seasons pantomime, revue, ballet and musical comedy. The best possible in resident artistes and the names you know from screen, radio and television.

An intimate theatre; a courteous staff and a café-bar where refreshments are cheap and you can chat with your friends between acts.

So give it a try and remember – a night at the theatre is a real night out!

There were also plans to create a Junior Theatregoers' Club which would be open to all school children whose small annual subscription of 1/- would pay for a badge and a membership card. They would be able to attend any performance and sit anywhere there were vacant seats for nine pence.

The idea for this club was first suggested by 11 year old Alison Wide, Michael Wide's daughter. Ann Winchcombe, a pupil at South Wilts Grammar School, was elected as its first Chairperson. It proved to be very popular and the target of 600 members was soon reached. In a programme note Ann wrote:-

> The theatre benefits from the club, because we fill up many seats which would otherwise be empty; and of course the fact that we pay only such a small sum of money to see a really enjoyable play is of great advantage to us poor school girls and boys, whose financial resources are invariably shaky and insufficient for our many needs!... We are hoping that our idea is going to be taken up by other repertory companies because we feel that if there were more clubs like ours, the interest in plays and theatre work generally amongst young people would be considerably increased. In addition we are building up audiences for the future.

It was later reported that Alison Wide, the founder member of the club was invited with several of her school friends to make a tongue twister of a record with Max Bygraves. He was extremely charming, giving all the children sweets and promising to send signed photographs. He also gave the entire orchestra cigarettes!

So was the name 'Arts Theatre' really putting some people off attending performances, thinking it was not for them and perhaps a night at the cinema would be more suitable? Certainly there had been letters in the paper suggesting a change of name and perhaps that huge prospective audience, the soldiers on the Plain might also be thinking that perhaps it was not for them. There was also the continuous lure of the cinema to tempt people to spend their money and evenings. As one critic wrote :

> The cinema is cheaper and its programmes are longer. Secondly the cinema gives three performances a day which are continuous. The cinema visitor has considerable latitude in timing attendance. The theatre should concentrate not on polite, well mannered nonsense which has received so much attention in the past and which interests nobody but should concentrate on something like 'A Streetcar Named Desire' which has a more psychological appeal.

(The writer would have approved of Reggie Salberg as he produced this play in 1964!)

So in 1953 the directors discussed the possibility of a change of name. Perhaps this would help to encourage more patrons.

There were many suggestions including: 'The Lyric', 'The Empress' even 'The Windmill' However, it was decided that 'The Queen's' was the favourite as it was Coronation year. Unfortunately the Home Office did not approve and in a letter received from the Under-Secretary of State it regretted that: 'In accordance with established practice in matters of this kind, he was unable to recommend Her Majesty to grant permission for the use of 'The Queen's.' The recommendation was that the theatre could be called 'The Salisbury Coronation Theatre'.

This was discussed several times by the directors and the name 'Playhouse' was their choice.

In the local *Journal* it was reported that:-

> Mr. Wide said that the change of name was thought to make a better appeal to the ordinary business man passing through the city and the soldier serving on the Plain, 'Arts Theatre' to some people sounded a bit 'snooty' and 'The Playhouse' would tell them exactly what to expect. The company and the firm would still be known as 'The Salisbury Arts Theatre Company.

During the summer the Theatregoers' Club with a little financial help from the Arts Council and the directors, re-decorated areas of the building including the coffee bar and the dressing rooms ready for

Redecorating the old Playhouse by the theatregoers, July 1953 (Salisbury Journal)

the big opening of 'The Playhouse.' It was also reported that:-

> The front of the stage has been altered to remove the unsightly pipes that were such an eyesore and the front of the balcony has been altered to give patrons a perfect view downstage to the footlights without leaning forward.
>
> There are also alterations to the seating on the balcony and those sitting in the front row will now be able to put their programmes on the plush balustrade!

The theatre was duly re-opened as 'The Playhouse' in July 1953 with a performance of 'Lilac Time.' with 'Full London Company and augmented orchestra.' Another milestone in this old unique building.

6

'IF THERE ARE NO HIDDEN REEFS AHEAD, WE SHOULD CONTINUE TO SAIL IN FAIRLY CALM WATERS'

Michael Wide

IN THE EARLY FIFTIES there was much frantic action by those running the Arts Theatre and those who supported it in an eventually successful campaign to keep the theatre open. But what about those who worked there – the producers, the actors and those working backstage and in the offices, what about them?

In October 1950 Peter Potter left for a tour of some of the continental theatres – Sweden, Denmark, Germany and finally to Paris, studying artistic developments and methods of administration. This was very useful for him and the theatre but unfortunately he continued to be in considerable pain with his injured leg and in March 1951 it had to be amputated.

However, this did not stop him working and in May he surprisingly announced to the company that he would be leaving to take up the post of producer of the Citizens Theatre in Glasgow. Though not before in July he produced his piece de rçsistance , a performance of '*Our Lady's Tumbler*' in the cathedral. As the *Salisbury Times* reported:

Superbly lovely is '*Our Lady's Tumbler*' which had its first night in the cathedral on Tuesday evening. The simple story of the circus clown turned monk who gives all he has to acquire grace, preaches an eloquent truth more forcibly than many a wordy sermon. Ronald Duncan who has written the play specially for Salisbury Festival in fact economises in words and relies on the great strength of the situation for effect. He has too, the advantage of having the best of the Salisbury Arts Theatre Company to enact the tragedy, the very imaginative direction of Peter Potter, the colourful décor of Cecil Beaton, the majestic music of Arthur Oldham and above all the natural beauty of the cathedral itself. It was an unforgettable experience.

The timing of the evening production had to be between 7 and 9 when the sun added its own uniqueness to the lighting effects as it beamed through the high cathedral windows.

A while later the play was presented at St. Thomas's Church in London's Regent Street. Michael Wide had the task of taking the Madonna statue designed by Cecil Beaton on the top of his car. He drove very gingerly to avoid serious bumps and there were several pauses to avoid heavy rain showers. Judging by the faces of some London policemen there was speculation that he might be absconding with a body!

For part of his time in Salisbury, Peter Potter stayed at Crane Lodge where he would often host parties for his theatrical friends and occasionally garden parties for theatregoers. His wife Elspeth Cochrane remembers cooking meals for over 14 guests from the theatre on Christmas day! Peter became a friend of William Golding who was teaching at Bishop Wordsworth School. One summer he helped him to find time to finish 'Lord of the Flies.' 'You are always going on about writing a book' he said to him!

Another personality who stayed at Crane Lodge was Ronald Harwood. He described it as one of Salisbury's most impressive residences boasting both a Georgian and an Elizabethan wing. It was owned by a local eccentric socialite, Vivian Macan who took in paying guests as a hobby. Ronald Harwood recalled; 'He was a queenly gentleman, tall, thin and willowy with white hair and blue eyes. All domestic negotiations with his lodgers were conducted through the medium of his enormous tabby cat Poozey!

Young Ronald Harwood was impressed by the famous garden parties that were held there where such guests as Anthony Eden's wife Clarissa, Cecil Beaton, Greta Garbo and Augustus John were often entertained. On one occasion there was a Lord Vivian who had been shot in a sensitive part of his anatomy at a range of three inches by his paramour, Mrs. Wheeler who was then on trial at Salisbury Assizes!

A sign of Harwood's growing status was that he managed to persuade Donald Wolfit and his wife Rosalind Iden to stage Ibsen's 'The Master Builder' in order to boost the Playhouse's finances.

On leaving Salisbury, Peter Potter said: 'The theatre must live in Wessex and this is only possible by the continued and increased support, come rain or shine of every single one of you. Thank you for making my three years so very happy.'

There was a leaving party for him at the South Canonry where it was said: ' The disappearance of the familiar figure of the 33 year old ex-guardsman whose quiet enthusiasm has done so much for the theatre in this part of the world will leave a difficult gap to fill.'

The partnership with Denis Carey had already broken up as he had been appointed producer at the Bristol Old Vic Theatre where he helped to create the legendary musical 'Salad Days.'

The Arts Theatre Company, September 1951. Hugh Grant (Producer), Peter Bryant, Ray Purcell, Charles Hubbard, Catherine Campbell, Colin Ellis, David Besgrove in rehearsal. (Photographer Unknown)

In the early 50s, after Peter Potter left there followed a succession of producers. Whilst Peter Potter was on his continental tour, Joan

Swinstead joined the company from the West End as Associate Producer. Hugh Grant then took over from Peter Potter as first producer assisted by Val May. Unfortunately Hugh Grant decided to move on very quickly and only stayed for three months. Then in 1952 Frank Hauser and Guy Verney took over as producers with Frank Hauser becoming sole producer in 1953. Under their guidance and considerable expertise they raised the standard of productions to another higher level.

One young actor however, did not find Guy Verney to his liking. A young Kenneth Williams briefly joined the company in 1952 as Bastien in Siegried Geyer's '*By Candlelight*'. In 'Just Williams' he wrote:

> Since I got lots of laughs during the run, it all started going to my head and I began to develop a comic persona which wasn't always appropriate for the production.
>
> My second play was '*School For Scandal*' and in rehearsal, I sailed on in my part as Benjamin Backbite. But before I could get under way, Guy Verney who was directing, called out, 'Go back and make that entrance again – try coming on as an actor in a company and not as a star!' I can still remember the shock of hearing such sharp criticism from the stalls but it couldn't have delayed me overmuch because I walked down to the footlights and said: 'I don't take that kind of cheap contumely from you or anyone else,' and walked off the stage.

He obviously was not very enamoured with Salisbury because he later wrote:

> Salisbury is madly cathedral and smug little self-conscious houses, freshly painted. All terribly disinfected and utterly boring. Huge notices asking for silence and telling dogs not to foul the paths because the church won't like it. It's all so mock. Pubs are all old fashioned and quite unconvincing.

Needless to say he didn't stay in Salisbury for very long and soon moved on to higher and greater successes!

One actress who certainly enjoyed her stay in Salisbury was

Prunella Scales. She joined the company in August 1952 and had her first role in Ben Levy's 'Return to Tyassi' earning the princely sum of £8 a week At Christmas she appeared as the oldest shoe child in 'Babes in the Wood'. and it wasn't very long before theatregoers and critics realised the gem they had in this 20 year old actress.

In March 1953 she appeared in Rose Franken's 'Claudia' and one morning, rehearsals were interrupted by the author and her husband who were on their way to see friends in Bournemouth. They watched the rehearsals for over an hour and afterwards the author commented that 'Miss Scales is the best Claudia I have ever seen. I think that was a wonderful performance. A little later Prunella appeared in 'A Doll's House' and a local critic wrote: 'She is the perfect changing doll, and by this latest example of her skill she can lay claim to being one of the most valuable assets the company has had in years.'

However, like most young actresses it didn't always go to plan. She was chosen to play Desdemona in 'Othello' with Pat Addison playing the main role. This was a huge, demanding role for such a young actress as Prunella remembers: –

> When I was playing Desdemona at Salisbury, Othello, who was played by Pat, a rather large actor took a long time over the last scene, after he had killed me. We'd done a matinee and I was quite tired and I fell asleep only to wake with a shriek when Othello had killed himself and he fell across me. As he'd already smothered me once, he had to do it again!

Pru's husband Timothy West did not join the company until 1957 when he was appointed as stage manager. They did not appear together at the Playhouse until 1999 when they appeared in Pinter's 'The Birthday Party.'

To boost the reputation of the Arts Theatre Company and also to help with the constant problem of finance, Michael Wide organised a season in Carlisle for the company in 1952. So to a certain extent the company was touring again but this time just to one theatre, Her Majesty's Theatre in Carlisle. Their first play was J.M. Barrie's 'Quality Street'. The company was an immediate success and soon playing to full houses. 'You must raise your hat to them for first class entertainment.' wrote the local critic. Of course it helped when they changed the matinee times from 2.30 to 5.30 to catch the punters attending the Carlisle races! The 10 week season was extended to 13 and the local critic expressed the views of the Carlisle public:- 'It is good news that what Salisbury has to be almost bludgeoned into supporting, can prove so popular elsewhere.' More than 7,000 people a week were seeing the Salisbury company.

Guy Verney and Frank Hauser were both involved in producing in Salisbury and Carlisle. Looking back it seemed that, these times also became a training ground for several actors who went on to achieve success and fame in both theatre and in the cinema. Leslie Phillips directed two of the early plays:- '*Harvey*' in which George Baker and Rachel Roberts appeared and '*To Dorothy a Son*' in which he acted alongside George Baker.

In Carlisle Leslie Phillips' first part was as Patrice in '*Ring Round the Moon*' in which he had to dance a fantastic tango with 'Lady India'. Kathleen Shiach, a local theatregoer spoke with great affection :- ' I still remember Leslie Phillips' wonderful tango. I saw the play several times.'

In his book 'Hello' Leslie Phillips wrote:-

I enjoyed working in Carlisle. Her Majesty's Theatre was a beautiful building in a pleasant setting. Next door there was a good old pub beside an ancient bowling green. We would often have a few drinks and a game of bowls before going into rehearsals. It was a marvellous company to work with and we put on very few duds as a result.

When he was stationed in Winchester, George Baker saw a poster advertising the Salisbury Arts Theatre and he had an intuitive feeling that he would one day, be working in Salisbury,. Fate played its hand and it wasn't too long before he had an audition with Guy Verney who chose him to work with the company in Carlisle.

In his book 'The Way to Wexford' George wrote; 'It was a splendid company, working for it had the feeling of being on summer hols.' He enjoyed working with Leslie Phillips who taught him a great deal about acting, particularly comedy and the theatre in general. He found Rachel Roberts 'full of wit and bubbling over with laughter. She

'May I Introduce': clockwise from top left: Gwen Watford, George Baker, Kenneth Williams, Prunella Scales, Timothy West.

was an explosion of talent. She is one of the souls I often recall with great joy.' He felt she was always destined for stardom.

He speaks of good days in Salisbury and working with Frank Hauser although he was a hard taskmaster. Above all though, he recalls the pleasure of working with Prunella Scales.

> I was terrified of Pru Scales, she was so clever, but I loved acting with her and remember our playing *'While the Sun Shines'* with the deepest affection… *'Home and Beauty'* with Gwen Watford and Prunella Scales; the cup runneth over.'

In an interview later he said: ' 'I was in awe of her but she is a very clever woman; very sharp; very business like; a wonderful comedienne'.

Whilst in Salisbury, Pru lived at Crane Lodge and George would often go over on a Sunday to do the cooking, to talk and to listen to music. George's lodgings were over the butcher's shop in Fisherton Street which was very useful in times of rationing!

Like most actors he frequented 'The King's Arms' just down the road from the theatre. He remembers their drinks being lined up on the counter ready for them as they rushed down to the pub before closing time.

One particular character he remembers sitting at the bar. He was a local cobbler who had just had his eighth child. 'Yus sir, I may be small, but I treads well!' he said with pride!

A company from the Arts Theatre continued working in Carlisle for two years and then in 1954 they branched out to play a season in the Hulme Playhouse in Manchester which proved to be just as successful.

 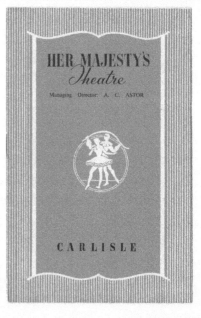

Carlisle and Manchester programmes, 1954.

The *News Chronicle* reported: 'Manchester – the city where 50 years ago the famous Miss. Horniman established the first English repertory theatre – is putting 'rep' on the map again. Putting it on the theatrical map again is the Salisbury Arts Theatre.'

The first play chosen to launch the season was '*The Angel of Montparnasse*' by Jean Giltne which was considered rather a risk in the eyes of Michael Wide: 'But that is as it should be' he said: ' I'm all in favour of the man who plants his footsteps off the beaten track – and the man who's not too sure before the curtain goes up.'

He need not have worried, as the company, which already had such actresses of the calibre of Avril Conquest, Dulcie Bowman and Joan White, and strengthened by the addition of Robert Eddison from the Old Vic and Carol Marsh who starred in 'Brighton Rock', was very quickly, a huge success. A local critic wrote: ' A touch of artistry has upgraded Mr. Brenna's Hulme Playhouse to Repertory Theatre Class One. The debut last night of a fine new company in a brave new comedy '*The Angel of Montparnasse*' was distinctly different.... Now it is up to keen playgoers to give the new company a welcome. They're worth it.' Geoffrey Edwards, Salisbury producer, remarked; 'The most encouraging thing that has happened over our first play is the very considerable number of people who have not been to this theatre before but have come to see us.'

During the early fifties as well as the burgeoning talent of Ronald Harwood, a stream of other young actors and actresses joined the company with many putting down a marker for a successful future; such as Gillian Raine, Ronald Allen, Heather Chasen, George Selway, the local actor, Daniel Pettiward and the man who soon became the Playhouse's 'matinee idol', Gerald Flood.

John Mullen, a theatregoer of the time recalled:

The ladies loved this actor and I always said that nobody could sneer quite like Gerald Flood. It is a great asset for any actor to have a great sneer. When he left, the ladies of Salisbury went into mourning.

The men were well catered for too at this time by the alluring presence of Nancie Herrod. I was very much in love with Nancie but I was not short of competition as all men who saw her fell under her charm. When eventually she too left, we all wept!

Nancie Herrod was a very talented and versatile actress, who, given the opportunity, could easily have become a national figure, but family life was more important to her. Noel Coward once said to her: 'Never mind Salisbury, you must come to London and you'll be a star.' Salisbury theatregoers were grateful that she didn't but instead decided to stay to entertain them for many a year.

Nancie Herrod was married to Stan Rixon, (known as Rick) the set designer, who with his two colleagues, John Scutt and Alan Daniel managed to create many excellent sets whilst working in very cramped conditions behind the theatre in the cottages. Though, Stephanie Cole particularly remembers the set he created for 'The Tempest'. 'He gave us a set which looked like the desert after the Taliban had raised it!' Rick had quite a fiery temper, perhaps because he had been a fighter pilot during the War. He had already worked with Reggie Salberg and Oliver Gordon so he was part of Reggie's 'family'. It was said that the set was always much better when Nancie Herrod was in the play and apparently he was a dab hand with a spray gun which annoyed Roger Clissold when he started directing plays as he felt it was a lazy way of painting, so he kept trying to hide it from him!

One of Gerald Flood's most noticeable appearances was in May 1954 as Lancelot in the world premiere of Jean Cocteau's play 'The Knights of the Round Table.'

The local *Journal* wrote: ' A Jean Cocteau world premiere at a small weekly repertory theatre is akin to the F.A. Cup being staged at the city's Victoria Park.' and their drama critic wrote: 'If any further proof is needed that Salisbury possesses one of the most enterprising repertory theatres in the country 'The Knights of the Round Table' this week will provide it.'

Of course for such a prestigious occasion there had to be a gala opening night attended by the high and the mighty of South Wiltshire. Amongst them was Cecil Beaton, a huge supporter of the theatre.

He once said: 'To live in Broadchalke and to be able to see an interesting play, well acted and intelligently produced each week in Salisbury – for what more can one ask?'

When talking about actors during this time, mention must also be made of two largely unknown actors who in 1953 during Salisbury's Shopping Week. became 'Playhouse Percy' and 'Playhouse Peggy'. They would walk around Salisbury in disguise and if shoppers spotted them they had to approach them and say' You are Playhouse

Percy (Peggy) and I claim today's voucher prize'. This was a voucher for a guinea. They would also hide three cards around the town which entitled the finders to a voucher for 5/-.The disguises were very varied and included being a decorator, a bus conductor, a girl guide and a vicar. The strange rule was that Percy could only be challenged by a woman and Peggy only by a man! Many people remembered a similar stunt by a national newspaper, people argue that it was the *News Chronicle* while others say it was the *Daily Mail*, that had a character called 'Lobby Lud' who wandered around seaside resorts doing the same thing. The Salisbury version proved to be very popular and gained a lot of publicity for the theatre.

The backbone of any theatre company though, are those people who do not share the limelight, but work backstage and in the offices. Henry Graveney and Neville Dickin the set designers whose talents and ingenuity created many outstanding sets in amazingly cramped conditions and Kate Servian the wardrobe mistress who often had to rely on material contributions from the general public but who managed to create so many realistic and often beautiful costumes, all were backstage heroes.

Often mentioned are Charlie Salter, known affectionately as 'Old Faithful' who did so many different jobs around the theatre and was always there when needed and Roberto Petrarca known as 'the fastest carpenter on two legs' or 'the singing carpenter' as he loved to sing opera as he worked. He was a very versatile and strong man. Timothy West remembers him pulling a nail out of a piece of wood and then straightening it!

One theatregoer, Peggy Belgrove remembers a production of '*Hamlet*' when Hamlet's father's ghost played the first scene with a nail stuck in his foot, left on stage by a carpenter. Nobody knows if it was one of Roberto's!

Also often showered with praise was Harry Brooks who used to drive one of the theatre's lorries but also played small parts in the pantomime. It was once said of him that 'he was the kind of man without whom the theatre would fall to pieces.'

Pride of place though, must go to the Astins, Stan and Pauline. Stan started at the Arts Theatre in August 1949 as Master Carpenter and Pauline signed on at the same time but before becoming Box

Stan and Pauline Astin, October 1966 (From the Salisbury Journal Archive)

Office manageress. She then spent three years working in the bar, as yet unlicensed, chiefly preparing teas for the touring company. In 1954 Stan became Stage Director eventually becoming Resident Stage Manager and Electrician. The former title covering miscellaneous activities such as locking up the premises, unblocking the drains and acting as, he used to refer to himself as 'Can Carrier in Chief!' However, occasionally his unfortunate stutter landed him in dangerous situations such as when his call for help was misinterpreted and he nearly electrocuted himself!

Pauline's motto was 'service with a smile' and she always made sure that she watched every Dress Rehearsal so she could advise customers what to expect. Sometimes she could be very direct: 'No dear this is not suitable for you, come next week, it's a much better play!' was often heard! She would sometimes have the task of locking up and would often be heard rattling the keys at the back of the auditorium if a Dress Rehearsal went on far too long! They were a much loved couple and when they retired in 1972 Daniel Pettiward wrote: 'The atmosphere behind the scenes at the Playhouse will be much impoverished without Stan's ebullient personality' and the knowledge and experience he was able to pass on to others. Equally Pauline's kindly presence in the Box Office, not to mention her remarkable efficiency, will be sorely missed by thousands of grateful playgoers.'

There are of course, so many more people without whom the Arts Theatre would not have survived.

And what about the ubiquitous Michael Wide – Director, General Manager and Playwright. A personality who had already figured largely in the Arts Theatre fledgling success and history? In April 1955, the 10th anniversary of the theatre, he said to the theatregoers: 'It has been an uphill fight but I do think that Salisbury has at long last warmed to its theatre and its most talented company and providing there are no hidden reefs ahead we should continue to sail in fairly calm waters.'

Then later that month still using a nautical theme, he said that as the theatre was 'on the crest of a wave' it was time for him to venture into a wider field and he announced that he was to leave the Playhouse.

In his six years he had seen many changes. He had played a prominent part in the fight for the theatre's survival and had helped considerably in developing the profile of the theatre and its popularity and respect throughout the theatrical world. With Peter Potter and Anthony Bavage the Touring Manager he helped to plan and organise the various schemes involving the different companies as well as working on the touring policy and he also helped to organise the successful seasons in Carlisle and Manchester.

The Board expressed to him 'its warm appreciation for his devoted service to the Playhouse and to the promotion of first class dramatic work in the city over a period of six crucial years.' Little did Michael Wide realise though, that by leaving, he opened up the way for the Playhouse to move into its most important and successful era because he mentioned that he was about to leave to an old friend, to see if he would be interested in coming to Salisbury. That old friend was Reginald Salberg.

In one of his last programme notes Michael Wide wrote: 'I am very glad to be able to announce, on behalf of my directors, that my old friend Reginald Salberg is to succeed me as General Manager of the theatre when I leave on 16th May. We are very lucky to have secured his services and I know that the management of the theatre will be in good hands.'

Enter the Playhouse's Godfather.

ACT TWO

The Salberg Years

7

'I HAVE FALLEN IN LOVE WITH SALISBURY AND I WOULD LIKE TO REMAIN HERE FOR A LONG WHILE'

Reggie Salberg

MICHAEL WIDE'S DESCRIPTION of the Playhouse being now 'on the crest of a wave' was somewhat exaggerated. It had certainly weathered many a storm and the sea had certainly been very rough and unfriendly at times but despite all the trauma during those early years, the theatre was functioning successfully and it was beginning to earn a deserved reputation for excellent and enjoyable productions. However, its future still remained very uncertain. There was much that needed to be improved and many plans needed to be made if the Playhouse was to continue to develop into a regional, repertory theatre that could face a confident future.. The hopes and the dreams were definitely there, it just needed someone with inspiration and a clear vision to bring these hopes to fruition and to make these dreams come true. That man proved to be Reginald Salberg.

On Michael Wide's suggestion, Reggie Salberg invited himself down to see if Salisbury was appropriate to add to his collection, having managed several theatrical companies in the past including Preston and Hull. His brother Derek once remarked that 'he went through repertory companies as some people go through pocket handkerchiefs.' For the past eight years Reggie Salberg had been running a company at the Hippodrome Theatre in Preston. With the closure of Preston's other theatre, the Hippodrome then became seasonal, only doing repertory for part of the year. He had also run a second company in collaboration with his brother Derek at Hull.

Reggie Salberg was part of a theatrical dynasty. His father Leon, a Polish Jew started out by running a furniture business but at the age of 40, the Alexandra Theatre in Birmingham came up for sale and Leon decided to buy it. This was eventually taken over by his son Derek. Another son, Stanley went on to run cinemas and theatres in the north of England whilst Reggie's younger brother Keith became a theatre agent. His cousin Basil Thomas ran the theatre in Wolverhampton.

At his interview the applicants were whittled down to just two. Reggie Salberg was given the job by one vote. However, it was a fluke as one of the directors thought he was voting for the other candidate when he cast his vote for Reggie!

When he arrived at the Playhouse on 16th May 1955, it was operating on the basis of weekly repertory which meant over forty different plays a year and the box office takings such as they were, were supplemented by a nominal grant from the Arts Council and much smaller grants from local authorities. But for the continued support of the Theatregoers' Club the Playhouse would certainly have closed down.

In one of his programme notes Reggie Salberg commented:

When I arrived in Salisbury in 1955 we were a weekly rep and under threat of closure. On more than one occasion the directors had to lend money out of their own pockets to pay the wages. In 1955 the company consisted of 8 actors and 3 stage management who also occasionally acted. The total cost of running the theatre was £22,000. The scenery was often transported by a wheel barrow from an old garage up the road.

At the age of 39 he knew he was about to face his greatest challenge.

Reggie Salberg was born in Birmingham in 1915. Growing up in a theatrical family, theatres soon became part of his family life and was an important part in his childhood development. The annual visit to the pantomime fired him with a love of live theatre and the family home was often filled with theatrical people and he once said: 'My father used to invite members of the cast home for a meal and I developed a taste for theatre people which has never left me.'

In a later interview he commented: 'Theatre people are like circus people. They just can't keep away from the smell of the greasepaint, and eventually it gets into your blood.'

He was very close to his older brother Derek and they would often play at 'theatres' together in the holidays.

Derek remembered: 'I can only recall one quarrel with him. When he was about five, we decided one night, when we were sharing a bedroom that we would each make up a story. His was about a county cricket match, a game to which he is only slightly less devoted than I, in which he kept referring to a batsman scoring boundary twos.

I pointed out that boundaries counted either four or six which he hotly disputed, insisting that he had seen many boundary twos scored. This caused such a violent quarrel between us that we had to be forcibly separated!'

Reggie Salberg was educated at Clifton College in Bristol where he was a keen sportsman and was regularly drafted into the school plays under his mentor Mr. Toms. When it came to deciding on a career his father thought it would be a good idea if he got away from the theatrical environment and he persuaded him to take up Law.

He duly qualified as a solicitor gaining his B.A. at Oxford. He enjoyed his four years there inasmuch as he did any work at all. He claims to have attended 12 lectures during his time at Oxford as the sports field became more of an attraction than the lecture hall and he became an excellent rugby player. He then hated being articled and working in a solicitor's office.

In an interview at the Playhouse he once freely admitted that he'd forgotten most of his law 'But even now it's quite useful when one is dealing with the bigger theatrical sharks, to drop in the conversation that one is a lawyer!'

He was playing for Moseley when war broke out and interrupted what could have been a promising career. As well as being a first class rugby player he also excelled as a cricketer, and he invariably appeared at matches in an array of splendidly different coloured caps, which greatly impressed the opposition who were not to know that he had won them, not on the cricket field but for drinking during his days at Oxford!

During the war he served in the Army and appeared in small roles in ENSA shows. His stage debut as the 'Fairy Queen' in a Middle East concert party nearly proved to be his last appearance! Apparently the Padre told him that one soldier had written home saying how much he enjoyed the show but that his illusion had been shattered during the interval when stepping outside he saw the Fairy Queen lift 'her' skirts to spend a penny in the sand!

After the war the 'smell of the greasepaint' proved to be irresistible and he forgot all about being a solicitor and he became the lessee of the Savoy Theatre in Kettering where he set up his first repertory company.

Derek Salberg wrote: 'One good thing certainly emerged for Reggie whilst at Kettering, he engaged an actress named Noreen Craven whom he eventually married in 1948. She brought with her an additional bonus in the person of her mother Lady Anna Craven, a delightful but somewhat eccentric lady, who would elegantly serve her guests with tea out of a lovely china teapot. Her table would be covered with a beautiful lace tea-cloth and the floor with somewhat ancient dog excreta!'

Noreen Craven (Photographer Peter Brown)

Noreen Craven trained at the Guildhall School of Music and Drama and spent her early years in repertory at Coventry, Bournemouth and York. As an actress she appeared in many Salisbury plays, notably as Mrs. Higgins on '*Pygmalion*' and as Madame Kapek in '*Bitter Sanctuary*' but it is as a very respected director that she will be remembered. Although, even after many years of successful directing, first night nerves would still affect her. She would be worried that it wouldn't be 'all right on the night'; a feeling that would continue to mount as the house lights went down and the opening night finally arrived. 'It's always the same', she once said, 'I would probably be happier sitting at home watching television but I couldn't do that. These actors are doing it for me and I couldn't let them down by not being there.'

The company knew that with Noreen directing, together they would be able to create an excellent production, although occasionally she would worry the cast by arriving at rehearsals carrying a pile of books saying: 'Well, I don't know what's it's all about but it's in here somewhere!'

Together they made a very incongruous couple. Noreen, tall, outgoing with a strong, clear, forceful voice and Reggie, short, reserved and with a quiet, measured but memorable way of speaking which actors loved to imitate. 'Like a salt and pepper cruet set an actor once remarked!

When Reggie Salberg arrived in Salisbury he said: 'The Salisbury Arts Theatre enjoys a national reputation for its high standard and its enterprise and it is my earnest endeavour to see that such a reputation remains undiminished.'

Reggie couldn't do much about the building but he could certainly improve the standard and the quality of performances. One of his main aims was first to increase the amount of rehearsal time to two weeks and then eventually to increase the performance times. Weekly rep was a hard taskmaster. As Sir Peter Hall once remarked: 'In weekly rep all you can do is sympathize with the actors and make sure they don't bump into each other!'

Like a successful football manager Reggie also needed to get a good team around him. As well as finding new talent, this also meant persuading people he had worked with before and knew he could trust, to come to work in Salisbury. It also meant scouring the drama schools and the theatre world for the talent he needed to make his successful company. He was excellent at spotting emerging talent although at one RADA performance he wrote 'No!' in the programme notes against the name 'Albert Finney'!

One of his most important early acquisitions was someone who became his most loyal and talented colleague and very close friend. A man who became a much loved character for the company but also for the theatregoers – Oliver Gordon. Ollie, as he was affectionally

Ollie Gordon in dressing room, January 1969 (Salisbury Journal)

known as, was not only a very talented director but he also achieved great success and admiration as being the best pantomime Dame ever to appear at the Playhouse.

Oliver Gordon was born in September 1903 as Oliver Gordon Battcock. One can perhaps appreciate why he dropped the surname. He developed his skills as an actor and director in many theatres including the Theatre Royal Windsor where he worked with Ralph Lynn on the Ben Travers farces and where he honed his skills as a farceur. He also worked at the Alexandra Theatre in Birmingham with his younger brother Henry Marshall and for a while in West End theatres.

It was whilst working in Hull though, that Reggie Salberg was able to appreciate his many talents and he was delighted when Ollie came to Salisbury to take over the production of the annual pantomimes.

Reggie Salberg's first Salisbury pantomime was 'Robinson Crusoe' and Reggie commented: 'Frankly, it was not very good.' This is despite it being written by Henry Marshall and having Ronald Harwood as Billy Crusoe in the leading role. By the time they reached the third week they were playing to half empty houses.

However, his second pantomime, again written by Henry Marshall, was a great success mainly thanks to the appearance of Leonard Rossiter as 'Len, a not very bad robber.' The total seal of success for Salisbury pantomimes came though in 1957 when Oliver Gordon arrived to produce '*Aladdin and his Wonderful Lamp.*' Ollie played 'Wishee-Washee', Ian Mullins was 'Abanazar' and Timothy West played the most important part of 'Genie of the Lamp'!

Ollie then continued to produce the pantomimes and to appear in them as one of the main comedy characters such as 'Idle Jack' in the 1959 pantomime: '*Dick Whittington and his Cat*' and 'Silly Sammy' in the 1960 pantomime '*Jack and the Beanstalk*'. He first 'went into skirts' in the 1964 pantomime '*Cinderella*' where as one of the Ugly Sisters, he played 'Fifi' alongside David Daker's 'Mimi.' It was a never to be forgotten duo!

His last performance as director (the title from producer to director had been changed) and Dame was in the 1969 pantomime: '*Aladdin*'. He had been ill for some time but insisted on going through the run despite often being doubled up with pain in the Wings. He even insisted on going through the mangle during the laundry scene.

Before his last performance, his doctor said 'I'll meet him in the King's Arms afterwards for a pint.' That meeting sadly never happened.

Actors loved working with him and his rehearsals were legendary. He liked to give people nicknames. Stephanie Cole was 'Dame Cole'; Barbara Wilson, the Wardrobe Mistress was 'Madam Barbara'; Christopher Biggins was 'Sunflower and Sunshine',

Cinderella: Ollie Gordon as Fifi and David Daker as Mimi, "The Ugly Sisters", December 1964 (Photographer Unknown)

Sonia Woolley, who often did Ollie's make up when he was the Dame, was known as 'Auntie Son' and he could never remember Suzanne Peverill's name so poor thing was known as 'Miss. Vesuvius'! Knight Mantell was known as 'Chloe' and he never really knew why! But most people were simple known as 'Cock!'

When rehearsals were extended to three weeks he initially didn't know what to do with the last week; 'Better go off to the cinema I suppose.' Michael Stroud said that Ollie could bang out 'King Lear' in a week.

Ollie was of the old school and kept his directions simple. In his book 'Mr. Home pronounced Hume', William Douglas Home wrote: 'Once whilst directing *Romeo and Juliet* he halted the rehearsals while he went to do what he was always pleased to call 'a weasel'. On retuning he called out to Romeo: 'OK cock – finish what you've got to say and then piss off left!'

Robin Ellis recalled:

> For me – not long out of Cambridge and accustomed to discussion and dispute at rehearsals – to be told to 'piss off left, cock' and 'get your laugh in here' were pieces of direction both novel and refreshing. I did as I was told!

Chris Harris also recalls a time when the villain in the pantomime asked Ollie 'But why do I have to enter down left?' To which Ollie replied: 'Don't ask me cock, it's near your dressing room, so don't complain!' Chris recalls one of Ollie's rehearsals:

> He would sit in the stalls, light up his pipe and dim the house lights. You would see this towering inferno and then you would hear this deep snoring. At one rehearsal the actors went through the whole run through and then tiptoed out for a cup of tea. On returning they called out: 'We've finished Oliver!' Ollie then woke up suddenly, came up to the stage and then promptly started to give them notes on their performances!

If an actor asked him what was the motivation he would be told: 'your motivation is your pay packet!'

He also had his own sayings: If he was not sure what to do he would say; 'It's a matter of complete imbuggerance to me old cock!' and if he wasn't happy with a performance he would say to Reggie: 'she is a complete non-offerer old cock!'

Both Henry Marshall and Ollie Gordon adhered strongly to the traditions of pantomime and would not tolerate any young actor who thought that pantomimes were a good excuse to be lazy or to 'muck about.' Any last night gags always had to be passed by Ollie first.

Cricket was Ollie and Reggie's other great love and Ollie would insist on having the Summer months off so he could play cricket. He made his debut for Buckinghamshire in 1925 and played Minor Counties cricket from 1925 to 1951 apart from the war years. He captained Datchet for 25 years and in the early sixties he captained a talented group of cricketers known as the Incogniti Club.

In his speech at Ollie's funeral Reggie said: 'In the Summer he turned to his even greater love, cricket at which he excelled and he still struck terror in the hearts of opposing batsmen even when in his sixties.'

At auditions an actor would often be asked: 'Are you a batsman or a bowler?' It paid to share this interest. One actor was asked: 'Are you right handed or left handed? By the way you're playing Laertes in our next production of 'Hamlet.'

Lionel Guyett remembers being directed by Ollie when in two days they had read through, blocked the moves and were working on Act One.. Ollie then announced that he was going off somewhere important for three days and that the cast were to have learnt their lines by the time he came back. He actually disappeared to attend a three day cricket festival!

Trevor Taylor, a theatregoer at the time recalls: 'In what I think was probably 1963, the Incogniti were playing a two day match against Southern Command at Tidworth and we were billeted at the School of Artillery Officers Mess at Larkhill. At Oliver's suggestion we attended a performance of 'Emma' at the Salisbury Playhouse as he had led us to believe that the play was based on the somewhat licentious activities of Lady Hamilton. On the night, what transpired to be Miss. Austen's wordy and genteel prose, proved too much for we cricketing proles and realising we had been duped, we departed the theatre en masse at the end of the first act and adjourned to the nearest hostelry. Next day back at the match, as revenge we hoisted Oliver's tattered blazer to the top of the flagpole and ceremonially burned his old plimsolls!'

Above all though, Ollie was a much respected and much loved man. Chris Biggins spoke of him:

'He was the kind of Dame that would throw himself through a trapdoor. He was a big influence on me. He was a good old fashioned director.'

'Stephanie Cole said of him: 'I adored Ollie. Everyone learnt so much from him. There was not one ounce of malice in him. Never bitchy, never judgemental. He was much older than us but he never talked down to you. You never noticed the age difference.'

And at his funeral Reggie said: 'He was a wonderful man and hadn't an enemy in the world. We will miss him, but can console ourselves with the thought that few people can have enjoyed their lives so much.' He finished by saying, 'Goodbye Cock!'

After his death at the far too young age of 67, a fund was set up in his memory which would provide the money to allow children, who could otherwise not afford to go, to attend the pantomime each year.

Henry Marshall (Emma Battcock, with permission)

Reggie's other early trusted lieutenant was Henry Marshall who wrote all the pantomime scripts from 1955 to 1985. He once wrote:' No one ever grows up completely. There are pockets of childhood in us all and it is in one of the larger pockets that many of us keep pantomime.'

Henry, born in February 1920 was Oliver Gordon's younger brother. For a while he worked as a stage manager but soon found his love of writing for the stage and in particular pantomimes. He worked in many theatres including the Theatre Royal in Windsor where he worked with his brother Oliver. He also had the opportunity to work with the Lupino family and later included several of their routines in his pantomimes. He also became an eminent fight director which became very useful in the rough and tumble of pantomime land. A skill he continued to teach at RADA until his retirement in 1995. His wife for several years, Stephanie Cole, became an expert sword-fighter herself and had a memorable sword fight with Brigit Forsyth in the 1964 production of 'Cinderella.'

Like his brother, Henry took the traditions of pantomimes very seriously. Stephanie Cole writes: 'Henry's writing was based in historical fact or legend, so the pantos are rooted in our past and our myths. The routines in Henry's pantomimes, based as they are on centuries of knowledge, are foolproof if all the instructions are followed. Panto is a very disciplined art-form – not a free for all as some imagine.' She performed in four of Henry's pantomimes and reflects: 'there is no doubt that they were the very best, written and directed by a master.' Henry also gave strict instructions to his actors and like Ollie, did not like acting ad-libbing or wandering about. He also gave very detailed set descriptions which had to be carried out to the letter. Changes were few and only if Henry agreed to them.

He would spend many hours travelling to other theatres to watch pantomimes and he would collect jokes and routines which were then put into his 'Gag Book' which eventually became a pantomime bible. Every possible joke and routine from the Salisbury pantomimes can be found here and it is an incredible source of material should anyone wish to put on a traditional pantomime. The Henry Marshall Gag Book can be seen in the Theatre Collection of the University of Bristol and has been written out in detail in Chris Abbott's excellent book about Henry Marshall's Salisbury pantomimes: 'Putting on Panto to Pay for the Pinter.'

Henry though, often had to be aware of Reggie acting as script editor and there was one line in Henry's 'Dick Whittington' that Reggie told him point blank he simply could not use. Alice Fitzwarren is distraught at Dick Whittington leaving London and cries out: 'Oh,

Dick, Oh, Dick, I do miss my Dick.' Henry couldn't understand why Reggie was so insistent!

David Ryall recalls his time in 'Cinderella' playing one half of the Broker's Men double-act with Michael Poole: and 'the voluminous rehearsal schedules pinned on the board and conducted it seemed all over Salisbury were reminiscent of the D-Day landing orders.' He asked Reggie's permission to throw sweets out to the children. He reluctantly agreed with: 'As long as I don't have to buy them.' so

> I bought some from the sweetshop by the entrance to the theatre and duly tossed some to the children during our duet singing number. As we danced and sang I felt something hit me and discovered to my astonished disillusionment that they were then throwing them back.!

Theatregoers and critics alike were often amazed at the versatility of the company. A critic wrote after one production of 'Aladdin' -'An inevitable pleasure to be derived from post-pantomime productions is that of marvelling at the many astonishing changes of sex and status that have occurred. A Chinese policeman miraculously appears this week as a silver haired maiden aunt and here is perky Aladdin himself, looking ravishing in a bustle and being tempestuously wooed by his ex-genie!'

Henry's pantomimes were of an era and eventually the Playhouse moved on to other writers especially David Horlock and Jack Chissick but his pantomimes have left an indelible mark at the Playhouse and are an important part of its rich history.

In his obituary for *The Stage*, Stephanie Cole wrote: 'Marshall was a great teacher, an eccentric who entertained while he taught and was much loved by those who worked with him….He was passionate about the theatre and cared deeply about those working in it.'

So Reggie now had two experienced lieutenants to work with and to share the heavy burden of running the theatre. The next task was to build up a talented and reliable company of actors and Reggie was certainly an expert in doing just that.

8

'GO AWAY AND HAVE A SANDWICH AND A PINT OF BEER AND WE'LL TRY AGAIN LATER'

Reggie Salberg

A S GENERAL MANAGER of the Playhouse, one of Reggie Salberg's many tasks was to scour theatres, go to drama schools, attend end of term shows, look in on summer seasons and talk to dozens of managers and directors in order to find members for his Salisbury company. He had inherited a talented company but Reggie knew he had to continue to find a group of actors who would not only add to the success of the present company but move the standard of acting always that notch higher. It was soon quite obvious that he had the Midas touch.

Many of Reggie's interviews took place in Sally Spruce's Costumiers in London. This shop had a family connection and interviewing in London would save the poor actor having to pay out for the train fare all the way to Salisbury. The shop was always full of people and costumes and actors would often have difficulty in locating Reggie, who was small in stature, amongst all the clothes.

David Simeon remembers seeing Reggie's long nose first, poking through a rail of costumes and one actor remembers sitting down amidst rows of costumes looking over at a little man who was also sitting down and staring back at him. The actor asked: 'Are you waiting to see Reggie Salberg as well?'

'No,' came the reply. 'I am Reggie Salberg.'

Lionel Guyett recalls his interview at Sally Spruce's when Reggie conducted the whole interview looking out of the window! On one occasion the shop was so full that the only space Reggie had to interview an actress was in the toilet and he didn't quite know the etiquette of whether or not to offer her the only seat!

Sometimes it also pays to know people. Reggie Salberg was getting desperate as he was casting around for an actor to play Tyballt in the 1966 production of 'Romeo and Juliet'. Barbara Wilson, the wardrobe mistress suggested Frank Ellis. Reggie approved of him and he stayed on as part of the company.

Familiarity though, was always very useful as it was in the case of Ollie Gordon and Henry Marshall. So some of Reggie's early appointment were people that he had worked with before. One such actor was Leonard Rossiter who worked for Reggie Salberg at the Preston Hippodrome. Reggie remembers: 'We had to cast a small part in Joseph Colton's 'The Gay Dog' and he read it pretty badly'. Reggie told him 'to go away and have a sandwich and a pint of beer and we'll try again later'. Reggie however, sensed a talent and persuaded him to read it again. 'This he did equally badly but very differently, and reluctantly Alan Foss the director considered casting him. Impressed with his dedication, Reggie offered him a chance to continue with the company in the role of assistant manager.

The Bespoke Overcoat, November 1955. Leonard Rossiter as Morry, Fredrick Peisley as Fender (Photographer Unknown)

Reggie always spoke of him with affection. He recalled:

Len was a very loyal man and always acknowledged his debt to me.
Not only because I launched him on his career but because I once
talked him out of giving up the stage at a time a few years later when
he felt his career was not making sufficient progress.

On 'Desert Island Discs' Leonard Rossiter said that he owed everything
to Reggie Salberg.

Knowing his hidden talent, Reggie invited him to join the
Salisbury company and his first performance in 1955 was in Wolf
Markowitz' '*The Bespoke Overcoat*' with Freddie Peisley. The next
month he appeared in Colley Cibber's '*She Would and She Would
Not.*' – a rarely performed 19th century comedy which sent many
London critics heading towards the Playhouse. Len Rossiter was a
great success and *The Times* wrote: 'The real life of the revival is Mr.
Leonard Rossiter who gave the plot real animation.'

Babes in the Wood, December 1956. Leonard Rossiter is 5th from the left playing
"Len, a not very bad robber", Josephine Tewson played Robin Hood
(Photographer Unknown)

However, it wasn't until December of the following year that
the Salisbury theatregoers took him to their hearts and appreciated
what an incredible comic actor he was developing into. In '*Babes in
the Wood*' he played Len, 'a not very bad robber.' In a very talented

cast it was his performance that everyone was talking about. The *Salisbury Times* wrote that he 'gave a magnificent performance; he is an absolute natural and quite steals the show.' and *The Stage* wrote: 'There are so many good things in this show but nothing better than Leonard Rossiter's performance. It is a real gem.'

People remember the mad duel the two robbers had using every conceivable weapon including guns, swords, scimitars, water pistols etc. After one particularly mad duel Ian Mullins, who was playing 'The Sheriff of Nottingham', said to Len: 'Please stop making me laugh so much, I'm supposed to be the villain!' Ian also remembers the occasion when Len's wig fell off during one scene. He quickly picked it up but instead of putting it on correctly he put in on back to front and played it like that for the rest of the scene!

Also in the cast of '*Babes in the Wood*' was Josephine (Jo) Tewson. She had arrived in Salisbury just before Leonard Rossiter, having been seen by Reggie Salberg in Morcambe, and he had cast her for a part in the comedy '*Clutterbuck.*' with the princely salary of £8 a week. 'A kittenish part' said Miss Tewson', and I've never been suitable for kittenish parts – never.'

However, her role in '*Babes in the Wood*' as Robin Hood suited her perfectly. The *Salisbury Times* wrote: 'Josephine Tewson, the charming and vivacious principal boy turns out to have quite a pleasant singing voice and her duets with Maid Marian are clear and tuneful.'

It was three years though, before she was to appear in another pantomime. This time she played 'Dick Whittington' in the 1959 production of '*Dick Whittington and his Cat.*' Once again she was surrounded by rising talent. The play was produced by Oliver Gordon who also appeared in it as 'Idle Jack'. Nancie Herrod played Tiddles the Cat ; Ronald McGill played Sarah the Cook, Philip Madoc, the Sultan of Morocco and Ian Mullins was once again, the villain – this time the evil King Rat.

Jo particularly remembers one of her earlier performances when 'I strode on to the villagers of Highgate Hill, feather in my cap, bundle over my shoulder, Puss at my side saying: 'Well, my lasses and lads, do you know who I am? To be greeted by a loud voice from the Circle – 'It's my Auntie Jo!'

Earlier, when she was appearing as Robin Hood she had two rather more important and influential people watching her – Julian Slade and Dorothy Reynolds who liked what they saw and what they heard and offered her a part in 'Free As Air' at the Savoy, which was intended to be a following up to their incredibly successful revue: 'Salad Days'. Leonard Rossiter was also given a part as an understudy. A romance slowly developed between them and they were married at St. Nicholas' Church in Harpenden. Sadly though the marriage did not last very long as Jo said: 'We were two frightened rep people, thrown together in London. If we had stayed at Salisbury we might not have got together. We admired each other's work and took that as love. He was lovely to work with , a smashing company man but not a good husband.'

At Salisbury Jo became know as a very talented actress. 'I once played three cookery charwomen on the trot', she remembers. For her performance in 'Small Hotel' alongside a veteran of comedy plays, Leslie Henson, The Salisbury Times wrote: 'Jo Tewson, whose character studies are always quite brilliant, makes a terrifying harridan of the kitchen cook, Mrs. Gammon.' Jo once said that they all basically the same character. The ambition is to hope that the audience doesn't recognise you.

In 1956 the audience certainly recognised the rain constantly dripping onto the stage during a performance of Agatha Christie's 'Black Coffee'. Jo remembers the rain dripping on the head of Brian Kent who was playing the Inspector; rain was dripping on Ken Keeling, who was the body lying on the floor; there was a puddle forming on the sofa which Doreen Andrew had to sit on; Jo's dress was a slinky red crepe de chine number which began to shrink and change colour; Graham Armitage was nearly electrocuted when he tried to switch on the standard lamp; and to crown it all the piano was floating in the orchestra pit much to the consternation of those sitting in the front row!

One week's rehearsal was a punishing schedule: Read through the play Tuesday morning; Learn Act One Tuesday afternoon; Rehearse Act One Wednesday morning; Learn Act Two Wednesday afternoon; Rehearse Act Two Thursday morning; Learn Act Three Thursday afternoon; Rehearse Act Three Friday morning; Friday

(left) Reggie Salberg cartoon (Daniel Pettiward)
(right) Reggie Salberg seated at rehearsals (Photographer Peter Brown)

afternoon run through the whole play; Saturday morning run through whole play. Sometimes the first performance would be later on that day. The unforgivable sin was to have your script at rehearsals.

Helen Dorward remembers the pressure: 'I was being measured for my costume for '*Jane Eyre*' and I hadn't yet read the script!' Hardly any time for a social life. The occasional visit to the local pub or a meal with friends, time to take the dog for a walk and if you were lucky a trip to the seaside if someone had a car but no further than 20 mile radius from the theatre, but don't be late back for rehearsals! – as Jo once was and incurred the wrath of Ollie Gordon! You weren't allowed to be ill either. Jo once played Rosalind with a broken Achilles tendon and Maggie Denyer recalls being very ill with flu and Reggie crawling up to her bedroom saying 'Oh, you'll be alright won't you?'

But it was a very happy time for a young actress; like Jo Helen learnt so much about acting being in so many different roles and being able to work with such masters as Ollie Gordon.

It was also a time to secure life long friendships and Jo recalls with great affection working with Maggie Denyer, Derek Smee, Angus

Mackay, Janet Hargeaves, Bob Mcbain, Ronnie McGill, Helen Jessop and Maggie Jones.

RADA was one place where Reggie Salberg often went to in order to search for new talent for his company. It was here that he saw Maggie Jones appearing as Mrs. Dawson in 'Frieda'. He was so impressed that he immediately engaged her to join the Salisbury sister company that was working in Hull. Her first appearance in Salisbury at the age of 23, was as the nanny in 'All For Mary' – 'a delightful cameo' according to Reggie.

After a succession of these cameo roles she soon became one of the company's leading ladies specialising in playing characters that were much older than her real age. Richard Findlater wrote after seeing her in 'The Walled Garden'. 'Margaret Jones, excellent anchor-woman'. I jotted down to discover later that she was half the age of the character she played and ten years younger than I imagined.'

She went on to play many memorable roles including that of 'Miss Prism' to Peggy Mount's Lady Bracknell in 'The Importance of Being Earnest'; Donna Lucia D'alvadorez in 'Charley's Aunt'; Emilia in 'Othello' and Madame Arcati in 'Blithe Spirit.'

In 1957 she played the part of Maria Helliwell in Priestley's 'When We Are Married.' to excellent reviews. She must have enjoyed the experience because in 1988 she returned to the new Playhouse to play the same part! This was a happy reunion for her because the play was directed by Hugh Waters with whom Maggie had worked at the old Playhouse 25 years before. However, she was a little fearful in returning to Salisbury in case ' round every corner I would bump into a memory!' But they were good memories such as the eccentric arrangements backstage at the old Playhouse which involved an outdoor dash through all weathers if one needed to cross from one side of the stage to the other out of sight of the audience. She recalled: 'We did 'A Midsummer Night's Dream' and I have never seen so many blue fairies in my life. They were having to sprint through freezing rain, pour things!'

Jo Tewson also became very close to Ian Mullins and his wife Helen Dorward. Ian had been seen by Reggie whilst he was working in Seaford and afterwards he received a letter late in 1955 from Reggie offering him 'the possibility of special weeks in Salisbury' – the special weeks turned into four years and eventually he appeared in the grand total of 114 plays. For a long while Ian kept that letter framed in his entrance hall. After his debut in 'Busman's Honeymoon' in 1956, Reggie grew to admire him and eventually trusted him to be one of the Playhouse's regular directors. His directorial debut was 'The Chalk Garden' in 1958 – not the easiest of plays to start with.

Sometimes he acted and directed in the same play, as he did in 'The Rivals.' Ian always had an ambition to run his own theatre and it is no surprise that he eventually managed the Everyman theatre in Cheltenham as well as Farnham and Basingstoke.

Reggie had obviously forgiven him his *faux pas* when in 'Double Image', playing a particularly unpleasant villain, he entered the stage from the wrong window and apologised to the audience. He went off and re-entered the correct window to an immediate loud round of applause. Apparently Reggie then promptly left the theatre without saying a word!

When Ian arrived in Salisbury, he found the quality of the company 'outstanding.' – 'the atmosphere was wonderful, warm and friendly with everyone mucking in.' It wasn't long before Reggie employed Ian's wife Helen who joined the company later in 1956 in 'The School For Spinsters'. For a while they lived in a flat above Reggie's office for a £1 a week. Lying in bed they could hear the clapping of the audience at the end of the show.

At this time Reggie was also managing the theatre in Hull and actors would often be sent there if there wasn't a suitable part in Salisbury. Actors would refer going to Hull as 'being dispatched to the salt mines.' Reggie soon realised though, that trying to manage Hull as well was too much. Financially it was being run at a loss and often Reggie would not be taking a salary.

Maggie Denyer was often banished there if the part involved singing and if Reggie had to sack someone he would immediately travel up to Hull so he wouldn't have to face the consequences!

It's the strong circle of friends they had at the theatre that Helen remembers most.. Times happily spent with Jo Tewson, Timothy West, Derek Benfield, Doreen Andrew, William Gaunt and Christopher Benjamin.

Helen remembers with pride when she played the girl in 'Hot Summer Night'. This was the first appearance of a black actor on the

Salisbury stage – Keefe West. The young girl originally chosen to play the part told Reggie that as she came from Zimbabwe she could not kiss a black man. Helen had no such qualms and played a memorable role.

Ian and Helen both remember, with mixed affection, Geoffrey Lumsden. In Ian's words: 'He was a very fine actor but could be very wicked on stage!' Ian remembers a scene in '*Flare Path*' in which he played the film star and Geoffrey Lumsden played an officer. The dialogue between them was supposed to be brief:

Lumsden: 'Do you know Alice Faye?'

Ian : 'Yes, I do.'

And that was supposed to be that, but Lumsden would not let it rest and he tried to corpse Ian:-

'What is she like?'

'Who else do you know?' and so it went on until other characters broke up the scene!

Jo Tewson remembers two unforgettable occasions. In one play Lumsden walked around the stage with a plaster cast on his arm that said: 'Don't Corpse!' and in '*Witness for the Prosecution*' the cast could not understand what the awful smell was on stage, until they found out that Lumsden had nailed a kipper underneath the witness box!

During his time at the theatre he used to donate a bottle of gin each season to be awarded to the actor by common consent, who had given 'The Worst Performance in a really Good Part.' Apparently Timothy West won several bottles!

Lumsden was also a successful playwright and one of his comedies: '*Gwendoline*' transferred to the West End under its new title '*Caught Napping*'.

Timothy West was in that production, one of 58 plays he was to appear in at the Playhouse during the short period of March 1957 until April 1960. He was initially appointed as Stage Manager but like so many people working backstage he was soon offered an acting role. His break came in '*Mrs. Dane's Defence*'. His first review came in '*The Cherry Orchard*'. The local critic wrote: '….another outstanding piece of work amongst a galaxy of talent, is that by Timothy West, as Firs.' He seemed to be playing a lot of policemen at first but over the short time he was at the theatre he played a rich variety of characters, ranging from the second soldier in 'Romanoff and Juliet' through to Archie Rice's brother in 'The Entertainer' by way of the Genie of the lamp in 'Aladdin' and he would often speak of his time at Salisbury as his apprenticeship.

His pièce de résistance though, was to come later when he returned in 1979 and gave a virtuoso performance as Sir Thomas Beecham in 'Make the Little Beggars Hop'. The Guardian wrote:

> Timothy West is confirmed as the supreme actor-impersonator of the Seventies. He not only looks like Beecham, he has expertly acquired the withering look and the flick of cigar ash off the lapel. Every word, including the marvellous stage whisper, carries irascible nuance...

Both Timothy and his wife Prunella Scales have never forgotten the happy time they had in Salisbury and retain a great amount of affection for the theatre. They have returned several times either together or in solo productions and in 1995, when the Playhouse was saved from closure, Timothy West was the popular choice to perform the re-opening ceremony.

Another very versatile member of the company who arrived in 1960 was in her own words, 'a young and very bouncy girl, who probably got on everyone's nerves' – Patricia Brake. Reggie wanted someone to play the part of Paula in 'Five Finger Exercise.' and like many actors before her, she soon stayed to become part of the company. One of her most important roles was that of 'Betzi' in the world premiere of William Douglas Home's play about Napoleon's love for the young girl Betzi. Or perhaps it was as the carrot in a vegetable ballet or the front part of the cow in the pantomime where she had considerable problems because the girl playing the rear end suffered from claustrophobia?!

Helen Dorward recalled, as well as so many friends amongst the company, a very important member of the theatregoers – Mrs. Margaret Blacking of 21 the Close. Every first night she would sit in the middle of the front row but what was more important was that she would regularly invite members of the cast to her house for meals and allow much of her expensive furniture to be used on stage, although

Betzi, March 1965. Cast included: George Waring (Napoleon), Stephanie Cole (Mrs. Balcombe), Patricia Brake (Betsy). World Premiere (Photographer Unknown)

she did once say no to a request to borrow her grand piano! As she lived by herself in this large, old house, she would often allow cast members to stay there if accommodation proved to be a problem.

Lodgings or 'Digs' were a very important part of an actor's life, as it was imperative to find one where an actor could relax in comfort after strenuous days and nights rehearsing and performing. Christine Edmonds remembers: 'There were several places where we lived such as Truda and Henri Panet's house in Wilton Road and a house in Nelson Road where several of us had rooms.'

Lodgings were also often with Mrs. Thornton and her son Simon who was a stalwart volunteer at the present Playhouse.

For a while, David Simeon, Michael Poole and Robin Ellis shared rooms at a house called 'The Mount.' just off the Old Blandford Road. Stephanie Cole described it as 'an extraordinary tip.' Needless to say, all sorts of activities went on there, including many parties for the whole cast, plus Reggie and Noreen of course. When food was short they would live on 'Mount Stew' which was basically all the leftovers from the week.

Nicholas Lumley recalled his digs above the Indian Takeaway in Fisherton Street. 'For weeks all my clothes reeked of curry!'

Derek Smee remembers lodgings in Fowler's Hill run by a strange landlady who always kept her hat on. On showing him his room she said: 'Guess who slept in that bed last week!' 'Oh, God,' thought Derek, 'she's going to charge me extra!'

Patricia Brake first lodged above a sweet shop in Fisherton Street but then a lady who lived in the Close offered her a room and insisted that she didn't pay anything. She had a housekeeper who made chutney and jam as if she was feeding the whole of the Close. When Patricia came back from the theatre there was always a glass of milk in her room with a muslin cloth placed over it.

David Ryall remembered an incident with his landlady when Reggie came to the rescue: 'I had a romantic attachment at RADA whom I persuaded to come down to Salisbury to spend the night with me in my digs – a bed-sitter at the back of a big house near the theatre owned by a family with high religious principles. I slept the night on the floor with the young lady in my bed as the relationship was platonic but the lady of the house was extremely shocked and loudly irate with me in the morning when she discovered my guest. As Reggie had found me the room himself, in fear of losing it and gaining his disappointment, I followed my father's dictum of 'Always get your story in first' and rushed straight to the theatre and into Reggie's office, blurting out my story – 'She was furious, Reggie and honestly nothing happened at all….' He looked at me as I regained my breath and then said dryly: 'Bad luck!' He then promptly phoned and put things right with my landlady!'

Equally important was to find friendly families where an actor could enjoy the occasional square meal. Robin Ellis recalled: 'the warm welcome of some of the faithful theatregoers who invited me into their homes. Sunday evening dinner at the Braddocks was a welcome regular respite in my first year.' Beryl Bainbridge recalled:

> The whole company was given endless hospitality by an Italian couple who ran a restaurant near the theatre. There was also a very rich man living in the area who would take some of the company up in his plane on Sunday afternoons!'

Christmas was always a very happy, sociable affair as most of the actors had to stay in Salisbury because of the Boxing Day performances and it was not easy to get to London and back quickly. Many remember Chris Biggins being in charge of the entertainment!

Reggie and Noreen would often hold 'open house' and their parties were often legendary. David Simeon recalls being invited by Reggie one afternoon to go swimming in his outdoor pool. 'You don't need a costume,' explained Reggie, and there they all were 'skinny dipping.' David remembers Reggie looking like a little pink hippopotamus wearing nothing but a little straw hat!

Christine Edmonds also recalls:

> The point about Salisbury in those days is that we lived, worked and socialised as a company. It was in fact our family. We used to go 'en masse' to the pub after the performance, for ages it was the Railway Tavern then it was the King's Arms. Of course in those days pubs used to close at 10.30 and often if the play overran or was exceptionally long there would be a panic as to whether w would make it on time, and many a curtain call was given with our daytime clothes beneath our costumes, faces devoid of makeup!

Another very talented actor/playwright who worked for Reggie at this time was Derek Benfield who worked for Reggie at Preston, Hull as well as in Salisbury. He recalled: 'Reggie was one of the best repertory managers of all time – caring, encouraging and also critical. I remember after the opening night of my second play for him – a farce called '*While Parents Sleep*' – he came into my dressing room, stood silent for a moment, and then said, 'Well, at least we know that you can't play farce!'

However, Derek recalled: 'We all learned our craft under Reggie – sometimes playing parts beyond our range – but he believed that experience in a wide variety of roles was the best training ground for an actor.'

Derek's first play in Salisbury was '*Reluctant Heroes*' alongside Ronnie Harwood.. Later he was to appear in a similar farce: '*Worm's Eye View*' where he came up against that wicked Mr. Lumsden! As they were waiting in the wings to make their entrance, their cue was just about to come when Lumsden turned round to Derek and said: ' Come on Benfield – let's show these youngsters how to dry!'

Derek's strong affection for Reggie was evident when he wrote:

I always look back on my days in Salisbury – and Hull and Preston – as some of the happiest of my theatre life. Reggie Salberg was a wonderfully inspired manager, and those who have worked for him have a strong bond. To be an 'old Salbergian' is to belong to a unique club, and we only have to open the doors of that club to bring back a host of happy memories that will stay with us for ever.

A sentiment echoed by Peter Robert Scott and his wife Christine Edmonds (known affectionately as Peter Bob and Crusty!) who in a letter wrote:

It is no coincidence that most actors working in the old Playhouse in the sixties and before still remain friends today. For many of us Salisbury Playhouse was our theatrical Alma Mater. This was due to the atmosphere that Reggie Salberg generated by his generosity and fairness to us and the excellent choice of plays and actors in the company.

The letter ended with:

When you work against time there are always things that can go wrong, the odd wobbly scenery and the dries and the corpses but generally we remember a sort of golden time with lots of laughs, a lot of hard work and friendships that have endured through more than 34 years.

Reggie had succeeded in his first important task that of appointing a company of multi-talented actors, many of whom were beginning to develop star quality.

But what about the building? You may remember that this was not built as a theatre but as a Methodist chapel and that the Methodists moved out in 1915 because the building was in danger of collapsing due to flooding. What was it like to work there and what could Reggie do about it?

9
'PLEASE DO NOT RUN HOT WATER DURING A PERFORMANCE'

T HE ANSWER to the last question is simply not a lot. When Reggie Salberg took over the Playhouse in 1955 he did not take over a purpose built theatre but a converted Methodist chapel that had already been condemned by the Methodists. Not for him the luxury of a purpose built stage, adequately comfortable dressing rooms, a beautifully seated auditorium, excellent backstage facilities and offices for the front of house staff to work in. On the contrary he inherited a random collection of facilities that had been shaped and moulded piece-meal over the past ten years. However, these facilities had been shaped and moulded with great care and above all with a great deal of love and affection. People who worked in this little old building began to love being part of its life ; it felt comfortable to be part of it and the building became a character in itself. It is this fact that helped to maintain and enhance its reputation. There is something special and magical in being entertained in a West End theatre but there was equally something special and magical about this quaint old, converted building, this unique character that actors and theatregoers warmed to. Despite all the problems associated with the building, the Playhouse became like a friend that you looked forward to meeting and being part of its day to day story. Reggie Salberg recognised this and used the character of the building to develop the Playhouse's reputation. To improve the building and the facilities would take a great deal of money and that was certainly not available. There were also many other pressing problems.

The auditorium may have had a quaint charm of its own but conditions, particularly backstage were very bad. Reggie once described the building as a 'theatrical slum' and in one advertisement for a staff appointment he described conditions in the theatre as 'Dickensian.' In 1964 he wrote:

> Those of us who work backstage know how difficult it is to present a play satisfactorily in the cramped stage conditions. The dressing rooms are not worthy of the artists they house; the scenic department work under conditions which would cause strikes in many a business or factory. The stage is draughty and cold in winter and unbearably hot in summer. In the front of house Mrs. Astin works in a Box Office which could hardly be called luxurious. We labour to provide drinks in a bar which is too small. We attempt (unsuccessfully in hot weather) to keep the theatre ventilated and at the right temperature. We can only offer a limited cloakroom space and lavatory accommodation. We would like to give you more leg room in the Circle and a bigger rake on the floor of the Stalls to ensure a good view if you are not very tall. We know for example, that to buy a cup of coffee can be something of an ordeal in that queue at the back of the Stalls but it is the best we can do in the space at our disposal.

Roger Leach recalled: 'Backstage at the old Salisbury rep was dreadful. It was like the wartime spirit. Coal was kept in the corridor on the left hand side of the stage so we had to be careful of our costumes when we made an entrance. We used to get in and out of the Wardrobe through a window which was always full of pigeon droppings as the roof needed fixing.'

For a while entrance stage left was open to the elements and Stephanie Cole remembers standing in the passageway there in the pouring rain waiting to go on as the Nurse in 'Romeo and Juliet' wearing wellingtons and holding an umbrella over Juliet's head and they both had a fit of the giggles just before they went on stage!

When it was eventually covered with corrugated sheeting, Roger Leach recalled that when it was raining outside it sounded like gunshots ringing throughout the theatre.

The corridor linking both sides of the stage was often full of water and Jo Tewson remembers during one performance, Lucy Young exited down the corridor and something fell on her. She never returned on stage and they simply continued the play without her. Actors in the pantomimes vividly remember Ollie Gordon resplendent in his Dame's costume thundering from one side of the stage to the other yelling: 'Out of the way Cock!'

Backstage was a maze of small rooms, corridors and confusion. Actors had to squeeze into the small dressing rooms and share the basic facilities. There was a Green Room but it doubled up as a store room and general purpose room. In it was one sink, in which you washed the paint brushes and prepared food fortunately on different occasions. Two umbrellas were always strategically placed in this room for emergencies. There were no extractor fans and very basic heating. There was one basic shower with only tepid running water; sometimes the actors would shower wearing their costumes!

Jonathan Cecil once remarked: 'We were budding young actors, enjoying ourselves; we would have dressed in the loo.' However, Robin Ellis was often caught smoking liquorice cigarettes in the toilet. 'They looked just like rabbit pellets' recalled David Simeon grimacing!

Outside, a row of cottages was purchased which served as offices for the likes of Reggie Salberg and Alan Corkill. Approaching from the station you could still read in faint white lettering on the grey slates of one building, the legend 'Front Stalls 6d' a reminder of the days when the building was a cinema. The workshop was very small and the ceiling low, so in some cases the scenic artist had to paint the flats sideways. Often to get the scenery into the theatre the crew had to enlist the help of the police to hold up the traffic in Fisherton Street.

People would talk of the rickety stairs that led up to Reggie's office, having climbed them to see him, you hoped that the stairs would still be there when you came down. One actor remarked it was never a good idea to be blacked up as there were few places to have a good wash and backstage you weren't allowed to use the toilet during a performance because the cistern was above the stage!

There was precious room backstage and one actor remembers during the run of the farce 'See How They Run' that there was such much running around that they had to have catchers in the Wings to catch the actors in case they crashed into the side walls! An appropriate title for the play!

Seven small photos of the old building (from top left to bottom right): Theatre looking from the stage; The Box Office; Entrance Stage left; Chapel Place Entrance; The Workshop; The "Infamous" Toilets; A Dressing Room.(Photographer Peter Brown)

Rain was always a problem and on the opening night of the Salisbury Amateur Operatic Society's production of '*The Quaker Girls*' in May 1955, it was raining very heavily and the new general manager of the Playhouse, Reggie Salberg, was amazed to find a lady in the second row of the stalls holding an umbrella over her head. He knew there were problems with leaks from the roof so he politely asked her to move to a drier part of the auditorium. 'We have solved the problem today,' he said, 'but only by climbing into the loft below the roof whenever it rains and putting buckets throughout the theatre in strategic positions.'

The floods of 1960 brought several inches of water slopping around the feet of the players in the orchestra pit. The carpenter, unrehearsed, had to join them for the entire performance one evening. His instrument, a stirrup pump, was fortunately inaudible to both actors and audience.

Fisherton Street flooded, 1960s (Photographer Unknown)

However, in 1956 Reggie remembered the amazing spirit of the theatregoers who braved a torrential downpour to see the first night of '*The Whole Truth*'. Reggie remarked: 'It was quite a sight to see them arriving shoeless, having paddled across the street. It is truly amazing that we played to over 50% capacity in such conditions.'

In 1975 Roger Livingston from Southern Arts wrote:

My tour of the premises coincided with the aftermath of gales and heavy rain. Dressing room, workshops, administration offices – all sported buckets to contain the worst of the roof leaks. The sound technician was busy clearing plaster from his desk and equipment. One of two rooms had been evacuated because the ceilings had fallen. Costumes had been stored off premises as the damp would surely ruin them.

In his book 'Just Biggins' Christopher Biggins, who joined the Playhouse in 1966 recalls backstage vividly:

I'd always adored the glamour of the lights, the thick velvet curtain, the plush carpets and all the trappings of the theatre. I had always dreamed that to go backstage would be like going to some kind of Narnia. And so it was – in reverse.

It was chaos. Backstage certainly wasn't quite the magical world of glamour and beauty that I had imagined. Salisbury Rep was falling apart. There was a tiny set of different stairs and rooms and corridors but there was nowhere to pick up a cat, let alone swing one. And yes, there was the high, intoxicatingly rich scent of make-up and hair spray but there was also the smell of mould, mildew and damp.

The roof leaked all over and most of the buckets were used to protect the seats in the auditorium. Backstage water just drained away wherever it could. Water soaked into almost everything and however, much our big old radiators banged out, it was never enough to dry it out. Backstage the light bulbs died and weren't always replaced. Old sets, old costumes, long forgotten props piled up in corridors and corners. Who knows what crawled amongst them. But who cared?

The actors certainly didn't. Those who were part of Reggie Salberg's company could turn a blind eye to the conditions. The important factor was that they were being employed. Today an actor will be employed for one production, two on the trot if they are lucky and if they are what the director is looking for. In the past though, if you were part of the Playhouse company then you would be employed for the season which meant being part of a whole range of plays. Timothy West has said it and many other fledgling actors would agree, it was their apprenticeship. Christopher Benjamin once remarked: 'One week I was the butler, the next week I played Othello.' If Reggie Salberg liked you then you could be re-employed for another season and so on, some actors staying for several years, until in some cases Reggie felt it was time for you to move on, as he once said to David Simeon after he had been at the Playhouse for several seasons: 'I've had enough of looking at you Simeon I think it's time I sent you off to work for my brother in Birmingham.' said of course with considerable tongue in cheek but also with a modicum of truth as he knew it was time for David Simeon to develop his career.

David Simeon was in fact one of Reggie's favourites and was often at the end of Reggie's barbs. David was about to appear in '*The Philanthropist*' and was told by Reggie: 'no one will ever come to see this Simeon.' It actually ran to packed houses and David said it could have run for ever! David soon proved to be a very versatile actor playing a whole variety of roles from comedy in '*Thark*' through costume productions such as '*The Importance of Being Earnest*' to serious drama as in '*The Birthday Party*', often considered to be one of his best performances.

David was great friends with Jonathan Cecil who often played 'the silly ass' parts but Reggie knew his strengths and would often give him much meatier roles. Unfortunately, the regular theatregoers would occasionally recognise him and start laughing as he came on in a serious role such as the Dauphin in '*Saint Joan*'.

He said that in Reggie's company, 'you learnt how too make an entrance and an exit. Simple things but so important to an actor and to the audience.' Jonathan was also a very versatile actor who wore many different roles with consummate ease. Both were excellent company people.

Like all actors they had their fair share of supporters, dare one say 'groupies'?! Jonathan remembers meeting a young lady at a party who told him that she was at school near Salisbury and that 'as young teenage girls we always used to come to see your plays at the Rep and we all thought that you were young, slim and great and we all used to love coming to see you on the stage.' It was Christine Hamilton!

There were occasional improvements backstage. In 1956 Reggie wrote:

> Builders have been busy backstage for several weeks now, making improvements to the dressing rooms and stage amenities. In addition the open passage from which the artists have to make their entrances on one side of the stage is being covered and this will prevent the icy draught which has blown over the front rows of the theatre in previous winters. We are most grateful to the Arts Council, out of whose funds these very necessary improvements are being made.

However, it was very important to keep the auditorium and front of house looking presentable as it was these areas that the theatregoers see, use and remember. Reggie went on:

> We realise that our next task is to make the auditorium more comfortable and we hope plans laid will be put in hand if and when our bank balance allows. Meanwhile we are making a start by moving the green seats to the back of the theatre where the added height will not impede anyone's view. We are also spacing out the other seats downstairs in such a way that they will not be directly behind one another and everyone will get a better view of the stage.

He also thanked the Junior Theatre Club who were raising funds for the purchase of new curtains.

Once again there was a reliance on the Theatregoer's Club not only for funds but also for physical help. In one of his programme notes in 1960, Reggie wrote:' The Theatregoer's Club are helping by re-decorating the bar out of their funds. The work is being done by some of the members and we are very grateful to them.'

It was the money raised by the Theatregoers Club and the Patrons' Fund set up with their contributions that helped save the theatre in the mid-fifties and the theatre continually needed this financial re-assurance to survive. In 1958 Reggie Salberg wrote:

Our reserve Fund now stands at £1,740. This sum has been raised by the social activities of the Theatregoer's Club. But believe me, £1,740 is a dangerously low reserve on which to operate. Thank goodness no crisis is in the offing, but even so it was only the amount of money raised by The Theatregoers' Club which enabled us to make ends meet, even in a successful year such as 1957/58.

Later on in the year he wrote:

I feel a deep gratitude therefore, to those of you who contribute towards the patron's Fund and to those members of the Theatregoer's Club who actively raise money for us. By these means a reserve of nearly £2,000 has been built up, but of course this is a pitifully small sum to put by for a rainy day...and in the theatre it can rain very hard indeed! These efforts illustrate the extreme goodwill of Salisbury towards its theatre.

These reserves were not only needed to help keep the theatre alive but were also very useful when Reggie Salberg saw a bargain. In 1958 the Empire Portsmouth closed its doors for the last time and Reggie went to the auction of its contents. There he purchased some luxurious seats for the costly sum of £500. This then needed another plea from Reggie in his next programme notes for more theatregoers to take part in the Patron's scheme!

Finance was of course, always a huge problem. In one of his 1958 programme notes Reggie Salberg vividly described the continual financial problem the theatre faced:

Patrons will have read with interest that the Salisbury City Council has decided to give the theatre a grant of £200. If the Arts Council grant stays at its present level of £1,000, we will thus be subsidised to the tune of £1,200 p.a.

Why must we be subsidised at all? Let me emphasize the fact that it is a miracle that Salisbury, with its population of 33,000 has a theatre at all – it is even more miraculous that this repertory company ranks amongst the dozen best in the country. This fact should fill all local hearts with pride. But is pride enough? Well, apart from the fact that the theatre should be an integral part of any community, I believe that as Salisbury is a tourist centre it is a matter of hard business to supply visitors with suitable entertainment.

'But,' cries your hard headed business man, ' a theatre should be self-supporting. Increase your prices.' Ignoring the fact that higher prices may mean fewer patrons; when you point out to him he will very likely say 'Well you must cut your coat according to your cloth.'; but lower standards may also mean less patrons.

This theatre seats 400 people and the most it can take at any performance is £80. Out of the receipts we have to find the salaries of the company, the managerial and box office staffs, the usherettes, the stage staff, the carpenter, the wardrobe mistress and the scenic designer. On last week's payroll there were 36 people and believe me, everyone works harder for less money than in the great majority of jobs.

From the balance of receipts, after paying this very considerable wage bill and after paying the author his percentage (on average about 9%) we have to find enough to pay rent, rates, taxes, insurances, advertising, printing, postage, stationery, fuel, electricity, gas, professional fees, rental of the scenic stores and offices, wardrobe costs and wig hires, and also keep the theatre clean and in reasonable condition.

Something of a miracle, but it is done.

Reggie Salberg was always concerned about keeping seat prices as low as possible and in 1956 he apologised for having to make a small increase in the seat prices.

It is with some regret that we announce a small increase in the price of our seats. As from next week prices will be 5/3, 4/3. 3/3 and 2/- except Mondays when the will be 4/3, 3/3, 2/3 and 1/3. This is the first increase since the theatre was opened ten years ago, and I am sure that you will all agree that it is a very small one.

No theatre can rely on Box Office takings alone and grants from the Arts Council and local authorities were vital to keep the theatre open.

Having returned in 1960 from a visit to theatres on the continent Reggie was amazed to see the discrepancy between what was available to theatres in England compared to the continent. In 1959 the Arts Council was able to give £83,000 to be divided between some thirty theatres. In Munich he visited two theatres each of which received about £130,000 per annum. The director of one of the continental companies said to Reggie: 'In England you have the actors and the tradition to establish the most splendid Theatre in Europe, if only you were given the money to do so.'

Reggie once commented: 'After all one rates Beethoven and Shakespeare as more important to civilisation than say Concorde and they cost much less.'

However, looking back in 1965 Reggie Salberg was able to report:

> Little of this progress could have been achieved without the added grants available from the Arts Council. In 1955 the grant was £500 – today it is £7,500 In addition the Salisbury City Council now make us a grant of £500 whereas no grant was made in 1955. We are grateful to them and to the other nine councils who help us. We have also received generous help from Southern Television.

Grants from the Arts Council were given regularly as it recognised the bourgeoning success of the Playhouse and the little theatre could not have survived without them. Grants from local authorities were not so regularly forthcoming but again were a very necessary part of the financial pot to keep the theatre open.

In 1961 the lease of the building, which was still owned by the Rank Organisation, was due to run out. Rank wanted to sell the site freehold. and the asking price was £7,000. As Reggie Salberg wrote:

> To purchase the freehold at a time when the provisional theatre is experiencing great difficulty is an act of faith. To provide the sort of entertainment which woos people away from their firesides, a good

deal of money has to be spent and no small theatre such as ours can hope to be self supporting these days. When we decided to go ahead with the purchase we believed that more support for the theatre would be forthcoming – and our faith has been justified.

This came in an extra grant from the Arts Council, support from the theatre world and huge financial support from the Playhouse theatregoers.

Such comments as these were received with donations: 'For goodness sake do purchase the freehold. It would be terrible to have another theatre turned into a warehouse.' Alex Atkinson.

'I am very grateful to you for the way you have presented my plays with distinction.' John Mortimer.

And from a local theatregoer: 'I have seen many other repertory companies but it was not until I came to Salisbury a year or two ago that I was lucky enough to see work of the highest quality.'

The *Evening News* wrote: 'The Salisbury Arts Theatre is appealing for funds to buy the Salisbury Playhouse. This little theatre has been serving its people well. At a time when repertory is said to be dying the Salisbury Playhouse has gallantly put on a number of lively productions. One or two plays first seen there have later come to London. It deserves all the encouragement it can attract.'

It felt that this theatre somehow now belonged to the theatregoers of Salisbury and when the appeal funds to purchase the freehold was announced there was no way the theatregoers were going to let their theatre slip away into oblivion like so many other local theatres. The money was of course found and a tablet was put up at the front of the theatre commemorating the purchase of the theatre by the citizens and actors of Salisbury. This triumphant achievement was celebrated by a Gala Performance of Noel Coward's '*Brief Encounter*' and '*Family Album*.'

Reggie Salberg quickly became the linch-pin of the Playhouse and he soon became a very powerful figure. Every decision, every plan, every idea, every policy, every agreement, indeed everything that happened in the Playhouse went through him first. It sounds as though he had become a dictator. Far from it, everything that Reggie Salberg did was simply for the benefit of the theatre and for those who

Gala Performance cover, November 1960

worked in it.; how it could survive the present and how it could face the future. He knew that to keep the theatre flourishing in the present and to see that it faced the future with optimism, it needed one man at the helm and he knew that he was that man.

In an interview, he actually once said: 'Yes, I'd like to be a theatre dictator, but then I'd also like to be Eccles!' With such power, some people could easily have turned against him but through his unique personality (Betty Anderson once said of him: 'He always pretended to be rather taciturn and overly serious but this was to cover up the fact that he was as hard as a marshmallow inside.') it was the fact also that no one worked harder than he did, and most people simply wanted to work for him. They loved the little theatre but they also loved worked for Reggie Salberg.

As Barbara Wilson, the wardrobe mistress once put it:- 'Sometimes you want to wring his neck. Sometimes you want to hug him to death. He's the most amazing man I've ever worked for in my life.'

One of his greatest achievements was in keeping the books in the black. To achieve this there were enormous demands on him and his working days usually started at 8am and finished at 9pm including of course, Saturdays (not Saturday afternoons though, if Southampton were playing at home!) In his early days he said he had a recurring dream: 'I used to cycle in my sleep and wake up feeling exhausted and the funny thing was, I didn't have a bike!'

One of his first duties in the morning, was to attend to the mail, which meant he would have to separate official letters from those intended for the actors and stage management. Robert Aldous recalled: 'He would make no bones about reading the backs of postcards, but he also seemed to possess X-Ray eyes, for he would sometimes know the contents of the letters as well! He would tell actors their next engagement even before they had read about it themselves!'

When he was budgeting he had various ceilings. He would start with the basic budget for the play then if someone came to see him with a good idea or if they were needing something important for the production then he would break that ceiling and move on to the next.

Occasionally at the end of a season there would be a profit which he would add to the actors wages. At Christmas, Maria Heidler remembered Reggie being just like Father Christmas handing out small brown envelopes which the other actors told her was 'our Christmas Bonus.'

Reggie had to be careful not to make too high a profit otherwise the Arts Council would deduct it from next year's grant. Alan Corkill remembers Reggie saying: 'It looks as though we're going to make a profit this year so will you go and buy some stamps or some spirits for the bar.'

In interviews Reggie would talk about what his job entailed:-
The choice of plays was largely his. He once said: 'There isn't any one
audience. At least one in three productions has got to be what we call
a W.I. play. There must be at least three classical plays a year and we
also try to do the best of the modern works. On top of that you have
the pantomime, a Spring review and an Old Tyme Musical Hall. If in
doubt, put on Shakespeare or Agatha Christie.' To him reading plays
though, was the ultimate chore.

> They come dog eared onto your desk, and you know they've been
> round every theatre in the country. Most of them are frightfully bad
> but every so often you find one that is exciting…even then you have
> to ask yourself whether you dare do it.

He was also responsible for choosing the company of actors and
as a rule no actor would be engaged unless his work had been seen
generally more than once. He said that on average four nights out of
every week would be spent watching a play and about 30,000 miles a
year travelling to do so.

In addition, of course, there would be a good deal of routine.
Many letters had to be written every day, he had to cost every show
and prepare a profit and loss account after its production. He had to
make out the salaries, prepare the programme and the advertising,
keep various account books, attend meetings of the Board and the
Theatregoer's Club', give talks to local clubs and societies; help out
at the Box Office and solve all the day to ay problems of running a
theatre, including seeing how the rehearsals were going!

He also had to deal with all the actors: 'One has to deal with all
their problems and these might not only be artistic. Actors obviously
believe that nothing else can interest you quite as much as their own
problems!'

How grateful he must have been in 1960 when Peter Cregeen
was appointed as his assistant. Reggie reported:

> He will be here to welcome you most nights looking resplendent in
> dinner jacket – I always felt a bit guilty about not wearing one myself
> but as my day starts so early and finishes so late, my directors felt it a

bit hard to make this final demand.

Anyway Peter looks much nicer in a dinner jacket than I do!… Even with Peter to help, I still hope to be in the foyer to welcome you most nights…nevertheless, it will be nice to get home occasionally in time to see the children off to bed!

Reggie would always be looking very smart when standing in the foyer greeting theatregoers but actors often recall that backstage he always seemed to be chewing something, his tie, a handkerchief or even a piece of cotton wool and of course, there was always the almost permanent cigarette!

Reggie Salberg loved and respected the patrons but there were many times when he wished they could behave better!

Back in 1958 he wrote:

I was standing at the back of the theatre during a performance of 'Jane Eyre' and was struck by the tension in the audience. You could have heard a pin drop. No one actually dropped a pin but at that point someone decided it was time to eat one of those delicious sweets wrapped in the crinkliest of papers. It must have been a particularly difficult sweet to unwrap, and after about 30 seconds the attention of at least 5 or 6 rows of the stalls was divided between the stage and the sweet lover. One could almost hear a sigh of relief when at last the dainty morsel was popped between the jaws. Alas there was to be no peace, for the offender was a nervous sweet eater and could not bring herself to throw away the crinkly paper, which she then rolled between her fingers until the fall of the curtain. As a result of this one person's actions the scene lost quite a lot of its effect and unwittingly she made many enemies. Might I suggest to all sweet lovers that they either confine their activities to the intervals or at least make sure that they do not crinkle paper whilst gourmandising! If you disobey these rules you are an even greater menace than the gentleman who lights a cigarette or even worse a pipe, during a tense scene. Incidentally there are on sale in this theatre chocolates packed by Kunzles, in their silent theatre pack; these you can eat to your hearts' content without any fear of annoying your neighbour!

He was never too concerned about smokers though, as he was a heavy smoker himself. But in 1956 under the heading: '*Burns Night*' he wrote:

> The new carpet has been much admired. So far only six holes have been burnt in it by smokers failing to use the ashtrays provided. Whilst on this tricky subject of smoking I would like to give reasons for the requests (no more than that) to patrons to refrain from smoking except during the intervals. Firstly it is hard on actors to have to play in a very smoky atmosphere and even harder for them to endure the coughing it causes. Secondly a smoke laden atmosphere is not in the best interests of general health and it is particularly hard on non-smokers.
>
> I might add that I am quite a heavy smoker myself.

As Ralph Richardson once said: 'Acting is the art of preventing audiences from coughing!'

Reggie particularly though, hated latecomers and in 1961 he wrote:

> There are others who push noisily through the entrance doors, talk loudly to the attendants, head straight for their seats without making any attempt to find whether a break in the play may not be imminent, push past those who are already in their places and slam their seats down with a thump that echoes through the theatre. Their thoughtlessness, which, amounts to crass bad manners, seriously disrupts the enjoyment of the play for the rest of the audience and has an inevitably deleterious effect upon the performance.
>
> Moreover, latecomers, are by nature, unlikely to respond to any kind of appeal. It is possible that the positively expressed disapproval of the remainder of the audience might have some effect and a well placed shoe on the toe of someone pushing past will at least provide grounds for regret!

Hopefully times have changed and theatregoers are now more considerate to others. Certainly theatres are so much better now that smoking has been banned but there will always be the minority of theatregoers who lack common sense and courtesy and think only of themselves and don't let's get onto the subject of mobile phones!

There were also many 'whingers', those who were never satisfied: In one programme note Reggie wrote:

> One must feel sympathy for the regular theatregoer who cancelled his seats for 'The Crucible' as he thought we did so few plays worth seeing. I am afraid he is going to have another theatre-less three weeks next February when we will be presenting 'King Lear!'

There was also the doctor from Winchester who wrote: 'We were in two minds whether to go or not (to see 'The Cherry Orchard') as none of the cast were named and the price of the seats so low that we could not expect anything but a very indifferent performance.'

Reggie replied: 'Perhaps if our prices were doubled then they would start to come and fill that quarter of the auditorium which on average is now unoccupied!'

There were also the occasional surprises though. Remembering how after a performance of 'Look Back in Anger' one angry patron beat him over the legs with a walking stick 'for daring to show such filth!' When it was revived in 1969, at one performance there were two parties from church organisations and one from the Mother's Union. Putting on metaphorical shin pads he walked to the foyer expecting the worst. The ladies of the parties all smiled at him as they left but one clergyman complained that the play was too old fashioned!

There are of course though, many stories of the loyalty of the theatregoers. One lady always bought two tickets – one was for her dog! David Simeon also remembers with affection Maudie who once told a friend: 'I love seeing that David Simmons. I've seen them all -James Maysonn, Googie Witheralls.. (Googie Withers)' She would go to the theatre every week, always sitting in the same seat and when the plays changed to two week performances, she still came every week, still sitting in the same seat!

But sometimes you never knew who would be sitting in the audience. At a performance of 'Maximillian', Margaret Lockwood was seen sitting in the 1/6 seats with the producer Henry Sherek and at a performance of 'The Birthday Party', Cecil Beaton was accompanied by Greta Garbo!

Members of the company became part of the community and were always very happy to meet their audience at the theatre and also around the town. Many an actor would be stopped whilst buying their weekly groceries at the market to be told by a theatregoer how much they liked or disliked this actor's latest performance. Sometimes though they never quite knew who they were talking to.

Richard Kane recalled after a performance during the 1980s:

At the theatre supporters' reception after the first night, everyone seemed very pleased with themselves. However, an accusing finger prodded a path through the throng in the foyer, to hover three inches before my nose. Behind it, below it, an elderly woman peered up into my face. Her eyes narrowed as she hissed: 'It's you! I always know it's you!' She turned on the proverbial heel, to disappear with her sheepish minder into the crowd. Then she paused, looked back and asked: 'It is you, isn't it?' Richard never did find out who he was supposed to be.

Reggie Salberg had gathered around him a loyal company and an equally loyal audience. He was becoming almost omnipotent and indeed omnipresent, but he always needed and appreciated the assistance and companionship of a second lieutenant, the likes of Oliver Gordon and Peter Cregeen. In 1966 Reggie appointed another person who was to prove to be an invaluable assistant to him. Someone who was to play an incredibly important role in the history of the Playhouse. Like Reggie Salberg he proved to be another much loved figure. Enter Alan Corkill.

10
'IN THE PAST MONTHS I'VE SOMETIMES LONGED FOR THE UNHURRIED EXISTENCE OF A LAWYER'
Reggie Salberg

O VER THE YEARS Alan Corkill had been given several titles including House, Theatre and General Manager but titles never bothered him. His main role was always to look after the customers. In fact he once referred to himself as the 'housewife' of the Playhouse and he was always happy to oversee all sorts of behind the scenes

(left) Alan Corkill outside the theatre (Photographer Peter Brown)
(right) Alan Corkill cartoon (Daniel Pettiward)

duties to ensure that the audience was safe and happy – whatever they may think of the play. Indeed one of his most important roles was to be in evidence in the foyer at the start and at the end of the performance, something he learnt from Reggie. 'You will never get the feel of an audience, if you don't get to see them.' Sometimes though, Reggie suffered from this dedication. Remember the theatregoer who attacking him with her stick. She would rather have seen 'Charley's Aunt' for the sixth time than the near the knuckle kitchen sink drama she had just sat through!

Alan always liked to hear what people thought about the performance and he would get upset when he saw people leaving at the interval. Then of course there are some occasions when they would vent their anger at him but he thought it was always a good idea for an unhappy customer to get it off their chest and complain to him before going home. 'An audience is different every night,' he once said. 'That's what gives the job such a wonderful variety and such wonderful pleasure.'

On leaving school Alan went into the bakery and confectionery trade and was a member of the local church choir. Indeed his first contact with the theatre was as a choirboy when his church was involved in a fund raising show at the local Barrow-in-Furness theatre. He was detailed to sell programmes and he enjoyed it so much that he virtually never left the place.

He became involved in all aspects of theatre life and on one occasion, when they were short of an actor they asked him to play the part of a custom's officer. They painted a moustache on his face but it made no difference because the audience soon recognised the baker's boy and they all roared with laughter! Alan couldn't get his words out and eventually they had to cut out his one and only line!

The theatre though, soon began to get into his blood and he decided that perhaps the bakery trade was not for him. In 1966 at the age of 23, on the suggestion of the theatre's manager, he applied for an Arts Council bursary to train in theatre management and he was sent to London for an interview. He got the job and Reggie Salberg entered his life. Alan didn't know it at the time but Reggie was on the interviewing panel and as Reggie owed the theatre manager a favour, it was suggested that Alan packed his bags to begin a new life down

South to join Reggie in his little repertory theatre in Salisbury.

Alan was given a six month training period in which he was to work in all the departments. Reggie told him: 'You can't be a manager if you don't know what all the departments do.' Alan was something of a liability in some of them but he enjoyed the challenges apart though from going on the stage.

He played a blind beggar in 'Romeo and Juliet' and Reggie insisted that he was killed off in the first ten minutes so he could then go and do his proper job of looking after the customers in the foyer!

Alan was rather frightened of Reggie at first but he didn't realise that Reggie was rather unsure of him as well. Alan was often referred to as 'that blunt Northerner.' Alan started by always calling him Mr. Salberg until the friendship and partnership firmly cemented and then Alan would often affectionately refer to Reggie as 'Dad.'

Alan confessed that he didn't always see many plays during a season. He wasn't keen on Shakespeare but had a penchant for a good thriller. He got on with most actors although there were some he had been glad to see the back of. He remembered with great affection working with Stephanie Cole who took him under her wing when he started at the Playhouse. When he was nervously working backstage and had to push on a chimney breast she would always tip him a wink when it was his turn to move into action.

Stephanie Cole was one of the many aspiring actors and actresses that were auditioned by Reggie Salberg at Sally Spruce's. She remembers the interviewing going very well when Reggie surprisingly asked: 'Show us your legs.' Remembering stories about the casting coach, she became rather worried but on raising her skirt a few inches Reggie commented: 'Oh, good, you'll do for the pantomime!'

Thus begun three special years in her career which she described as 'an extraordinary happy time.'

Her first play in Salisbury was 'Where Angels Fear To Tread'. However, the first rehearsal did not go very well and the director, Ollie Gordon was forced to confer with Reggie: 'It's no good old cock, she's going to have to go. She can't do it.' Fortunately for us all, Reggie saw something special in her and gave her another chance.

In three years until June 1967, Stephanie appeared in 55 productions ranging from Margery the Cook in 'Dick Whittington' through Miss. Marple in '*Murder at the Vicarage*' to Mrs. Malaprop' in '*The Rivals*'. She was often cast as characters that were much older than she really was. 'I suppose I had one of those faces that looked younger as I grew older, if that makes any sense!' Also she had a fine singing voice and appeared in many Music Halls and Revues often billed as 'The Songbird from the Hills' or 'The Mellifluous Mistress of Melody'.

To Stephanie, Rep was the most amazing training ground. 'You stretched every muscle of the actor's being. One was in plays with the most wonderful actors, now household names, giving amazing performances in the sort of parts they would never be called upon to play now'.

But of course she also remembers the many laughs. In one memorable production the stage management thought it would be a good idea to crunch up some toast to make a good, crunching gravelly effect for the path. On the fourth night Stephanie walked across the path, sat down on the sofa and crossed her legs. She suddenly noticed some laughter going around the audience and some pointing towards her stiletto shoes. Looking down she saw a whole slice of toast speared on the end of each shoe. That evening the management, in their hurry had forgotten to crunch up the toast!

On another occasion Stephanie remembers one play which had the usual drawing room set – French windows, fireplace, telephone. At one point in Act One the phone was supposed to ring and there was a terrible, terrible pause – no sound. So the cast improvised and suddenly they heard from the Wings the young assistant stage manager making frantic telephone sounds: 'Brr, Brr, Brr!' Stephanie recalled that the cast all started to laugh and then they couldn't find the telephone! They were all lurching around the set pretending that they weren't looking for anything, when suddenly a hand appeared through the fireplace holding up the phone! At that moment cast and the audience all burst out laughing

In the early days of rep, the Prompt was a very important member of the backstage crew, as actors, who had precious little time to learn their lines, would often have to be prompted. Stephanie remembers suddenly forgetting her next line and she casually wandered over to prompt corner only to find the prompt girl was busy doing her knitting with the page of the script open on Act One and they were in the middle of Act Two!

Knitting was also a problem for Jane Quy who, during one performance was prompting and in charge of the curtain. In a rush to close the final curtain, her knitting got caught up in the pulley system and went along the front of the curtain six times! An added enjoyment for those theatregoers waiting to exit!

Stephanie remembers her days in Salisbury with great affection and in her autobiography 'A Passionate Life' she wrote about the times out of the theatre

..Steak and chips on pay day at the Flaming O café; (The Flamingo Restaurant which is still open in Fisherton Street) sunsets at Stonehenge; trips to London, seven of us crammed into my little mini-van; sitting over cheap wine and Nescafe talking acting and philosophy, art and music until the sun rose; organising an egg and spoon race; cooking endless spaghetti bolognaise; the friendships, the quarrels, the laughter..

Easter Egg Race, Easter 1966. L to R: Chris Biggins, Chris Harris, Carolyn Moody, Brian Elwell, John Swindells, Sonia Woolley, Reggie Salberg, Jonathan Cecil, Michael Stroud, Jane Quy, Barbara Wilson (in hat), Stan Astin (in background), David Gooderson, Vivien Helibron, Ollie Gordon, Jan Booth. (Salisbury Journal)

Stephanie once said: 'Don't let anybody tell you that you aren't good enough or that you can't do it…you must follow your bliss.' Something that all young actors could remember.

The famous egg and spoon race was organised by Stephanie and Christopher Biggins during Easter 1966. To break up the occasional monotony of life in the theatre this pair would often organise different activities but this special race was also to raise some much needed publicity. The route was around the block of the Playhouse building. The whole company took part and each person had to have a different spoon and a different egg. Reggie drew the short straw being given a straining spoon and a raw egg! The race was won by Michael Stroud and the prize was awarded by Stephanie with Biggins of course, proudly looking on!

Christopher Biggins grew up in Salisbury, the family having moved from Oldham because of his health. He vividly remembers travelling on the back of a Pickford's lorry wrapped in cotton wool because he had pneumonia. The family moved into a small house in Sidney Street beside the railway line and his father opened a garage.

At the age of 13 Christopher played the Ethel Merman part in 'Call Me Madam' at his school, St. Probus. Thanks to Mrs. Christian, an inspirational teacher, he already had the acting bug and eventually he decided to join Stage 65 at the Playhouse. In an early Stage 65 diary note it states: 'and Chris Biggins was in charge of the gramophone!'

Christopher soon realised where his ambitions lay and one day in 1965 he went up to the Box Office, even though he was terrified of Mrs. Astin and asked to see Mr. Salzberg (he couldn't

Chris Biggins before he worked at the Playhouse (Photographer: Peter Brown)

remember Reggie's actual name) to ask for a job.

Reggie obviously saw something in this 16 year old boy and gave him the part of one of the servants in 'She Stoops to Conquer'. This was a four week contract but he eventually joined the company and stayed for two years.

He was known as a Student ASM and was paid £2 a week rising to £8 during the second year. Amongst his many early jobs was to sweep the stage before each performance and he often worked a 12-14 hour day. However, he recalled that he had joined a very happy and talented company and he would call his time in Salisbury: 'the happiest time of my life.' He appeared in nine plays and was given a whole variety of roles including his first tastes of pantomime, first as one of the rats in 'Dick Whittington' and then as P.C. Boggins in 'Jack and the Beanstalk.'

As an ASM he would recall moments when things didn't always go according to plan. At the beginning of one thriller the curtain opened to the sound of a phone ringing but the trouble was, the backstage crew hadn't put the phone on the set! As the actors wandered around not sure what to do next, the Company Manager decided to knock on the set door and say: 'Good evening, we've come to install your telephone!' Accompanied by Christopher he put a wire under the carpet, installed the phone, it started to ring, and the play started!

Always willing to help others, Chris remembers during the run of 'Lock Up Your Daughters' in 1966, Brian Protheroe had consumed two Newcastle Browns and a tin of peaches before he was due to make his entrance with the line: 'There is a plot afoot!' This time the line ended in 'Yeuk!' and the Newcastle Browns and peaches cascaded across the stage! Chris immediately rushed in from the wings, grabbed Brian's hat and promptly took over his part.

Sometimes though, without thinking, he could cause problems for the rest of the cast as in the opening scene of the 1966 production of 'Romeo and Juliet', Howard Southern couldn't understand why there was much laughter amongst the audience until he noticed that Biggins was doing his nails with his dagger!

One of Christopher's greatest loves was 'propping' scouring the city's shops for props, which could be used on the sets. He recalls that most of the furniture and ornaments in his house at one time or another would appear in one of the Playhouse productions!

He was soon very well known to Salisbury theatregoers as he would wander around Salisbury in a full length, mauve kaftan and flamboyant cape. The rest of the company soon warmed to this larger than life character and he was given the accolade of an Ollie nickname as he was usually known as 'Sunshine' and 'Sunflower!'

At school Christopher Biggins was very friendly with the Brown family and it was the younger brother Peter who will always be grateful to him. Peter was already beginning to make his name as a very successful photographer and when Christopher heard that the Playhouse photographer had just left and that Reggie was quickly looking for a replacement he mentioned this to Peter who hot footed it to the Playhouse for an interview. Unfortunately Peter arrived late but once again Reggie could see through the present problem and realised that the future was more important and he employed Peter who eventually became the Playhouse photographer for over thirty years.

Peter Brown with camera
Photographer: Henry Wills

In Peter's words:

In November 1965 as a freelance photographer my day started normally. I was in my darkroom checking which orders were to be printed when the phone rang. It was Chris Biggins, my brother John's best friend, to tell me that the Playhouse photographer was leaving and Chris thought that I might like to apply for the post. This was a call that was to shape my future for ever.

An interview with the manager Mr Salberg followed and it was agreed that I should photograph the next production, '*Semi Detached*',

Peter Brown with Chris Biggins on the set of: "The Good Old days of Music Hall" August 1989 (Salisbury Journal)

and provide front of house pictures for a fee of £2. After the first year I asked for a pay rise and was offered two guineas!

I have a lot to thank Chris for. My time spent at the Playhouse never felt like a job – it was pure enjoyment and pleasure and I made many friends over the years.

Playing Jack in that production of 'Jack and the Beanstalk' with Biggins was Chris Harris who remembers one painful performance when he climbed up the beanstalk at the end of the act to a slow curtain. He got stuck at the top and had to lie down across the ceiling so he couldn't be seen. Rather painful as at the time he was suffering from piles!

He later went on to become one of the best dames in the business. Stephanie Cole said that he was what a true pantomime dame should be. She also though, remembers his performance as Ariel in 'The Tempest' which she described as 'like Shirley Temple on Ecstasy!' He will though, be fondly remembered for many one man shows such as 'Kemp's Jig'.

The winner of that famous Egg and Spoon race, Michael Stroud, was another example of Reggie's golden touch when it came to discovering talent for his Playhouse company. 'Stroudy' as he became affectionately known as, arrived at the Playhouse in 1965 dressed in a smart suit complete with briefcase, bumped into David Simeon and enquired: 'Where do we report for duty? Thus begun an association with the Playhouse that lasted for nearly forty years which included 84 plays and as director of 6 others.

Michael grew up in Devon and studied English, Drama and Art at St. Luke's College where he became a prominent figure in the college drama society. After a period working for the British Council in the Colonial Service the lure of the stage eventually drove him to seek out Reggie Salberg who gave him a job for a week, to see if the company liked him. This was eventually extended to three years.

Michael once said: 'Reggie taught me everything. I owe him so much.' But like most members of the company he became a victim of Reggie's waspish tongue! Michael remembered when a group of W.I. ladies were invited to stay behind after a matinee for tea and questions.

'Could we ask the actors what parts they have enjoyed playing? asked one lady.

Reggie replied: 'No, ask them what parts they didn't enjoy playing!'

Michael thought for a moment and then commented: 'Well, I didn't enjoy doing 'Saint Joan'.

To which Reggie quickly replied: 'No, and we didn't enjoy you in that either!'

Michael particularly remembered a production of 'The Ghost Train' when events did not go according to plan: 'In one scene they were all stuck on a railway station in the waiting room and one of the characters was saying' Oh, dear we'll never get out,' and at that moment the door just swung gently open and the stage manager pulling her jumper over her head reached for the door and slowly shut it ! Another moment a person went off stage to go to the ticket office and he couldn't open the door to get back, so he did the rest of the scene with his head through the ticket hatch!'

Michael's stature as an actor continued to grow and he was often cast as important people – sirs, kings, lords, admirals, captains and mayors but he is often remembered for his wonderful performances as Sir. Peter Teazle in 'School For Scandal' and 'Antonio Salieri in ' 'Amadeus.' However, in an amazing list of characters he once played the Cannibal King in 'Robinson Crusoe' and the Turkey in 'The Owl and the Pussycat Went to See'. He also played Fifi one of the ugly sisters in the 1970 production of 'Cinderella'. He was particularly proud of his one-man show 'Playing the Man' the story of Baden Powell but talking to him he would say that he was equally proud of winning that Egg and Spoon Race!

Also arriving in 1965 was Christopher Benjamin, who like Stephanie Cole was adept at playing characters much older than he really was. Although he yearned to play romantic leads, Reggie Salberg knew they did not suit him, and he proved it in a rather humiliating way. He cast him as 'the juvenile lead' in 'Mr. Pym Passes By' and even the actor had to admit he was 'quite dreadful. I wasn't a handsome young man so it was inevitable.' Reggie told him that he had cast him in that role because 'I wanted to have a good laugh!'

Christopher's giggling nearly got him the sack from Reggie. He often played husband and wife with Maggie Jones who was also an expert giggler. During one rehearsal she giggled so much that she had 'an accident!'. The director Michael Alexander, who was rather short sighted said: 'Oh, Maggie look, you've dropped your brooch!'

Christopher was never afraid though, to speak his mind. At one of Reggie's parties, Henry Marshall saw him across the room and with pipe in hand, poked him in the chest. 'Why were you so bloody awful in my pantomime?' he exclaimed. To which Christopher replied: 'Well. before the panto I had just done 'Long Day's Journey Into Night' and I was used to good writing and I didn't know what to do with your dialogue!'

Two years later in 1967 another stalwart of the Playhouse arrived. The Playhouse's own knight – Knight Mantell. He had decided early on in his career to change his name from Christopher. Knight Mantell certainly had an impressive ring about it. Reggie discovered him and offered him a job on one of his many visits to the Liverpool Playhouse.

Knight did not know Salisbury at all and was not sure whether or not to take the risk as the Liverpool Playhouse was housed in a fine building and it had a national reputation. Fortunately for Salisbury he decided to take the risk and he soon became a popular regular of the company.

Early on, like most company members, he had to dip into pantomime. He was not a great lover of children but he loved the general anarchy of pantomime life. During 'Aladdin' when he was playing Mrs. Twankey, if the director wasn't around he would often slip in rude jokes and during one kitchen scene he threw dough at the audience and some of it hit a lady's glasses! Twice his antics led to visits to Reggie's office for 'a quiet word!'

During 'Robinson Crusoe' the ship's wheel came off in his hand and he walked off with it sideways which the audience appreciated even if the director didn't!

He was however, building up a reputation as a very talented actor and during the next two years he was given several important roles including the Headmaster in 'Forty Years On'; Vinnie in 'The Odd Couple' and Truscott in 'Loot'. He also revelled in 'The Good Old Days' particularly when he was the Chairman! His greatest passion though was for Henry Irving and his farewell performance in 1969 was playing Irving in his own production: 'The Life and Times of Henry Irving'. Needless to say, he was also given an Ollie nickname and was known to all as 'Chloe!'

Old Time Music Hall, November 1975. Knight Mantell (Chairman) and Olivia Breeze, Jill Graham, Maria Heidler, Patience Tomlinson, Sonia Woolley, James Charlton, Derek Crewe, Alex Johnson, Jeffery Perry and the Lynx String Ensemble under the direction of Chris Littlewood (Photographer Peter Brown

Having a talented company around him was thus very important but without adequate rehearsal time this would be a waste of their talents and ultimately detrimental to the Playhouse. Adequate rehearsal time was always one of Reggie Salberg's main ambitions. In 1958 he wrote:

> When I arrived, no production ever got more than a week's rehearsal, but we now give extra rehearsal time to over half the plays presented. This inevitably means higher standards. The actors become far less tired and the producer is given time to add some touches which might well be lacking with less time at his disposal. Above all it becomes possible to persuade actors and actresses of good standing to work here, despite the lures of television.'

In 1960 he wrote:

> In these days when TV tempts so many actors away from the stage, it is increasingly difficult to persuade artists of quality to play in repertories which rehearse only a week. They demand a reasonable rehearsal period and an interesting programme: these together with the artistic satisfaction of playing to a live audience, offset the higher rewards of television.

However, in March 1961 television did play an important part in the story of the Playhouse as the play 'The Master of Arts' was shown as part of ITV's 'Comedy Matinee' series direct from the stage of the Playhouse where it had made its debut. The story was about a young schoolboy trying to blackmail his housemaster.

David Garth, a familiar face on television, played the housemaster and the sister of the blackmailing schoolboy was played by Nancie Herrod. David Hemmings played the boy with the camera, five years before his most famous role as a photographer in what many people consider to be the definitive 'swinging sixties' film, Michelangelo Antonioni's 'Blowup.'

Later in 1961 Reggie wrote: This theatre is in the forefront of the battle to improve conditions for the repertory actor who must not be asked to learn and rehearse a part in seven days unless absolutely necessary.'

Initially a policy was developed of two week's rehearsal for some plays and then it was decided in 1960 to put on occasional runs of a fortnight as an experiment. The results were promising but it was three years later before the bold step was taken of trying a period of three months when every play ran for two weeks. This continued until August 1967 when the theatre changed over to three weeks for each play. Then in 1976 plays were given four or even five weeks runs. 'Cowardy Custard' ran for five weeks and played to nearly 80% capacity.

In 1975 John Bavin in his book 'Heart of the City' wrote:

> Each increase in length of run has brought an increase in attendances, which is no doubt partly attributable to the fact that is easier to find a dozen or so plays with audience appeal, rather than having to find forty eight each year. Standards of performance have risen as rehearsal periods have lengthened and coupled with improvements in the standard of design at Salisbury over the last five years, the Playhouse productions have reached new heights.

Robin Ellis who was at the Playhouse for a short time in the early sixties would have welcomed longer rehearsal times and longer runs. In a letter he wrote:

> It was fortnightly repertory – with about 10 days rehearsal for each play – I'd arrive at the theatre just before 10am with barely enough time to grab a cup of coffee before stumbling into the rehearsal room, masking my lack of preparedness with a display of coughs and splutters and stories of friends having persuaded me to that extra pint after the show the night before. I was putting off the awful moment when rehearsal would start and exposure begin. I must have been enjoying myself though. I remember thinking our production of 'Murder at the Vicarage' had a touch of Chekhov to it! Though I was brought to earth with a bump on the first night, getting up from the dinner table to make the opening speech as the curtain rose – and drying stone dead. It was a punishing schedule which took its toll.

Reggie once said: 'In the past months I've sometimes longed for the unhurried existence of a lawyer.' But despite all the hard work and the traumas of running a repertory theatre there is no way he would swap this busy life for any other world.

Reggie Salberg had many personal favourites amongst the plays during his early years at the Playhouse but it was later when there were longer rehearsal times and longer performance runs that he would occasionally speak affectionately of certain productions, such as 'The Royal Hunt of the Sun', 'The National Health', 'Saint Joan', 'Becket', 'Victoria Regina', 'Long Days Journey Into Night', 'Who's Afraid of Virginia Wolf', 'Equus' and 'Chips With Everything'.

Peter Cregeen's production of 'The Royal Hunt of the Sun' was amongst the theatre's most ambitious productions, with scaffolding all over the proscenium arch to represent the Andes! However, it was a great success and played to 90% capacity. Reggie will never forget this production though, because Robert Powell, who was playing the Inca Sun God, Atahuallpa, was delayed in London before one performance and the only way to get him to Salisbury in time was for him to hire a plane to the nearest airport. This then meant a hair-raising journey by Reggie to collect him. Fortunately Robert Powell was only on in the second act, his voice in the first act had been covered by another actor. He got to the theatre by the interval and six people backstage rushed to cover him with body make-up. Alex Romanes spoke of her claim to fame as being the one that blacked up Robert Powell's left leg!

A very special production was 'Oh, What a Lovely War' and Reggie would often talk about the time the audience was so stunned that some left the auditorium in silence or in tears. Although Robin Ellis recalls that during some performances of this play you would 'often hear seats in the auditorium slamming up as the Colonel Blimps of Salisbury left in disgust!'

Reggie would always though, keep a watchful, fatherly eye on each production and usually after each performance there would be a post mortem, often in the King's Arms or perhaps in the Flaming O. After the last night of one particularly turgid thriller, Reggie commented: 'I didn't like the fact that there was more clapping and cheering behind the curtain than there was in front of it!'

This local author was not very popular amongst the company and they offered a prize to anyone who could write a better ending. The prize was won by a schoolgirl from Godolphin School!

Reggie also talked about the worst production of 'Macbeth' ever to be staged anywhere. A lady asked him if the production was suitable for children. 'Oh yes,' he replied. 'It's the grown ups I'm worried about!'

Trying to please everybody is of course impossible but in his choice of plays for the season Reggie had to make sure his choices would keep the patrons happy but he also had to keep his company happy and not exhausted. He would also want to introduce the theatregoers to the best of the modern works even if occasionally a play such as 'Look Back in Anger' would shock some theatregoers from the shires. Indeed one disgusted theatregoer after seeing this revolutionary play wrote that 'the play and Reggie Salberg should be consigned to the nearest sewers!'

Like Mrs. Astin in the Box Office, Reggie was very honest if he felt a group of theatregoers would not appreciate a certain production. But he occasionally did like to shake up the Salisbury theatregoers. At first he found that he had to keep looking over his shoulder at The Close and they were very upset when early on he decided to present 'A Streetcar Named Desire,' but in an interview before retirement he said: 'But they've seen much worst since!'

It is interesting to note that although he selected all the plays for the season, Reggie never directed. His wife Noreen Craven, a respected director herself put a stop to that, she once said to him: 'The company still has some respect for you. Why not keep it that way!'

In his retrospective account of his first 21 years at the Playhouse Reggie wrote:

> With longer runs, we were also able to find time for many other activities. For example work in schools started in 1966, and from it has sprung our very busy Theatrescope Company which tours schools, Arts Centres and theatres over a wide area.

Before then though, in 1965 an incredibly important part of the Playhouse was launched – Stage 65, which fortunately is still flourishing today. Michael Pugh, then Drama Adviser for Wiltshire initially saw it as an extension of the Junior Theatre Club and it was immediately taken under the wing of the Playhouse.

The club's activities began in a modest way with occasional play readings but in the summer of 1965 under the direction of Richard

Gregson it mounted a successful revue in the theatre. A leading light was Brian Jones who after changing his name to Brian Protheroe eventually joined the Playhouse company and went on to appear in the West End.

When Roger Clissold arrived at the theatre as an Associate producer the club started to flourish and under his command the club's membership soon passed the hundred mark. For his highly regarded production of 'Noyes Fludde' in the cathedral, Stage 65 supplied the Assistant Producer and most of the animals!

In 1969 Bernard Krichefski was appointed full-time Director of Youth Work. During his two and a half years in that role, Stage 65 membership and activities continued to increase and there were some notable Playhouse presentations such as Peter Terson's 'Zigger Zagger' and Barry Rockford's 'Skyvers.' Stage 65 has had a rocky history but today, the Playhouse would not want to be without it.

Theatrescope, May 1966. David Simeon, Roger Clissold, Chris Harris, Sonia Woolley. (Salisbury Journal)

From the first few tours of schools, 'Theatrescope' was formed. As well as modern productions such as 'The Caretaker' and 'Under Milk Wood', and plays specifically for children such as 'The Bear that likes Geraniums', it also presented in schools and village halls,

The Company, September 1966, on the set of "The Creeper" (Salisbury Journal)

In the front row: Noreen Craven, Oliver Gordon, Reggie Salberg, Roger Clissold

social documentaries on such issues as racism, violence and corporal punishment. The Playhouse policy was that the casts of Theatrescope touring productions would be drawn from the main company and then re-absorbed at the end of the tour, thus avoiding any feeling of a reserve team, and it meant that people in the local community would be seeing the same performers as they would see when they visited the theatre.

'Play Days' were also created for schools which involved a morning session when the director and cast would demonstrate aspects of putting on a production and then this would be followed by a complete performance of the same production.

In 1964 an event happened that brought the Playhouse national recognition.. '*Twelfth Night*' was chosen to open the prestigious new Nuffield Theatre within Southampton University. Technically it gave the Salisbury players a whole new dimension within to act.

Lock Up Your Daughters, October 1966. David Simeon: Faithful, Politic's Servant; Stephanie Cole: Cloris, Hildret's Maid. Cast also included: Jonathan Cecil, Howard Southern, Michael Stroud, Sonia Woolley, Christopher Biggins. (Photographer Peter Brown)

The Bishop of Salisbury declared it a wonderful production as did the local press. *The Times* critic however, found 'his pleasure in the new theatre dampened by a production that made little use of the splendid new stage of the Nuffield.' A view contradicted by the *Financial Times* critic who thought the Salisbury company were 'inspired by their new surroundings and used the opportunity offered by the open stage to transform the best loved but most worn of Shakespeare's comedies into really super revels!' Whatever the critics said, it was a wonderful opportunity for the Salisbury company and many must have had thoughts of the possibility of acting on a larger, and better equipped Salisbury stage.

In 1966 the Playhouse celebrated its 21st Anniversary and a special photograph was taken of the company on the set of '*The Creeper*'. In it you can see a young Christopher Biggins at the back on the left and a young Alan Corkill at the back on the right.

'*Lock Up Your Daughters*' was a splendid production to celebrate this special anniversary. No curtain was used so the audience arrived to see a wonderful set in full view.

However, one lady was heard to remark: 'Oh dear, where are the curtains?' To which her friend replied: 'Oh, don't worry my dear, I expect they're at the cleaners'!

It was a time to pause, to look back, not in anger but in pleasure, and to give a broad smile of satisfaction at the success the little theatre in Fisherton Street had achieved over the years. But it was also however, a time to look forward and for Reggie Salberg to wonder if in the years to come, that dream of a new building for the Playhouse would ever come true.

11

'HOW MUCH LONGER CAN THE POOR OLD LADY BE EXPECTED TO LIVE?'

Reggie Salberg

THROUGHOUT THE 60S AND 70S 'The little theatre with the big reputation' continued to flourish. Reggie Salberg was a formidable captain of the ship and thanks to his tenacity, belief, sheer hard work and yes, sheer bloody-mindedness he was beginning to create the theatre that he had always dreamed of.

The Little Theatre With the Big Reputation advert

Eventually there were longer rehearsal times, longer performance runs, a wider range of productions to suit all ages and tastes and a company to match any regional or repertory theatre. There were always going to be financial problems; you could not run a theatre without the ogre of financial restraints constantly appearing. The old building was also going to keep giving problems as it just managed to hold itself together with the occasional structural and aesthetic help from occasional grants, spare pennies at the end of a season and the considerable support from the theatre's Fairy Godmother, the Theatregoers' Club. One day, there may be a new theatre appearing in Salisbury and it was important to hold on to that dream, but in the meantime it was the people working in the theatre that created its reputation and kept it in the local and national eyes.

(left) Roger Clissold (Photographer Unknown)
(right) Roger Clissold cartoon (Daniel Pettiward)

One such person was another of Reggie Salberg's second lieutenants, Roger Clissold, who first arrived at the Playhouse in 1965 after winning an A.B.C television scholarship for trainee directors. He left after a year to widen his experience but was invited back in 1970 to become Director of Productions.

Roger had been educated at Kings School in Gloucester and studied Law at St. David's College Lampeter. He went on to train at the Birmingham School of Speech and Drama.

His first play in Salisbury was '*Oh, What a Lovely War*' in November 1965 which also starred Stephanie Cole and Robin Ellis. That year he also played King Richard II in '*Dick Whittington*'. and pantomimes eventually became an important part of his life whilst he was at the Playhouse.

In 1966 and 1967 he was the Associate Director of the Playhouse and also lectured in Speech and Drama at the Salisbury Theological College.

*Old Herbaceous, November 1979. Roger Hume as Bert Pinnegar, World Premiere.
(Photographer Peter Brown)*

In 1970 he became Director of Productions and these ranged from his mammoth cathedral production of '*Noyes Fludde*' for the 1966 Festival of Arts to the much acclaimed one man play '*Old Herbaceous*' which starred Roger Hume as the old gardener Bert Pinnegar. This play eventually toured Britain, Australia, Zimbabwe and had a short run in the West End. It was also performed at Windsor Castle in front of the Queen and other members of the Royal Family as part of their Boxing Day entertainment.

Roger's wife Sonia Woolley remembers that they were not allowed to tell anyone about it and it wasn't until Christmas that the family was eventually told. She recalled that the entrance hall to the Castle was thick with dead birds, presumably the result of the Royal Boxing Day Shoot. The play was to be set up in the Drawing Room and the guests were given a room in which to change and to wait. Roger, Sonia and Anne, Roger Hume's wife, were able to watch the performance from a special balcony. After the show, in evening dress, they processed to a dining room. Sonia sat between the Duke of Kent and the Duke of Gloucester whilst husband Roger sat next to Princess Alexandra. It was a special performance for the Queen Mother who would ask: 'I wonder what Mr. Pinnegar would think of this plant?'

Sonia remembers Princess Margaret saying to her: 'You must come and use my loo!'

In his programme notes Roger described the seeds of 'Old Herbaceous': -

Shortly after my father's death, I cleared his workshop and sorted the carpenters' tools which had formerly been used by my grandfather. As a non handyman I had the melancholy task of placing these beautiful old objects into temporary storage after a century of active service, and was struck by the thought that our present generation is seeing the last of the old craftsmen who were trained in the Victorian tradition. No longer are skills passed from father to son. This suggested itself as a worthwhile theme for a one man play and so the search began for a suitable story line. For some years my family has rented as a holiday home a cottage formerly used by the gardener of a large house, and it was here I idly began to read 'Old Herbaceous' whose author ironically had been born within a mile or so from my parental home and I knew that I had found my subject.

During the play's interval, Roger Hume would walk amongst the audience giving them gardening tips. However, in reality Roger Hume was not apparently a gardening expert and one theatregoer recalls when he was invited by her for tea before a performance in Warminster he had much pleasure in telling her that he had brought some lupins for her – they were in fact sweet williams!

It was a very busy time for Roger as he took on more and more responsibilities, helping to run the theatre as well as directing. Gradually though, he was able to maintain a larger audience than average for a provincial theatre and he once said: 'The Playhouse policy has arisen from an awareness that you cannot please all of the people all of the time. Someone was once unwise enough to say that the W.I would never come to see Shakespeare and insulted half of England.'

His wife Sonia said:

He was very good at creating stage pictures and making the story move along. He was very good at creating a company and casting people to bring out the best in them, making people feel that they mattered. Unfortunately he tried to be all things to all men and he wore himself out.

Sonia reflected: 'he found it impossible not to take his work home and he would often say: "I'll just pop into the theatre". Actors talked about him as being a 'safe director' and that perhaps he was better at running the theatre than he was as a director. Whatever the thoughts, he was very well respected and eventually a worthy recipient of the keys to the new Playhouse.

One of his great successes, was Stage 65. When he arrived in Salisbury he took part in the first schools' tour. 'One of the things I am sad about is that the school work has been neglected.' he commented. So he helped to develop and to work on Theatrescope which toured many local schools and he helped to establish Stage 65 as an important and rich seam amongst the Playhouse's treasures.

In 1974 Roger wrote:

Our Playdays have proved to be a vital factor in the developing relationship between the Playhouse and schools in the area. These are occasions when a young audience is given an insight into all aspects of bringing a play's text to life in the theatre. We now have a full time Drama leader working with Junior and Infant schoolchildren. Members of our staff serve on local, regional and national committees, as well as carrying out a full programme of adjudicating, lecturing and advising school, dramatic societies and other organisations. This is not mere window dressing but is all part of a modern theatre's responsibility to its audience, present and future. It is an end in itself rather than a means to an end and it carries with it its own rewards. Nevertheless we must confess to a sense of gratification when we receive letters such as those printed below.

One letter from a teacher contained the comment:- 'They were really interested and said how much they had enjoyed it. And I assure you being able to capture and retain the interest of so many children for so long is no mean achievement!'

There were often interesting and amusing comments from the children themselves: 'When I first entered the hall I felt very unhappy as I had seen frogs killed in the biology lab and I felt sorry for them. By the time I left the hall I had forgotten about the frogs and was in a good mood.'

And: 'The acting was fab (the ladies particularly) and the whole group had talent. Some of our teachers had never laughed in their whole life but they had a good laugh this morning!'

And: 'All the boys at our school enjoyed the play I am sure, especially when she had a cigarette and kissed him on the lips (lovely) wish it could happen to me!'

However, Reggie recalled: 'When I was young, school parties were usually only organised for the classics and we somehow gained the impression that actors always wore knee britches!'

As a child, going to the theatre for the first time can be a magical occasion. Betty Anderson recalls taking her niece and her two children to one of the Polka Theatre shows.

Kimberley was three or four and my niece said 'get some seats on the end of the row, littl'un will never last out.' Well, littl'un was hooked the moment she came through the door. She just sat and looked at the stage. It was some Russian Folk Story and there were tall trees: 'Mummy, mummy, the trees moved! Did the wind blow them?' So then the strobe light and smoke effect started: ' Mummy, mummy, it's snowing!' she shouted.

At the interval we gave her an ice cream and when it had run down to her elbow and she hadn't licked it, we took it away and she sat looking at the stage again and shouted 'Come on!' When we got to the end we said 'Right, home now!' but Kimberley said ' No! I want another story!' She is now PA to the artistic directors at Birmingham Rep!'

Like all directors not everything went according to plan for Roger and in a performance of 'Our Town', the actors were standing respectfully around the grave. It was raining and they all held umbrellas. Roger was delivering his eulogy to his dear departed friend. He was supposed to say: 'Yup, that was a real smart farm.' Unfortunately it came out as 'Yup, that was a real fart smarm!' Suddenly the umbrellas all started to shake and the sound of the rain from the sound engineer slipped into a much faster gear! It didn't help of course, that one of the actors standing around the grave was one Mr. Biggins!

Coming from London, Sonia didn't know where Salisbury was but Reggie Salberg was quick to see that she was not unoccupied for too long. Roger and Sonia had only recently married and initially Roger was on a low salary. Reggie would always find jobs for Sonia to do and she helped out with publicity, party bookings and a whole variety of tasks, backstage and in the offices.

Reggie of course soon realised that in Sonia he had a very versatile actress and it wasn't long before she appeared in a whole variety of plays. 'In my first few years I played everything from fairies in pantomimes to octogenarians – that's terribly good for you.' she once remarked. Amongst her favourites she recalls: 'The Farmer's Wife', 'What Maisie Knew' and 'A Handful of Dust'.

She remembered playing in 'The Tempest' with Stephanie Cole and Carolyn Moody. The wardrobe mistress, Barbara Wilson, had made them Elizabethan costumes which looked good but they could hardly move in them.

> We had to enter down the corridor to stage left passing the coal store. We had to walk in the correct order along sideways in case we got our costumes covered in coal. Already tightly restricted we became hysterical and had to control ourselves before we could enter the stage. It was like going in and out of a weather house.

It was sometimes difficult if Sonia was in one of Roger's productions. She would always make a point of not talking about it when she got home; it was important to her not to go back with 'tales.' 'If you have a problem', she would say, 'you must talk to Roger, he would want to know, but not from me.'

In an interview she once commented:

> Haven't I been lucky – whatever you were doing at the time totally absorbed you – kept you fresh. Every play had its own challenges – they could be exciting, emotional, intense. In some plays you could be playing several parts, some you would like and possibly some you wouldn't but it was all excellent experience. Music could also be very evocative, some pieces or some songs could instantly take you back to a particular production.

Like many actors in repertory Sonia had to get used to Agatha Christie plays. Some years ago she commented: 'If you put on a Christie play now, many people would be surprised at how much it creaks and how bad some of it is.'

Roger Leach commented: 'It's very difficult to learn Agatha Christie and those Inspector's lists – lists and lists of questions to ask and if the Inspector dries, then you're buggered because no one else can ask the questions!'

Recently there has been a revival of her plays after a drop in popularity as television versions took over. Her plays though, were once part of the very fabric of most repertory theatres; in fact there have been 30 productions of her plays at the Playhouse. In 1956 there were three Christie plays and '*Spider's Web*' has been produced five times. Other old favourites have included '*Murder at the Vicarage*' and '*Witness for the Prosecution*', which many consider her best play.

Prunella Scales believes that there should be a place for Agatha Christie in good theatre companies as her plays are an important element of English theatre. However, Timothy West believes that audiences are now not so much interested in the 'whodunit' as in the 'howdunit' as represented by such plays as '*Wait Until Dark*' and '*Dial M For Murder*'.

Annette Crosbie never knew how anyone could get through an Agatha Christie. She once said: you'll find if you watch carefully.... that no one is meeting anyone else's eyes, particularly if you are working with someone like Roy Kinnear who was a terrible corpser as he would deliberately forget his lines!'

Michael Stroud painfully remembered his first role as Dr. Haydock in '*Murder at the Vicarage*' when nerves got the better of him when he had to look at a corpse on the floor and had to say; 'She's dead and beyond my arts.' At which point the audience always burst out laughing. He asked Stephanie Cole who was playing Miss. Marple what to do. 'Kill it darling, kill it.' she recommended. So for the rest of the run he just mumbled the line and nobody laughed.

Stephanie Cole once said: 'If you can perform well in Christie then playing *King Lear* is a doddle!'

Timothy West has many memories of playing in Christie plays at the old Playhouse. In the last act of '*The Unexpected Guest*' the Inspector (played by Tim Hudson) comes into the library and asks as always, the usual batch of questions, ending with: 'And who has the key to the gun cupboard?' The Governess then sheepishly replies: 'I have!' There follows more surprises, more questions and then the identity of the murderer is revealed. Before the second house one Saturday, Timothy West looked at his watch and saw that the play was running late which he mentioned to Tim Hudson. They were both known to like their Guinness in the King's Arms after the play so agreed to speed up the action. When it came to the scene in the library, the Inspector asked all the usual questions but no mention of the gun cupboard. Isobel Rennie, playing the Governess panicked and said in a shocked voice: 'But don't you want to know who's got the key to the gun cupboard?' To which Tim Hudson replied: 'No, I don't think so, I must get back to the station.' Somehow the play was concluded, the murderer was announced, the audience went home satisfied and more importantly the two Timothys had their Guinness!

Touring with '*Murder at the Vicarage*', Timothy West remembers that they had a set but no backcloth. On the night of the first performance there was a huge round of applause when a character went to the window and announced: 'I see Miss has been watering her garden.' He opened the curtain to reveal not a garden, but the backcloth of the previous week's production which was a ship in full sail from 'HMS. Pinafore'! Now what would Miss. Marple have said about that?!

Perhaps the most dramatic event during an Agatha Christie play was on 22nd November 1963 when the Playhouse was performing '*The Hollow*'. It was the day of the assassination of President John Kennedy. Frank Barrie was playing a character called 'John' and he was shot during the course of the play. Patricia Doyle had to kneel over him whilst he lay on the stage and say: 'John, John, they've shot

School For Scandal, October 1983. Barbara Wilson (on the right) with Julia Chambers (Photographer: Peter Brown)

John!.' Patricia had heard the news of the assassination but Frank hadn't – he had been on stage when the news came through. As Patricia said her line, Frank was amazed to feel real tears falling on his face. At the curtain the audience was informed of the news – there was a collective gasp of horror and they all immediately stood up in shocked respect.

Not too many problems with costumes if you put on an Agatha Christie, unlike a Restoration Comedy. But whatever play it was, it was all in a day's work for the Wardrobe Mistress, Barbara Wilson, a stalwart of the Playhouse during the 60s and 70s. (known affectionally as Babs or Madam Barbara!)

Time, or lack of it was a huge factor in her life. In her early days, Reggie would announce which plays they would be putting on, the dates and so on but the cast and the director may not have been appointed so the wardrobe couldn't work too far in advance. There was never much time to go into too many discussions, so often frantically, she would have to get some designs ready for Monday rehearsals. The director and Barbara would have an initial chat, rough an outline of what was wanted and there would hopefully be a consensus of opinion. Then the actors would come along and put in their ideas and at the end of the day it would be a combined effort to finalise the designs.

Longer rehearsal times and longer runs would ease the pressure but it was something that the Wardrobe always had to live with.

Barbara trained as an actress. In an article in the *Journal* she said:

> It would be nice to act if I was famous enough to choose what I wanted to do but the trouble is that this profession involves being out of work so much that you have to take parts you don't really fancy. When I was in Birmingham it was suggested that I go in for costume design as it was something I could do well and it took over from acting.

Barbara joined the Playhouse in 1965 initially for three months. For some while she combined her work in the Wardrobe with playing small parts, until the full time pressure of costume designing took over. Initially she had to work in one of the old cottages down Chapel

Place, which was very often freezing, with her costume store next door.

Money, or lack of it would mean that Barbara and her assistants would have to go back to basics to make everything needed. This could mean dyeing material, improvising, cheating and above all working flat out to meet the deadline of a first night. Some outfits could be of so tricky and robust design that they could never be properly cleaned but they still demanded maintenance so a great many of the Wardrobe's department's working hours, especially for the assistants, would involve washing, ironing, mending and general running repairs. A blackboard was available for actors to leave messages about broken zips, popped buttons and so on.

Before the washing machines arrived Barbara remembers with horror the visits to the launderette. 'We used to have to do the washing in one big load in the launderette on a Monday morning. It used to cause some fights because we had to bag four or five machines at a time so we were not very popular!'

Barbara's reputation was legendary, not just for the excellent costume designs which she miraculously conjured out of nowhere in no time at all, but also because she was not very keen on actors. She also kept rabbits in her room which didn't go down very well with actors because of the 'messages' they would leave everywhere!

It was said that if she liked you, you were safe and so was your costume. If she didn't like you for some reason, perhaps because you argued with her, then you would often have a problem with your costume!

She once said: 'Very few wardrobe mistresses are keen on actors, if like me, they have been struck at by an actor, chased down the corridor by an actor, had violent arguments with an actor, then you can fully understand that it can be a brittle relationship.'

Frank Ellis recalls when he was playing the Lion in 'The Wizard of Oz' Barbara made a head for him to wear instead of making up his face. Unfortunately it was far too tight. ' I can't move in it! I can't breathe,' he tried to explain to Barbara, but not wishing to incur any more wrath from her, he went ahead and wore it!

Stephanie Cole remembers that Barbara wanted the in the cast of 'The Rivals' to wear genuine corsets. In this p sentences can be very long so you need plenty of breath. With her genuine corset pulling her tightly every time she breathed, Stephanie could not cope so after the first night, Stephanie deliberately 'lost' her corset in a pile of old costumes. Madam Barbara was not best pleased! However, Stephanie will always speak highly of her, saying that Barbara inherited a quite good wardrobe and turned it into a very good wardrobe.

Barbara remembers the 'groupies' that used to hang around the stage door. Desmond Gill was playing Absalom in 'She Stoops to Conquer.' Looking good in his costume he impressed the young girls watching the school's matinee performance. Many of them crowded round the stage door waiting for his autograph. 'Don't go out yet!' shouted the stage manager. 'Bugger that,' he said, and he opened the door and walked through the crowd. As he walked down Fisherton Street one girl shouted out: 'That's him!' and they all rushed after him, caught up with him and pinned him against a wall, tearing at him. Eventually he managed to break free and made a dash across the street to the Flamingo restaurant where he was a shaking wreck!

Tim Meats recalled the time when he had a difference of opinion with Barbara over his Prince Charming costume. The white, velvety trousers he was wearing had become rather black after sitting around on a painted tree stump for so long, so he asked Barbara if she would do something about it.

She was obviously very 'panto busy' because her repair took the form of a brand new rectangle of white sewn on the seat of the trousers that simply looked like a pillar box! Fortunately as this was Tim's first pantomime she took pity on him and repaired it properly before the next performance!

Tim Meats was another talented actor discovered by Reggie Salberg, this time not in Sally Spruce's but at LAMDA at their end of term show. Reggie was interested in Tim but he had already been offered a job in Farnham where Reggie's daughter, Jane was Stage manager. After a season there he went to Derby where Roger Clissold was Artistic Director. Reggie went to see some of his productions and eventually Tim received a letter in Reggie's minuscule writing that simply said: 'Dear Tim, give me a ring if you would like to come for the season.' So in this circuitous route, Tim eventually found himself in 1970 at Salisbury Playhouse.

He was first involved in Theatrescope where the local critic wrote: 'he gave a notable performance as Aston in '*The Caretaker*'. His first role on the main stage was as Prince Charming in '*Cinderella*' where once again he impressed the local critic: – 'an outstandingly personable and melodious Prince Charming.' For a while though, Barbara Wilson felt otherwise!

Tim soon became an important member of the company for two years, in which he appeared in 16 plays ranging from Shakespeare, pantomime, comedy, music hall with the occasional controversial play such as '*The Boys in the Band*' thrown in for good measure.

Later in '*Miss Leading Lady*' Tim was able to show the Salisbury theatregoers what an accomplished singer he was. He always had a great love of opera but wanted to be an actor who occasionally sings rather than a singer who occasionally acts.

He hugely enjoyed playing comedy. He once said: 'It is very exciting to hear an audience laughing. With a serious play the audience could either be showing rapt attention or be fast asleep but with comedy, you know if the audience is with you very quickly.'

He enjoyed being part of a company because 'you already knew who you were working with and you didn't have any 'getting to know you time.' It was his apprenticeship, and he learnt so much from such excellent directors as Caroline Smith and Noreen Craven and from close colleagues such as Michael Stroud and Roger Hume.

He had fond memories of the old theatre, such as after a matinee, when the doors opened at the back you immediately got a strong whiff of fish and chips from the Yorkshire Fisheries! Time for tea!

Tim's employment continued for many years and despite several departures he happily returned to work at the new theatre. He lived locally so the Playhouse always remained part of his life. Tim once said : 'I have had a wonderful life and I could never have been a regular 9 to 5 man in a suit. One day I'll grow up and get a decent job.' Tim did get a job, a more than decent job which certainly wasn't a regular 9-5!

A few years later Reggie Salberg raided another drama school, this time the Central School of Speech and Drama, where he saw a young student called Roger Leach performing in David Mercer's 'Flint'. He was sufficiently impressed to offer him a one year contract. Roger's first part was as the butler to Charmian May in 'Barchester Towers.' This one year contract was soon extended and Roger rapidly became one of the Playhouse's most popular actors and over the years he performed in more than 40 plays. Despite the many calls from radio and television such as his role in 'The Bill', like Tim Meats, Salisbury remained his home, to which he eagerly returned whenever possible.

Roger's versatility covered the whole spectrum of the theatre and theatregoers will have their own favourite Roger roles. Roger would talk with pride of his performance in David Horlock's production of 'A Christmas Carol' in which he played Scrooge. He said it was one of the few times that there was a black market in tickets, so popular was this production. The role of Lambert Le Roux in 'Pravda' gave him much pleasure, as did the roles of Inspector Karn in the controversial play 'Sus', as well as Pooter in 'Diary of a Nobody'.

He was equally at home with comedy and starred in several pantomimes which included an hilarious performance as Abanazar

School For Scandal, October 1983. Roger Leach: as Sir Benjamin Backbite; Venetia Barrett as Mrs. Candour; Howard Attfield as Crabtree (Photographer: Peter Brown)

alongside Knight Mantell as Widow Twankey! Although he would have liked to have done more Shakespeare, he did appear in a whole range of costume dramas. There is a photograph of Roger as Sir Benjamin Backbite in '*The School For Scandal*' wearing the most outrageous of wigs. David Horlock asked him not to go too far over the top in his interpretation of this particular character. Knowing Roger, his interpretation was probably most certainly, way over the top!

Roger said though, that serious plays were the most rewarding to do: 'When you're doing a real masterpiece like '*The Crucible*', it's actually very easy, it's very satisfying, and it kind of plays itself; you've

Neville Dewis, Head of Design (Photographer John Walmsley, with permission)

just got to go in and be true to it and you'll be alright.' Roger was at the beginning of the new Playhouse's life and very much part of it. Though he made the Salberg studio his own. To which we will return later.

So Reggie Salberg continued to be successful in recruiting excellent actors for his companies and despite the inevitable financial constraints in 1970 he could look back 'with a fair degree of satisfaction.' as performances averaged over 70% for the fourth consecutive year and the Playhouse continued to be one of the most successful small repertory theatres in the country. Of 34 provisional repertory companies, only four played to a higher percentage of capacity in 1969 than the Playhouse did. In his programme notes Reggie wrote:

Once again there was no production which made me want to hide my head in shame. Obviously productions of such masterpieces as 'The Cherry Orchard' and 'King Lear' will fall a long way short of perfection but both had some memorable performances, in particular Roger Hume, Christopher Dunham, Stephanie Cole and Charmian May in 'King Lear' and Roger Heathcott, Christopher Ravenscroft and Christine Edmonds in 'The Cherry Orchard'.

Setting up the stage at the old Playhouse, for "On The Boil", February 1973
(Photographer John Walmsley, with permission)

The pantomime 'Cinderella' gave more performances than ever before and still managed to play to 100% capacity. He also praised the work outside the theatre. The company played a total of 112 performances for children in schools and the newly formed Theatrescope Company gave performances of 'The Caretaker' to adult audiences from Swindon to Southampton.

He noted that taking into account the Playhouse's touring activities 'the little Playhouse has served audiences of over 150,000 people.' He concluded by saying: 'It can be seen that a repertory theatre is a busy place these days!'

In a report in 1971 he wrote:

No good repertory theatre can be self supporting. Greatly increased seat prices would make theatre available only to the comfortably well off and would probably mean many empty seats so our subsidies are vital. Our total annual grants amount to £27,350 of which £25,000 comes from the Arts Council. 14 local authorities contribute between them £1,850 and Southern TV gives us £500. This means that we still have to earn 65% of our total expenditure.

Reggie continuously tried to keep the seat prices as low as economically viable but in the early 70s he was forced to raise the prices by 1/- per seat for the following season. This was because Equity had agreed to an increase in actors' wages, longer holidays and better rehearsal payments. This could cost the theatre an additional £600 – £700 per annum. Reggie said: 'as I am constantly being told that our prices are too low, I'm sure our patrons will not resent this extra charge especially as the money will go to the actors they admire.'

In 1971 he sent a letter to the BBC after an 'Any Questions' programme where he concluded by saying: 'It is perhaps worth noting, that most civilised countries facing equal problems after the War gave (and still give) subsidies to the Arts on a scale undreamed of in this country without damaging their economies. In fact they seem to be doing rather better than we are – perhaps they have their priorities right.'

At the AGM of the Board of Directors that year, he reported: 'last year's accounts show a surplus of £400. Ever since 1955 we have managed to keep out of the red every year except 1962/63 when the blizzards affected us so badly. A proud record but it is the subsidies we receive that enable us to survive and extend our work. And costs are increasing much faster than subsidies!'

A good example of 'Peter paying Paul' were these notes in Reggie's programme diary:

Saturday 11th September 1971: 'Hadrian VII' continues to play to poor houses. We can only hope that four wonderful press notices will help.'

Sunday 26th September 1971: 'Worked out the profit and loss account for 'Hadrian VII'. The loss is £635 but luckily this is covered by the profit on '*French Without Tears*'. Such is the drawing power of revivals of popular comedies.

Reggie Salberg was now running a very successful theatre despite the constant nagging toothache of financial instability.

However, there was one 'elephant in the room' that was always being talked about and that was the state of the building and the need to see Reggie's dream of a new theatre come into fruition.

There was another scare when Reggie heard that there was to be a road constructed by the side of the theatre to enable cars to enter the new main car park. He was concerned that this would mean extra noise and therefore extra expense on sound proofing which the theatre could not afford. It was another reason to start planning for a new building. This road, which became Summerlock Approach, was eventually constructed during the 70s and it meant the destruction of three shops, Mr. Crow's wrought-iron works, Marie's sweet shop and taxi service and Mr. Payne's music shop. Marie's sweet shop and taxi service was obviously very popular with the Playhouse theatregoers.

In an article for *Southern Arts* in 1975, Roger Livingston wrote in support of the Playhouse

If theatre is to survive in Salisbury, the new theatre building is not simply desirable, it is a necessity:

What kind of building is it that has been fostered over the years? The Playhouse is a repertory company and with what I would describe as a repertory audience. While I was there a woman at the box office put down her basket of groceries to purchase tickets for next week's performance in the same way as she bought the weekly shopping, and I suspect that the Playhouse has a large number of such regulars. Audience figures would bear this out. For the past seven years attendance has exceeded 70%. In 1974, 83% was the average. Going to the theatre in Salisbury is not a rare treat, it is a regular date for most of the audience.

This is the achievement of Mr. Salberg's practical policy. He will not have a theatre half full, and argues that it is not serving its purpose as an enriching experience if it remains empty. His reward is a faithful audience, and an audience who give the theatre its remarkable good atmosphere. Somehow the dedication of the theatre management and the company's enthusiasm have been conveyed to the audience, creating an atmosphere which affects everyone connected with the theatre, from technicians who laugh off impossible conditions to box office staff who always have time to talk to callers about forthcoming productions.

The support for the Playhouse, both locally and nationally goes without saying but this much loved little theatre was suffering from a long list of ailments and each year the building was being granted its licence more or less on the understanding that this would be the last year it would be needed.

At last though, in April 1974 at the Theatregoer's Ball, an Appeal was launched for a new theatre. As Reggie explained:

We feel sure that theatregoers will enjoy their theatregoing more in a new building. No longer will they have to fight their way through our tiny foyer; to fight for coffee; to queue to spend a penny; to wonder where to put their dripping mackintoshes on a wet evening or to suffer the tortures of the damned on a hot summer's night when the thermometer in the Circle creeps up to 95°F.

He once exclaimed: How much longer can the poor old lady be expected to live? She needs a healthy offspring to carry on the good work.'

It was going to be a huge and difficult project that would stretch the energy, will-power, imagination and resources of all those involved and it would affect and indeed change the lives of many people. It was a mountain that had to be climbed. But where do you begin?

Perhaps a trip to Colchester may help?

12

'I BELIEVE THIS THEATRE IS MORE THAN A LUXURY, IT IS A COMPLETE NECESSITY'

Reggie Salberg

In 1915 the Primitive Methodists moved out of their chapel in Fisherton Street as there was the constant danger of flooding. The building then became a cinema, a drill hall and recruitment centre, a garrison theatre and it was now a flourishing and much loved repertory theatre. Reggie Salberg had worked miracles and the 'little theatre with the big reputation' was much loved by the people of Salisbury and beyond. However, in the early 70s, Reggie could do no more to improve nor indeed to save the building. It was very much on its last legs and it was certainly now or never to plan for a new theatre. Each year the fire officers gave the building its fire certificate on the understanding that a new theatre was going to be built.

So why visit Colchester? The reason being because it was one of the many theatres that were being considered as the prototype for the new Playhouse. In March 1973 a party of keen theatregoers and representatives of the Playhouse made a trip to Colchester to visit the newly opened Mercury Theatre. On the way, there were many people who were mourning the inevitable loss of their much-loved Playhouse. However, on the return journey there was much eager talk of how soon the new theatre might become a reality. The visit included seeing a production of '*The Liars*'. It was an excellent day out which cost the princely sum of £2.95 which included the ticket to see the play.

The visit proved to be fortuitous as this theatre was eventually chosen as the design for the new Playhouse and Norman Downie from

The Mercury Theatre Colchester, 1970s (Photographer Unknown)

Colchester, who was the architect for the Mercury, was appointed as the architect for Salisbury's new theatre.

Prince Philip once remarked that there was never a good time to ask for money. This was certainly true of Salisbury Playhouse. The Board had decided to raise the money for a new building but the Appeal was launched during Edward Heath's three day week and a time of economic and political crisis. However, with a building that had outlived its life what else could they do? The directors had to go ahead before the old building was closed down or at worst, collapsed.

The ideas of a new building had naturally been discussed many times at Board Meetings. Then in 1973 a suitable site had become available on very good terms, and assurances of financial support had been received from the Salisbury District Council, the Wiltshire County Council and the Arts Council amounting in all to £240,000.

This however, was half the £500,000 which was considered the required amount for the new building. The directors decided to go ahead with the planning for the new building, aiming to raise the balance of the money by an appeal to the public. In the autumn of 1973 the directors invited Craigmyle and Company Limited to organise the Appeal and John Musgrave was appointed as Appeal Director.

Insufficient space was available in the theatre's administrative buildings, so accommodation was obtained in offices owned by the South of England Building Society in Castle Street. Furniture and office equipment were either borrowed from people associated with the theatre or purchased. By the middle of November a secretary had been engaged and the office began to function.

The next task was to recruit an Appeal Committee. Sir Henry Langton (Calley) was invited to become Chairman and the successful and influential people of Salisbury were invited to join the committee. Forty two were invited and thirty accepted. Rather a large group of people to keep focussed and to direct!

To give the Appeal added status, a number of prominent people associated with the local area and the Arts were invited to become patrons – people even higher and mightier than the Appeal Committee.

All of these people however, were not just names on a list as they all gave financial support and active help to the Appeal.

The Appeal had therefore already started in the background and large donations were beginning to trickle in when on the morning of Friday 19 April 1974 a news conference was held at the Playhouse to announce that the Appeal for the new Playhouse was going to be launched that evening. The announcement was made at the Theatregoers' annual ball by the Chairman of the Appeal Committee, Sir Henry Langton who also happened to be the Club's President. In his speech he remarked:

> Half a million pounds are needed to build the new theatre. We already have promises of support from local and national authorities amounting to half this sum but the rest must be raised by our public appeal. At first we shall be concentrating on direct approaches to the more likely sources of gifts but we believe that there will be a wide response to the Appeal not only from Salisbury and its immediate surroundings, but also from the extensive area from which the audiences are drawn and indeed from the many friends and supporters throughout the country. Nevertheless, we shall need all the help we can get.

How very true, as the cost of this new building would soon begin to creep above the original quote of £500,000.

Reggie Salberg of course, understood that the bulk of the money must come from grants, trusts, businesses and organisations, but he was adamant that he wanted the new theatre to be built by ' ten thousand people' and 'the little men' should be able to play their part. In other words, everyone could make a donation however the money was raised or however much the donation was to be. This hope was eventually to become a reality as the 'ten thousand people' eagerly responded to the call and a minor miracle could be possible.

But first how to raise this sum? An appeal brochure was circulated with many ideas such as: -

1. Give a donation or sign a deed of covenant. Every gift of £150 or more (£15 a year under covenant) would entitle you to have your name permanently recorded on one of the seats in the new theatre.

2. Become a Founder. If you gave £50 or more (£5 a year under covenant) you would be entitled to a private viewing of the completed Playhouse and your name will be placed on the theatre's mailing list for two years and it would be recorded in the Founders Book.

3. Pay for some specific feature of the new Playhouse. A dressing room perhaps or the lighting equipment or the house curtains.

4. Contribute to the collecting box in the Box Office whenever you bought tickets.

5. Hold a coffee morning, a sponsored event or an entertainment for the benefit of the Appeal.

6. Join the Theatregoers' Club which was actively working for the Appeal.

7. Publicise the new Playhouse- talk about it, write about it and encourage friends to support it.

8. Invite your friends to one of the current productions (perhaps with a little supper party afterwards?)

9. Form a group and promote local fund-raising.

10. Ask relatives or friends in the business world to help.

11. Give personal support and publicity to the many fund-raising events the theatre was promoting.

The most advantageous way of making a gift was by Deed of Covenant. Over a period of at least seven years the donor undertook to make regular payments to the Appeal Fund. The Playhouse as a registered charity, could then recover from the Inland Revenue income tax already paid on each gift. Thus the total value of the contribution was increased by at least 43%. Over the forty months of the appeal some 700 Deeds of Covenant were formed giving a total value of over £146,000.

Many people preferred to make a single payment equivalent to the total of seven covenanted instalments, which meant that through such Deposited Covenants the theatre could enjoy immediate use of the entire sum as well as benefiting from the recovery of the tax.

Some people paid by Bankers Order and many benefited from the opportunity of having their name recorded on one of the seats.

The very wealthy and businesses donated for a specific item or room, for example, if you were feeling particularly generous you could have sponsored the theatre foyer for £30,000! In fact many groups did sponsor specific areas of the theatre; for example the Pilgrims Trust paid for the Green Room and the Theatregoers' Club paid for the Bar.

Becoming a Founder was very popular. Donors of over £50, plus seat holders, private donors, trusts, organisations and business donors could all have their names written in the Founders Book. This was originally hand written but that proved to be too expensive so it was to be 'electronically type written.'

This book was placed in a glazed compartment in the centre of the Box Office and was opened at successive pages from day to day 'where I believe it will be of widespread and lasting interest' remarked the Chairman of the Appeal. It remained there until the Box Office was relocated in 1996. It is now in the Playhouse Archives.

In August 1974 Craigmyle's contract was terminated. It had not been the great success that was envisaged and it had been expensive. However, it had made a start and the foundations for the appeal had been laid.

A member of that team, Jane Pearce carried on to be joined by Veronica Burrough and Nigel Ponsford and the Appeal Office moved to 22A Winchester Street.

When he left, John Musgrave remarked: 'The general impression after ten months of the Appeal is that the money can be raised, but to bring it in will call for long, persistent and sometimes repeated effort by all those already associated with the Appeal and by as many as possible who can be recruited to help. It will be a long and difficult struggle but it should eventually result in a most rewarding and lasting achievement.'

In October 1974 Louis Schuyleman, Treasurer of the Federation of Playgoers' Clubs spoke to the Theatregoers' Club's Annual General Meeting and issued this word of warning about asking for large sums of money. He believed that people would give large sums for medical research but that they related their level of theatrical appeal support to the price they paid for admission. He said that in famine conditions in wartime Holland he used to visit farms to ask to buy a single egg – and he usually got three. If he had asked for six he would probably have got none, and this experience had shaped his appeal philosophy.

Unfortunately after a three month trial period Nigel Ponsford and Jane Pearce lost their jobs because of continually rising costs, and the Appeal Committee was not happy with the amount of donations since they had taken over. Veronica Burrough was to remain and Pat Tozer and Brenda Wade joined the team. But who was to be in charge? After two false starts it was third time lucky, because a member of the Board, Robert Hawkings, became Honorary Appeal Director and the fund raising really took off in earnest. Robert Hawkings was local, he had the local knowledge, he knew people, he knew who to go to, he knew how to organise, he was influential and above all he was free! He was quite simply, the right man for the job.

The Appeal Office moved yet again, This time to one of the old cottages behind the Playhouse so at last, expenses were kept to a minimum. The first donation recorded was that by Julian Slade, the second by Robert Hawkings and the third by the Playhouse's Theatregoers' Club. Although many in the theatrical world had rallied round and made their donations, the Appeal had to go national. So in May 1975 a reception was held at the Haymarket, organised by Martini and Rossi where William Douglas Home made the official announcement. This prompted further donations from across the theatrical and business worlds but it was at grass roots level, particularly Salisbury grass roots that the fund raising really took off.

In 1977, in his final report to the main appeal committee, Robert Hawkings reported 'that there had been over 200 different fund-raising events, covering a very wide range and some showing great enterprise and imagination.'

Many naturally involved theatrical personalities. There was a Brains Trust chaired by Alfred Shaughnessy, which had Honor Blackman, Gordon Jackson, William Douglas Home and Evelyn Laye as the panel.

Bernard Miles came to do a one-man show entitled 'On the Wagon.' Timothy West and Helen Ryan exhibited their costumes from 'Edward VII' at Wilton House. Eleanor Bron, Timothy West, Prunella Scales and Robert McBain were involved in an evening's entertainment called: 'Behind the Scenes.' Local celebrity Christopher Biggins provided Christmas entertainment and Agatha Christie donated her fee after a performance of her thriller: 'Spider's Web'.

The Theatregoers' Club played a major part and raised a total of over £8,000. Their Annual Theatre Balls and Garden Parties being the star attractions.

There was also a 'Show Biz' Football Match at Victoria Park with Ed Stewart, and an Open Day at Wilton House where a team of pedlars in period costume, street musicians and Morris Dancers were in attendance.

A local firm, Wellworthy, held their Gala Day on the works and sports field at Netherhampron Road which included a Grand Tour of the factory including a demonstration on how pistons were made – how fascinating!

There was even a Slimming competition where the first prize was 1 piece of Crispbread and the second prize was 2 pieces of Crispbread!

Naturally the theatre staff was heavily involved in spreading the news and Reggie Salberg went to many a meeting to explain the need for the new building and to drum up donations. He usually took with him the model of the new Playhouse that was made by Bill Toop and Ken Lailey and Bill Toop's painting of his vision of the new Playhouse. Sadly the model is no more but the theatre still has Bill Toop's original painting.

Alan Corkill has lost count of the number of fundraising events he was involved in. From Coffee mornings to choosing the Tisbury Carnival Queen! The theatre also had two schemes to help the new building. 'Be a Brick and Buy a Brick' and 'Help to 'Cement' the future of the new Playhouse by buying a bag of cement!'

Bill Toop's painting of the new Playhouse from publicity, 1974

Various publications also benefited the Appeal: -

'Heart of the City' – the history of the Playhouse by John Bavin Price 70p.

'The Old Playhouse'- unframed prints by Michael Charlton. Price 30p each.

Stage production in the old Playhouse – signed and numbered by Bill Toop. Framed £7.50 or Unframed £3.50.

Whilst all this was happening, the 'little men' (the people of Salisbury) were busy organising coffee mornings, dance displays, sponsored walks, concerts, jumble sales, drinks parties, barbecues, flower festivals and jumble sales.

Old Playhouse showing thermometer, 1970s (Photographer Peter Brown)

There was also the case of a pensioner who donated the increase in his pension. to the Appeal.

However, some supporters were over enthusiastic. Mrs. Gertrude Smith held a coffee morning in Crane Street which made £50. Unfortunately a saucer from a treasured Dresden tea service was sold by an over zealous helper. The following notice appeared in the next programme: – 'If you are the purchaser please let us know at the Appeal Office as we would very much like to buy it back for Mrs. Smith'! It is not known if it was ever returned!

Unfortunately there were some people who objected to this money being raised for a new theatre. Such as James Watson who wrote from the South Newton Vicarage:

> Have we shut our eyes to the needs of the man in the street and are only concerned with the needs of an affluent section of society? Surely it is the man who gives us the everyday needs of life – the milkman, the coalman the farm-worker, etc who needs a roof over his head that should be our first concern. You can do without a Playhouse but not a house.

He had his supporters but they were outnumbered by the many that wrote to the local paper in support of the Playhouse, such as this old age pensioner:

> As an old age pensioner living in one room without a TV set I do not know what I would do without our wonderful theatre. It has given me hours of marvellous entertainment all for the price of 50p. One does not live by bread alone, one's mind has to be fed as well. My mite has been sent towards the new theatre and may it flourish.

The cost of the new building continued to rise above the original quote of £500,000, in 1976 it was creeping up nearer to £700,000. On mid-summer's day the Playhouse appeal entered its final and most crucial stage.

A generous business gift of £1,000 took the appeal total well beyond the £650,000 milestone so the shortfall was then £50,000. It was vital that this figure was raised before the opening of the new Playhouse because the management did not want to open with a debt hanging over them. Supporters rallied round for one last-ditch effort. There were demonstrations of landscape painting, a Bridge tournament, flower arranging demonstrations, a ballet display and demonstrations of haute cuisine cookery. South Wilts girls held a sponsored spell which raised £99 and two girls aged 8 and 10 raised £16 by doing a sponsored walk.

One big event was an exhibition held in the Library in the November. It was called 'Long Live the Playhouse' and was organised by Alec Fieber from the College of Technology. It consisted of stage designs and models, costumes and properties, and paintings of both Playhouses and a comprehensive collection of photographs of the two theatres. There was also a 'Pick a Picture Draw' of paintings by local artists and a silent auction of a splendid patchwork quilt made by the Mid-Wessex branch of the Embroiderers' Guild. This enterprise raised £660.

Then finally the £700,000 mark was reached just after the building opened and Elizabeth Medley from Grateley won six theatre tickets and six champagne dinners, as it was her donation that hit the target!

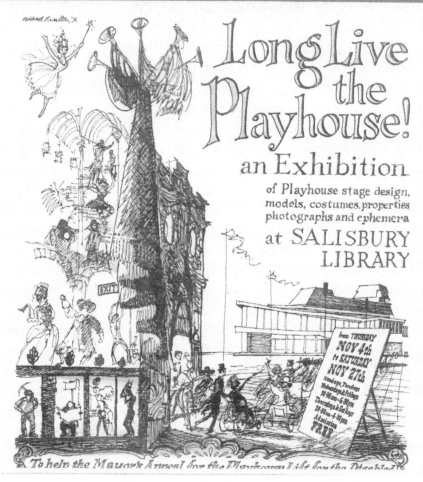

Poster for Exhibition for new building, 1976, Michael Charlton

In his final report to the main appeal committee, Robert Hawkings reported that grants from the Arts Council and various authorities came to £458,900 and that private and business donors, organisations and trusts donated £239,700. This was made up of some 2,030 separate gifts. Many of these donors had given on two or more occasions – many more had given anonymously and many thousands had supported the many fund-raising events.

The Appeal costs including professional and secretarial help over the forty month period, also expenses such as telephones and lighting, construction of the theatre model, engraving of 530 seat labels, provision of the big 'Benefactors Board' in the Foyer and other signs and notices came to just over £30,000. – or rather less than 5% of the entire sum raised.

. *"The End of the Appeal". Robert Hawkings, Roger Clissold, Brenda Wade, Jackie Martineau*

He added: 'By far the largest item was the fee paid to the professional fund-raisers engaged at the start of the Appeal.'

He concluded by saying: 'Possibly the biggest factor in the appeal's success has been the real love of the old Playhouse and the high regard for its management and company.'

In 1981, Robert Hawkings was awarded the OBE in the Queen's Birthday Honours List. At a celebration some years later on the occasion of his 90th birthday Alan Richardson spoke of Robert and his wife Francis: 'Pope Paul XIII said: 'Men are like wine, some turn to vinegar, but the best improve with age.' Robert and Francis are indeed Chateau bottled and are examples of a rare and very fine vintage.'

The minor miracle had occurred and the money had been raised. In fact the appeal raised more money by public support than any other appeal in the country. The Playhouse had scaled their Everest and it was time to wave the flags but not for long, because everyone was anxious to experience the excitement and the pleasure of their amazing new building.

The basic concept of the new building was arrived at in consultation with the head of design of the Royal Shakespeare Theatre, Christopher Morley. This was based on the principle of a small hexagon (the stage area) within a larger hexagon (the auditorium).

The auditorium walls (from the stage area to the widest point of the hexagon) were to be formed of screens or towers which would appear to be completely integral with the structure of the building and yet could be moved in and out to produce different forms within the theatrical representation.

As it was being constructed, Andrew Golden in an article wrote: 'the structure looking like two black hexagons sitting one on the other, jut out against the skyline like a giant beehive in silhouette.' A.J. Dunning and Son from Weyhill won the contract to become the constructors. The important people were now in place and the new theatre could start to rise phoenix like from the rubble of an old timber yard.

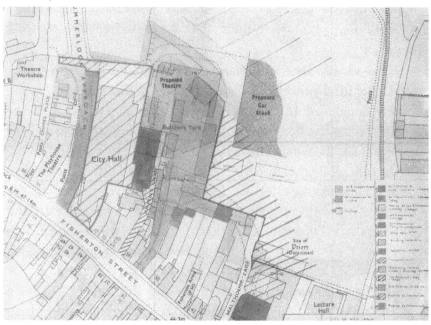

Plan of site of new building

Once the decision had been made to build a new theatre, one big question remained, where was it going to be built? The land behind

Fisherton Street, at the back of the old theatre had been developed in the form of a group of Maltings buildings owned by William Brothers and covering some three and a half acres.

At the back of the Maltings ran the smallest standard gauge private railway in England, which ran from the main station to the Market House, which eventually became the Corn Exchange and then the Central Library. Subsequently Market Walk which runs by the side of the Library was once part of the railway line. This track carried goods for the Electric Light Works, the Maltings and the Building Material Company. The railway closed in 1964 and the Maltings business was sold in 1961 to Way and Beazley for £30,000.

The original site for the new theatre - the builder's yard, 1970s
(original photo given by Richard L.K. Griffin)

Nearby was a timber yard owned by the Griffin family until the death of Fred Griffin in 1905. The Building Material Company carried on their trade until eventually much of the land behind Fisherton Street was purchased by Wort and Way of Castle Street. They sold the land to the City Council. Mr. Wort was on the Board of the Playhouse and the land was sold to the City Council on the understanding that the land where the timber yard once stood would eventually become the site of the new Playhouse.

There had been talk of building the Playhouse nearer to the river and the library which would have given theatregoers better access but the Maltings site was eventually chosen. The City Council provided the site to the Playhouse on very generous terms. The only proviso was that they asked in return that the old Playhouse and the cottages behind the Playhouse should be conveyed to the Council.

This was reluctantly agreed as the Board was hoping to sell the old Playhouse to help cover the cost of the new building. However, they got the site they wanted which was going to be close to the old building and near the centre of the city.

Having a new Playhouse building in the Maltings area was part of the council's plan, at the time, of creating a new civic centre, as the press release explained: 'There will be easy parking for cars and coaches and a large traffic free area surrounded by trees, shrubs and ornamental ponds, uniting the Playhouse with the City hall, the new Library and the proposed new Museum.' Sounds familiar?!

The new building was proudly presented to the public as being so much better than the old building. There would be more seats available in the auditorium and every seat would be within 60 feet of the stage. There would also be generous legroom. There would be dressing room space for 24 actors although more could be accommodated if the production required it.

There would be a much larger workshop on site. No longer would the scenery have to be constructed in cramped conditions. There would be a Bar and a Restaurant that 'would provide new sources of revenue and would enable the audiences to enjoy a complete evening's entertainment under one roof. The report continued: 'provision is also made for patrons to leave their coats in free self-locking devices. There will be neither wet coats in the auditorium nor any queues outside the ladies' lavatory!'

Roger Clissold wrote about the restaurant:

I hope that this theatre will be open for as much of the day as possible and I hope that the barriers will be broken down between the theatregoing and the non-theatregoing public. For example the restaurant will be totally classless. There's no reason why somebody wanting a cheese roll and a cup of tea shouldn't sit down next to someone eating smoked salmon and crepes suzettes.

It was also announced that the small studio alongside the main stage would be called 'The Reggie Salberg Studio' which would inevitably become 'The Reggie!'

Of course, publicising the new theatre started on a solid base because of the success and popularity of the old Playhouse. Attendance figures for the old theatre showed that audiences averaged over 70% capacity. The theatre served not only Salisbury but also the whole of the Wessex region. In fact two thirds of its patrons came from outside the city. The Playhouse also took productions to outlying areas by means of their schools' policy and the Theatrescope scheme. Reggie Salberg commented: 'The main factors in our success have been a carefully and varied programme which really caters for the community in which we live and an atmosphere of friendliness which always makes you feel part of us.'

When addressing the City Council in 1975 in a bid to obtain a further grant, Reggie remarked:

I believe this theatre is more than a luxury, it is a complete necessity. It is also a tourist attraction in the area in the summer when it is possible to come into the building and not hear an English accent.

However, we do not live in cloud cuckoo land. We have designed a theatre to run more cheaply than most other theatres and for the past twenty years we have been able to keep within our own budget.

We haven't been able to plan the building we would like to see as that would cost a million but we have already got a possible cuts list.

Roger Clissold said: 'Although the new Playhouse represents a great leap forward in comfort and convenience for all who use it and it will be a valuable amenity and tourist attraction for the area, it is a bare bones building without superfluous, wasteful features.'

One cost cutting feature was to dispense with one fireproof door. The saving would be £6,000, the exact price the old theatre paid for the freehold of the Playhouse in 1963!

The plan was that once the new theatre was up and running, extra items could be added at a later stage. A Development Fund was set up after the building was completed and under the astute chairmanship of Alan Richardson many items were indeed added.

Started in 1975 and then finished in 1976 the Playhouse was ready for an official opening. Subsequently it applied for a place in the Guinness Book of records because:

1. Its appeal raised more money by public support than any other appeal in the country.

2. The building was completed and the theatre opened three months ahead of schedule.

3. Its first season broke all box office records playing to an average of nearly 98%.

Quite an amazing success story!

13
'IT HAS BEEN THE CENTRE OF MY LIFE FOR 21 VERY HAPPY YEARS AND I LOVE IT, WARTS AND ALL'

Reggie Salberg

In keeping with tradition, it was decided that it would help to bring good luck to the new building if there was a ceremony when 'the first sod was turned.' It would also of course, be very good publicity if a celebrity could be found to carry out this special task.

As so often happens in the theatre world, someone knew someone who knew someone and it was eventually suggested that Derek Nimmo should be invited to the Playhouse building site to 'turn the first sod.'

In the 60s and 70s Derek Nimmo was a very popular television star, specialising in ecclesiastical roles such as the Reverend Mervyn Noote in 'All Gas and Gaiters' and as Brother Dominic in 'Oh, Brother.' He was also a regular panellist in the popular radio programme 'Just a Minute.' His face would therefore be easily recognised as would his often imitated voice.

The Appeal Committee worked out an elaborate plan of campaign which included a vintage car and a flight of pigeons! The ceremony however was kept much simpler but it still made a huge impact on all those who were present, and the Playhouse publicity machine made sure it was a very successful day.

The plan was to have an Open House coffee morning with the cast of the present production '*Barchester Towers*' in costume. The regular theatregoers as well as Playhouse dignitaries were to be invited. Tickets cost 50p each. Occasional rows of seats were to be left empty to enable Derek Nimmo and the Playhouse company to move more easily amongst the seated audience.

So on 19th July 1974 at 10.30 Derek Nimmo arrived at Salisbury Station having travelled first class and not on the footplate as was originally envisaged. He was greeted by Sir Henry Langton, Chairman of the Appeal Committee, Guy Jessop Chairman of the Playhouse Board of Directors and other members and officials of the Playhouse. He was then driven to the Playhouse, not by a vintage car, but in a dormobile.

For half an hour Derek Nimmo entertained the audience, ad libbing in his own inimitable way, speaking of his life in the repertory theatre and on television. He said that ever since his ecclesiastical series on television he has been asked to open nothing but Baptist Bazaars and Methodist Missions. 'It's awfully nice to be asked to do something that's not ecclesiastical at all,' he commented. Then someone reminded him that the original Playhouse in Fisherton Street was a Methodist Chapel and that the present production; 'Barchester Towers' had a religious theme!

He was delighted to be able to appear at the old repertory theatre at last – he said that it was 'a lifetime's ambition realised.' He went on to praise the people of Salisbury as the appeal target had now reached £300,000 of the required £500,000. 'I'm sure it will be a wonderful theatre in every way and I hope that this wonderfully ambitious plan will be completed in 1976. I hope that I can be there at the opening.'

After coffee he went to the site of the new Playhouse followed by many members of the audience, to perform the ceremony of 'turning the first sod'. This was to be in an area outside the building site so as to cause no disruption to the builders' normal work. It was a rather inappropriate title, as the building site was not covered in turf but with an assortment of broken bricks and rubble. However, it was all spruced up with the usual carpet walkway and tubs of flowers and Derek Nimmo, armed with a shovel decorated with a large bow, walked towards the rubble. Watched carefully by Roger Clissold, the Playhouse's Artistic Director, he vigorously tossed some earth into the air and declared: 'I have never turned a sod before – I declare this sod well and truly turned.'

Within an hour the ceremony was all over and he was whisked off back to the station, leaving behind an audience hoping that it

Derek Nimmo turning the first sod, July 1974 (from Salisbury Journal)

would bring good luck to the new building. After all it was carried out by a member of the cloth!

The next tradition was the Laying of the Foundation Stone. But who were they going to get to perform this important ceremony?

'Princess Alexandra cannot come so we suggest that Lord Olivier or Sir John Gielgud should be invited next.' This was reported at a meeting of the Appeal Committee in January 1975.

Many names had been bandied about at other committee meetings including the Queen Mother, Princess Anne, Alec Guinness and Ralph Richardson. Reggie Salberg also wrote to the Countess of Pembroke to see if Prince Charles was available. The ceremony had been planned for mid summer 1975 and it was getting urgent.

Amongst the many names suggested was Peter Hall, the Director of the National Theatre. As his theatre was also in the process of being built it seemed appropriate that he agreed to travel to Salisbury to be the main attraction. The ceremony was to be kept informal and only a few dignitaries, including the Bishop of Salisbury, the Chairman of the District Council and the Mayor of Salisbury, were invited to meet for coffee and light refreshments on the stage for 11.00 on Friday 6th

June.

Accompanied by his wife, Jacqueline Taylor and his two children, Edward and Lucy, Peter Hall then made his way to the building site where a small area had been cleared of building material to allow the ceremony to take place.

Peter Hall was introduced by Guy Jessop, as 'a true man of the theatre and as the sun shines on our new theatre we are very honoured that he should come down to Salisbury from his London theatre to our provincial theatre to perform this important task.'

In reply, Peter Hall gave praise all around. Praise for Reggie Salberg who had been the General Manager of the Playhouse for the last twenty years; praise for the choice of design of the new theatre and praise for the contractors who were six months ahead of schedule. The latter was particularly significant for him as he pointed out the difficulties of getting his own theatre finished on the left bank of the Thames in London.

He knew that this new Salisbury theatre would be successful because it was not for example, being grafted onto a new town. He commented: 'This theatre is here because of the old theatre over there.' Although he said that he had never laid a stone before and had had no

Peter Hall laying the foundation stone, June 1975 (Salisbury Journal)

rehearsal, he used the mallet to good effect and carefully knocked the block of Portland stone, inscribed with gold lettering, into the wall of the partly finished building. However, as he wrote in his diary later: 'I put the foundation stone in place, gratified I must confess by my billing and then the TV crew asked if I could lay the foundation stone again as they had a technical hitch. Reality these days is only on film!'

At the end of the ceremony, Guy Jessop announced that the appeal fund had been boosted that very morning by a cheque for £3,000 from the Grocers' Company pushing the fund up to £410,000.

The final act of the ceremony was a blessing from the theatre Chaplain, the Rev. Michael Hurst-Bannister for the building and for all those who would be working there. This was followed by a rousing fanfare from two trumpeters of the Queen's Regiment stationed at Bulford.

The theatre gods had given this short but important ceremony a beautiful sunny day and perhaps because the foundation stone had been laid twice, their intention was that the theatre building was going to last twice as long as was originally intended!

~~~

Before the move to the new building another important event was to take place and that was 'The Last Night of the Old Playhouse.'

The genial host and chairman, Mr. Elwyn Johnson bangs his gavel onto the table and welcomes the audience to the 'Famous Salisbury Thespians' performance of the Ninth Edition of 'Music Hall' and of course it was 'at enorrrmous expense!' Thus began the last performance at the old Playhouse in Fisherton Street on Saturday 23rd October 1976.

Of the nearly 500 shows that have been produced since Reggie Salberg arrived, Music Halls, revues and of course the pantomimes have been amongst the most popular – they are fun, full of variety and energy and with plenty of audience participation. So at a Music Hall the 'Playhouse family' could enjoy one last evening together.

There would be sadness that the old Playhouse was finally closing and the air would be thick with nostalgia, but the emphasis of this last show was to be one of happiness and enjoyment. Everyone involved with the theatre, the company and the theatregoers, could celebrate for one last time the enormous success of the old Playhouse even with tears in their eyes, because just around the corner a bright new future awaited them in the shape of the new Playhouse - a shell

Poster for Old Time Music Hall, October 1976

at the moment, but an empty building waiting to be filled with the same degree of happiness and enjoyment and the seeds of many more memories for the years to come.

The '*Music Hall*' show ran for nearly three weeks but the demand for tickets for the last show was obviously enormous and once the allocation of seats for VIPs had been organised there was a draw to see who could fill the remaining ones. Many previous members of Reggie's companies wanted to join in the celebration and the BBC came to film the show as part of a programme to celebrate Reggie's 21 years as General Manager.

Reggie took the BBC interviewer around the theatre to show him the desperate state it was in. He showed him the dingy cramped rooms backstage and into the catacombs that eventually lead to the stage, passing the coal hole stage left. He showed him the condemned buildings in Chapel Place that served as offices and workshops.

'These buildings are only fit for human habitation by theatre managers,' he commented. He then pointed out one roof that had caved in and his hope 'that the one that they were under would not cave in until after the new theatre was opened.' I like working with young people but I don't like working in an old building.' was his comment.

Despite the poor condition of the old theatre, the last season played to 80% capacity and there was usually a demand for tickets for most performances, particularly of course for the pantomimes, and the Music Halls.

Members of the cast were interviewed and they expressed their love for the old building despite all its problems. They said that the warmth of the old building would soon transfer to the new one and much would be the same although they would miss Reggie for his fund of stories, his gossip, his great theatrical knowledge and the fact that they would often tease him because of his easily imitated voice! One actress commented on another aspect of warmth when she said that they were forever complaining that the theatre was cold on a Monday because the heating was always turned off on Sundays!

The cast of eight were Miss Rosamund Shelley, Miss Jane Argyle, Miss Liz Moscrop, Miss Sonia Woolley, Mr. Chris Harris (Returning by Public Demand), Mr. Derek Crewe (Returning by

Public Transport), Mr. Anthony Millan and Mr. Graham Richards and the 'whole stunning spectacle' was supervised by Mr. Roger Clissold, Mr. Christopher Littlewood and Miss Liz Moscrop.

The whole show was a wonderful mixture of song, dance, comedy and true old-fashioned variety so loved by theatregoers at the time, although many today still hanker for that type of good old-fashioned entertainment. The audience loved joining in with such old favourites as 'Joshua' and 'Shine on Harvest Moon' and they loved laughing at three of the ladies of the company trying to outdo each other as cats in the wonderful 'Cat's Chorus!'

The Theatre Manager, Alan Corkill resplendent in top hat and tails, met the audience as they came through the door. He was naturally busy with refreshments and it stated in the programme: 'There will be one intermission during which our esteemed patrons are invited (at their own expense) to partake moderately, of intoxicating liquor from our well stocked Dress Circle Salon or to sample our excellent coffee at the rear of the Stalls. The proprietors particularly request that any incivility or overcharge on the part of the attendants be made known to our popular manager Mr. Alan Corkill.'

Also interviewed for the television programme were three ex-company members – Derek Benfield, Prunella Scales and Leonard Rossiter. The latter spoke of Reggie being a true gentleman and that often company members would find some extra money at the end of the week if they gave a particularly good performance. Once though, he was a little nervous of Reggie when just after he had joined the company and was working as an ASM, he met him wandering around the theatre 'like a little mole.' Len was busy making props when in came Reggie, playing with his loose change in his pocket: 'How do you strip?' he said. Len got rather worried and thought 'Oh, dear, here we go.' 'How do you strip?' repeated Reggie. 'You see we are putting on 'The Little Hut' and that Graham Armitage does not look right without his clothes on.' It transpires that Len never got the part because Reggie decided not to produce it!

After the final bow, many actors from previous companies joined the cast on the stage and then there were the speeches. Bernard Krichefski, a former associate director, presented Reggie with a certificate and there was a toast to the new theatre.

Photo of last Night at the old theatre, October 1976 (Salisbury Journal)

'For he's a jolly good fellow' was sung with great gusto, to be followed by three cheers for Reggie. The actors then danced a conga down the aisle and there was much cheering and waving of balloons.

Reggie was asked how he was feeling: 'I'm in a whirl at the moment, feeling rather punch drunk and in a few days time I will be feeling rather depressed.'

However, in the programme notes he wrote:

It is of course with mixed feelings that I see the old Playhouse close its doors. It has been the centre of my life for 21 very happy years and I love it, warts and all. To lift my spirits however, I have only to walk a few yards to the wonderful new building which is the culmination of everything for which I have worked: but for it, I would feel my work had been wasted, for my dearly loved old Playhouse would be under sentence of death, deemed unfit to carry on any longer.

Although Reggie was going into semi-retirement he would still be helping Roger Clissold with theatrical and financial matters, coming down to Salisbury twice a week. He said that he would be known as a 'consultant administrator' whatever that may be, working about 30 hours a week.

Building the new Playhouse, 1975 (Peter Brown and Salisbury Journal)

He said that his semi-retirement was a way of catching up on the soccer and rugby that he'd been missing, as well as his theatregoing, 'Although I worry a bit about that. Nowadays I find the first thing I ask when I get inside a theatre is the time of the final curtain!'

Roger Clissold would now be taking over the reins from Reggie and he said how delighted he was that the majority of the Salisbury theatregoers had accepted the fact that a new building was inevitable and that they were very optimistic about the future. 'Even the 'scoffers' and 'the nostalgic merchants' are beginning to look forward to the new season.' After the show, one lady remarked that they could still have their fish and chip supper after the performance as the new theatre was still near the local fish and chip shop!

It must have been very difficult for the theatregoers to eventually leave the old Playhouse that evening, but leave they had to and many continued their chats and nostalgic gossip as they made their way home probably humming some of the tunes they heard that evening. The gate in front of the old Playhouse entrance was pulled shut and locked for the last time. The Playhouse was finally left alone with its own memories but if they glanced up, was that a Harvest Moon shining down from a Salisbury sky?

ACT THREE

The New Playhouse

14
'HERE ON THIS SPOT SHALL HISTORY BE MADE.'
Daniel Pettiward

'Welcome **back** to Salisbury Playhouse!' With these words Roger Clissold began the official opening ceremony of the new Salisbury Playhouse on Tuesday 30th November 1976.

After so much hard work, the dream was becoming a reality as the building had finally been completed and all those involved could rest awhile and bathe in the joy and the glory of an official opening ceremony.

In his speech Roger Clissold began by praising the most important man in the audience by saying:

> When I heard that mine was to be the first voice to be heard addressing an audience from this stage, I made a resolution that the first name to be mentioned would be that of a man who has earned the affection and gratitude of us all and without whom there would be no Playhouse – Reggie Salberg.

He then thanked all the public and private benefactors who had earned the gratitude of all Salisbury theatregoers by making the new theatre a reality. Their fundraising was announced as a national record for any theatre appeal.

In particular it was important that two names were mentioned for special praise. The success of the appeal was largely due to the ceaseless hard work and devotion shown by the Honorary Appeal Director, Robert Hawkings, and also mentioned was the Chairman of the Board of Directors, Guy Jessop, who made the original decision to go ahead with plans for a new theatre.

It was then his proud duty to welcome the guest of honour by saying:

> Celebrated actors tend to fall into two categories. There are those who have become household names because of their recognition on film and television and there are those who have gained respect throughout the profession because of the quality of their work. Both these though are gross understatements when applied to our honoured guest. We are indeed fortunate and proud to welcome to Salisbury, Sir Alec Guinness.

As Sir Alec Guinness walked onto the stage there would have been many people in that audience who would have given a contented smile of satisfaction that all their hard work and commitment had finally come to fruition.

In September of that year Sir Alec had written to his friend Alfred Shaughnessy, who was an important member of the Appeal Committee:

> I am awfully bad at doing what you ask of me but unless you can find someone more suitable (which should be easy) I'll say yes. I can't do a Monday, Wednesday or Thursday so I think Tuesday November 30th is the nearest to December 1st which would suit me. But I must be back in London by 4.00 otherwise I shall talk rubbish at the evening performance at the Queens! Please take seriously my plea that you should get someone else, if possible – far from taking offence I would be relieved.

So that was one problem solved, after many discussions and many letters, the committee had finally got their man, even though he was a rather reluctant one. Finding an important guest to perform the opening ceremony had loomed large on the agendas of the appeal committee for many months.

Royalty was at first considered and a sub group, which included Jo Benson and Francis Pullen, came up with this list, in order of preference:

Queen Mother – popular and would do well.

Prince Charles – ideal (if we could get him.)

Duke and Duchess of Gloucester (He is an architect and might be specially interested.)

Princess Alexandra

Princess Anne.

Time may be too short to get any of them in which case we might try for a top theatre personality.

This proved to be the case. Lord Margadale, the Lord Lieutenant of Wiltshire, informed Guy Jessop that the Queen Mother was unable to accept the invitation and had advised against approaching any other members of the Royal Family.

Princess Alexandra would have loved to perform the ceremony but could not make any commitment until July or early August.

Robert Hawkings reported that the Duke of Gloucester had presented the cathedral's floodlighting trophy to the Dean and (reportedly) had done very well – but it was felt that he might not bring to the theatre the sense of occasion that they wanted and that they should try for a top personality in the theatre field. At the next meeting there was a general discussion when the following names were considered and turned down – Peggy Ashcroft, Ralph Richardson, Peter Hall, Keith Michell, Dorothy Tutin, Irene Worth, Bernard Miles and from the other side of the footlights – The Minister of the Arts, Lord David Cecil, Roy Jenkins, John Arlott, The Bishop of Sherborne and Lord Margadale.

Amongst leading theatrical personalities it was felt that Lord Olivier would be ideal but that he might have to decline for reasons of health. So it was decided that a carefully worded invitation would be sent to Lord and Lady Olivier. Failing acceptance, the committee would try (in this order) Peter Ustinov, John Gielgud and Alec Guinness. Olivier and Gielgud graciously refused and Ustinov was out of the country. The committee gave a sigh of relief when Sir Alec agreed!

In a letter to Roger Clissold, Alfred Shaughnessy wrote: 'I must say it's rather good news isn't it? For me, far better than minor royalty!'

The composition of the opening ceremony was also naturally very high on the agenda. In March the plan was to have a simple opening ceremony in the covered approach to the new Playhouse where there would be seating under cover for about fifty people with ample room in the open on either side for members of the general public. The ceremony would include the cutting of a ceremonial tape.

The invited guests could then see the new theatre in action with scenery being painted, lighting systems being operated and rehearsals taking place on stage followed by lunch or tea. If royalty was coming then the city might organise a formal banquet in the Guildhall.

The opening ceremony would be followed by a week of preview performances which could be in three parts-

1. A single singer at the back of the auditorium singing 'Prepare Ye the Way' from Godspell moving forward onto the stage to meet the company. Then a light-hearted dramatised documentary-history of drama in Salisbury down the ages to the present day.

2. A compere demonstrates the equipment of the new theatre – flying the scenery, operating the lighting and sound systems etc.

3. Company then returns and there would be a programme of singing and dancing with a medley from recent successes. The programme could be called 'Welcome to the New Playhouse.'

Nothing however, could be finalised until they knew who was going to perform the opening ceremony and precisely when it was going to happen, although tentative plans were in place for late Autumn before pantomime time.

Another big problem was who to invite if the ceremony was to take place in the auditorium because with so many dignitaries needing to be there plus members of the theatregoers club, architects and contractors, old friends and 'those who had given £50 or more' the theatre would be full to overflowing. The solution was to invite many of these people to the planned preview evenings.

Alfred Shaughnessy, a close friend of Sir Alec's, made the final preparations. The timing had to be tight as Sir Alec was appearing in 'Yahoo' at the Queens Theatre in the West End. Train timetables were checked and the plan was for him to arrive at the theatre ready for a 1.00 start.

In his speech Sir Alec said that it was a kindly tribute to his profession to invite an actor to open a theatre. 'Nearly all actors, whatever honours may be bestowed upon them, are deep down in their hearts merely rogues and vagabonds and may they remain so and not aspire to be civil servants.' He commented that 'the building is a great cause for much civic pride and that Salisbury stands very high in the theatre profession's esteem – happy is the actor who can say that he has a week in Salisbury and not a couple of weeks in Wigan!'

The people of Salisbury have taken a great step forward and the whole nation will be grateful to them.

He quoted Hazlitt, the 19th-century critic, who wrote: 'When a town has a theatre there is not much wrong with the world.' He also quoted Shakespeare when speaking about actors: 'Use them well for they are the abstract and brief chronicles of the time. After your death you were better to have a bad epitaph than their ill report while you live.'

Alec Guinness opening the new Playhouse, November 1976
(Photographer Peter Brown)

He concluded by saying that it only remained for him, as an 'ageing mummer' to wish those who would be working in this new theatre and those who would be in the audience, great pleasure, happiness and excitement as the theatre grows. The old theatre had a huge reputation and was much loved and he saw no reason why this new building would not continue in that tradition. There was a pause and he commented: 'I can assure you that this curtain will go up and the lights will go on...' And suddenly there was the fanfare by the trumpeters of the Royal Signals Regiment and the cathedral choir began to sing! Daniel Pettiward had written a beautiful ode for the occasion and Richard Seal had set this to music.

The final verse was very appropriate and struck a chord with so many people in the audience and throughout Salisbury when they got to hear it:-

> May all who serve here or were glad to give
> Time, toil or money they could ill afford
> And all whose love has made this theatre live
> Find in its presence infinite reward.
> Fly out the curtain – let the house lights fade
> Here on this spot shall history be made.

The commemorative stone was unveiled by Sir Alec and then Guy Jessop paid a tribute to his fellow directors, ordinary men and women who showed great courage when in the time of financial stringency, they voted unanimously to take the risk of building a new theatre and they had the courage to sign a contract for the building work to begin.

He also announced that Robert Hawkings had again 'pulled a rabbit out of the bag' and knocked a further £1,000 off the shortfall of £9,000. This had been donated by the Cave Foundation.

Finally, the theatre chaplain, Michael Hurst-Bannister blessed the new building and then the National Anthem was heartily sung by the audience and the company.

Time for drinks and refreshments in the Bar where drinks had been provided by Hall and Woodhouse and the food served by the catering students from the Salisbury College of Technology. The whole

Ceremony for the Opening of

SALISBURY PLAYHOUSE

1.00 pm November 30th 1976

Introduction: Roger Clissold, Theatre Director

Opening Ceremony: Sir Alec Guinness, C.B.E.

Fanfare: Trumpets of The Royal Signals Regiment

Ode For The Opening of The New Salisbury Playhouse:

> Text by Daniel Pettiward. Music by Richard Shephard
>
> Conductor Richard Seal
>
> The Cathedral Choir and Salisbury Playhouse Company
>
> *Fly out the curtain - let the house lights fade*
> *Here on this spot shall History be made.*
>
> *From Salisbury's oldest, best-loved monument*
> *Summoned by trumpets, we its choir salute*
> *With fervent hopes and friendliest intent*
> *Our newest, our most radiant recruit.*
>
> *Hail to this miracle of light and air*
> *These gracious promenades and magic screening*
> *Hail to the Company, without whose flair*
> *This Playhouse would be void and lack all meaning.*
>
> *May soon this stage, the city's shining heart*
> *Throb to new works of vision and inspire*
> *Great acting feats that lovers of true art*
> *Will gather from all quarters to admire.*
>
> *May all who serve here, or were glad to give*
> *Time, toil or money they could ill afford*
> *And all whose love has made this theatre live*
> *Find in its presence infinite reward.*
>
> *Fly out the curtain - let the house lights fade*
> *Here on this spot shall history be made!*

Reply: Guy Jessop, Chairman of the Board of Directors

Blessing of the Playhouse: The Rev. Michael Hurst-Bannister, Playhouse Chaplain

National Anthem: Company, Choir and Audience

Architect for the new Playhouse: Norman Downie, R.I.B.A.
Main Contractors: A.J.Dunning and Sons (Weyhill) Ltd.

Ceremony for the opening of the new theatre, November 1976

catering operation was of course, masterminded by Alan Corkill. Photos and presentations were made and then it was time to whisk Sir Alec off to the station when in a comfortable first class carriage

Roger Clissold, Alec Guinness, Reggie Salberg and Robert Hawkings toasting the opening of the new building, November 1976 (Salisbury Journal)

he could begin to turn his mind once more to his performance at the Queens Theatre.

The new building was now officially open and some people's minds may have drifted back to the opening of the original Playhouse in Fisherton Street when the actress Beatrix Lehmann said:

'We have a building. We have a company. We have an audience. Care for each other, love each other, watch each other critically and helpfully and may you work together for a long time and prosper in your work for many years to come.' No problem. The Salisbury theatregoers will certainly see to that!

~~~

Just after the official opening, the Theatregoers Club celebrated by having their traditional Christmas party on a Sunday afternoon organised by Roger Clissold and Ray Smith from the Theatregoers Committee.

A selection of local artists were invited to take part including the Downton Amateur Dramatic Society, the Studio Theatre, the

Downton Band and a group of local poets who called themselves The Company of Five. It seems appropriate that the Theatregoers Club, that had raised such a significant amount towards the building of the new theatre, should be amongst the first to use the new stage.

The week of preview performances however, eventually morphed into one show. It was to be called 'Welcome to the Playhouse', and as Roger Clissold wrote in the programme: 'The opening show is very appropriately a celebration – aimed to communicate and share our delight in our new building with the audience. This festive revue is a light-hearted documentary about theatre in the area and demonstrates in a variety of theatrical forms how the new Salisbury Playhouse came into being.'

The show ran from 1st December until 11th December and all seats were 80p. Elwyn Johnson and Tim Meats, who were already steeped in local theatrical history, wrote the script and Christopher Littlewood, already a great favourite because of his musical skills, wrote the original music and songs.

His group, Lynx, performed the music and one critic was led to comment: 'undoubtedly more will be heard of them.' The show was produced by Roger Clissold and directed by Adrian Reynolds.

Welcome to the Playhouse programme cover, December 1976

With photographic background shots, the company of ten – Olivia Breeze, Helena Breck, Mary Keegan, Jill Graham, Derek Crewe, John Bramwell, Graeme Malcolm, Elwyn Johnson, Graham Sinclair and David Shaughnessy – brought to life the story of drama in Salisbury, starting appropriately at Stonehenge and moving through various periods of history taking in many famous names including Shakespeare, Sheridan and Irving as well as many theatrical milestones such as Strolling Players, Music Hall and Melodrama –

leading up to the beginning of the Playhouse's story:-

> In Salisbury City, down by the station,
> They're building at high speed,
> With bricks and mortar, love and elation,
> A splendid little chapel, with a history great indeed!

There followed the story of how this chapel became a cinema, then became a garrison theatre and how it eventually became the first

Welcome to the Playhouse: Elwyn Johnson and Jill Graham, December 1976
(Photographer: Peter Brown)

Playhouse. The story then moved on to the struggle to build the new Playhouse.

Amongst the cast, Olivia Breeze gave a delightful cameo of Edith Evans who had appeared at the Garrison Theatre; Jill Graham, recreated Beatrix Lehmann's speech at the opening of the Arts Theatre and John Bramwell had the job of portraying various voices of doom and dissent. However, the star performance was that of Derek Crewe who gave a superb impersonation of Reggie Salberg, whose unique tone of voice was often imitated by fellow actors!

The huge struggle to create the new Playhouse was sensitively brought to life and like all good stories there was a happy ending as the cast celebrated the opening of the new building. In a highly spectacular climax, the voice of Alec Guinness was heard officially opening the building, and then a stream of banners appeared from above thanking all those who played their important part in seeing the dream of a new building come true. These included all the local councils, the many fund-raising groups, the architect and contractors and last but not least, the Playhouse appeal staff.

The production drew capacity audiences and the praise of local critics:-

> In an hour and a quarter, without any break, the story of the struggle to keep the Theatre going in Salisbury is unfolded in song, dance, mime and words in '*Welcome to the Playhouse*' which marks the opening of the new Malting's building.
>
> It is drawing capacity audiences and they are finding happily, that the general friendly atmosphere which was such a feature of the Fisherton Street theatre is still existing.
>
> It is a real joy to sit in the place and to see such a good, fast moving show.

So wrote R.M. Williams for the *Stage* and *Television Today*. Andrew Golden of the *Western Daily Press* wrote:

> If this is the sort of dynamic performance we can expect in the future, then many a television set will remain switched off during 1977. The emphasis was on happiness, and the obvious joy of the performance

at coming alive in a magnificent new theatre must have permeated through to even the most stony hearted theatregoer.

Of course you cannot please everyone, and one stony hearted theatregoer from Ashley Road felt the need to write to the *Journal*: 'The performance took the form of an end of term rag by the upper sixth.' Fortunately he was soon shouted down by the hundreds that did enjoy the show.

It was very much a time of celebration as seen in the last lines of the production:-

> Time of joy and celebration
> Nothing lost and all things found.
> Sing with joy and loud elation:
> Fill the air with boundless sound;
> Sing with joy that knows no ending
> Reach for the stars and touch the moon:
> Tragedy and Happy Ending
> Blend together in the tune.
> From our hearts we welcome you
> And welcome too, the new Playhouse!

The next production was to be the annual pantomime: '*Cinderella*'. The cast and the production team could now stretch their imaginations to so many new and exciting levels in this, their new building, and of course it would certainly play to capacity audiences!

There will no doubt, be more problems and challenges to face in an uncertain future; no road ahead would remain smooth and there will be many bumps and twists and turns to negotiate, but now, for the moment, it was a time to smile and to bathe in the warmth of an incredible achievement.

15
'LET THE PAST GO UP IN SMOKE –
AND SPARKS – AND TO ADMIT THAT
WE CANNOT TELL WHAT THE FUTURE
HOLDS.'

Roger Clissold

There was still one important question – what to do with the old building? It was now owned by the City Council and they had to make a crucial decision. The front of the building had been shored up; there were cracks in the walls and the roof leaked. It could potentially be a danger to the public and as Anthony Stocken, the council chairman commented 'Positive action is needed before the Playhouse becomes dangerous and a prey for squatters and vandals.'

There were two main trains of thought: The lease of the old Playhouse could be used for short-term warehouse use or it could become a joint leisure complex with the City Hall. This was a logical extension to the cultural and leisure activities planned as part of the Maltings redevelopment scheme. The other alternative, of course, was to pull it down and sell it for redevelopment.

The Conservation Area Advisory Committee considered the Playhouse to be a 'building of importance.' The design of any replacement would therefore be critical and the existing frontage would have to be preserved.

The Council decided to wait for the findings of a structural survey but as one councillor commented: 'We could end up with a load of rubble being tenaciously held together by cobwebs.'

Many locals certainly did not want to see the building demolished and they had their champion in Councillor Lynn Weeks who accused the developers of putting big business before the conservation of an historic landmark. He commented: 'There is considerable sentimental feeling for the old building. It is historical in its own right as a mid-Victorian structure and with the names associated with it over the years it also has a social history. He warned: 'We must be on our guard at all times, otherwise our historic buildings will gradually go and they will be replaced by something not worthwhile to look at.'

Demolition of the old building, 1979 (Salisbury Journal)

A petition was organised and over 300 local people signed it. They wanted the appeal money to be spent on repairing the old Playhouse and bringing it up to safety standards.

Gordon Industrial (South Western) of Salisbury quickly saw the potential for redevelopment of the site as a Freezer Centre but to pacify those who did not want to see the building demolished, their plan was to base their design on the Playhouse's original Victorian appearance.

Eventually though, because the building was deemed to be unsafe, the Environment Secretary, Peter Shore, made the final decision to demolish the building and this began in February 1979.

The redevelopers did a fine job and they kept the façade of the old building. Those many theatregoers who remember the old theatre can now stand opposite this new building and see in their mind's eye their old Playhouse and then surely memories will soon come flooding back..

As the building was being demolished, one reporter commented:

Walking around the old Playhouse today it's hard to believe it was full of life a few weeks ago. The carpet is up, the stage curtains are gone and the air is dank. On the backs of threadbare seats are the names of donors who paid two guineas for the privilege: Sir Ralph Richardson, T. S. Eliot, Anna Neagle, Sir Laurence Olivier and Terence Rattigan to name just a few. They read like a Who's Who of the theatrical and literary world. Outside above locked gates a plaque records how the theatre was bought in 1960 'with funds subscribed by the citizens of Salisbury.' The whole atmosphere would be depressing in fact but for one thing – about 100 yards away a magnificent new theatre has been built.

A magnificent new theatre had been built but the work is never finished. A Development Fund was set up soon after the official, opening, to provide a brand new three storey building at the rear of the theatre and also to provide a room which could be used for rehearsals and meetings. This was under the wise chairmanship of Alan Richardson, a member of the Board. Thanks to a generous interest free loan, the work was able to go ahead at a cost of £60,000. The theatre then had to pay the loan back and after two grants from

'Godspell' 1977: members of the cast
(Photographer Peter Brown)

the Arts Council and a local authority, the bulk of the money came from some three hundred benefactors both private and business. In appreciation, their names were also recorded in the Founders Book.

The three storey building was to house the Playhouse's huge collection of costumes and props as well as 'Togs' a fancy dress hire service which was inaugurated by Roger Clissold as part of the fund-raising efforts.

The new rehearsal and meeting room was created by filling in the covered area beneath the Bar which was originally designed as a through way for cars but which was never used for that purpose.

This room was then named The Hawkings Suite in honour of the man who had been responsible for raising so much money for the appeal fund.

The new building was built without a lift so the Mayor, Dr. Tym Hattersley decided to make it his Mayor's Appeal when he was in office. In 1977 the money was available to build it thanks to £7,563 being raised plus £1,206 which came from the local hospital fete committee. Mrs. Patricia Kidd had the privilege of being the first patron to use this new lift.

There were many other things on the Playhouse's shopping list including an air conditioning system but these had to bide their time.

The driving force behind the Development Fund, Alan Richardson was a very influential figure at the Playhouse for many years. In 1977 he joined The Theatregoers Club, becoming their Chairman in 1978 and eventually their President . He was an ardent fundraiser for the new Playhouse alongside his close friend, Robert Hawkings and when Robert retired from the Board in 1983 Alan took his place and served as a Board member for nine years. When sponsorship began to appear he became a hardworking member of the Sponsorship Committee and it was the

Alan Richardson
(Photographer Peter Brown)

Theatregoers that sponsored one of the early plays in the new building, the musical '*Gilgamesh.*'

Alan was born in Salisbury and spent his early years in Catherine Street where his mother owned a needlework shop. He recalls in his book *The Cinema Theatres of Salisbury* – 'One day when I was very small I dimly recall a visit to our house by a man with a very large Alsatian dog. He talked with my mother about buying our shop! It transpired that he wanted our home and garden to make an entrance to the front stalls of a brand new cinema he planned to build around the corner in New Canal.' This building became the Gaumont Palace which we now know as the Odeon Cinema housed in the beautiful John Halle building.

This incident must surely have planted the seed which gradually grew into a love of the cinema and the arts in general. He recalls seeing his first 'talkie' film at the Picture House cinema in Fisherton Street which eventually became the first Playhouse.

Alan initially wanted a career in the film industry and he decided to go to the top and wrote to David Lean, the famous film director. However, he eventually ended up at the BBC where he soon made his mark, a very large mark in fact, because at the BBC he created the biggest film library in the world even larger than the one in Hollywood.

A little known fact about Alan is that he was a First Lieutenant during the Second World War and helped to deliver a deadly cargo of ammunition from a landing craft to Sword Beach during the D-Day landings. He recalled: '

We nosed towards the land amid the gathering armada of ships. The grey thin shoreline ahead, some two miles distant was lit with the flashes of gunfire and bursting shells. Our world in that eastern extremity of the beach head was this barely floating steel box of high explosives that we had to beach and unload on a hostile shore.

After a campaign by friends and family, in 2016 he was eventually awards France's highest honour – the 'Legion d'Honneur'.

~~~

Cinderella: Jane Argyle as Cinderella, December 1976 (Photographer Peter Brown)

After the euphoria of the grand opening of the new Playhouse , it was soon back to business and to open with what is surely the highlight of any season, the annual pantomime, which this year was that all time favourite, 'Cinderella' starring Jane Argyle as Cinderella and Derek Crewe as Buttons. Seat prices ranged from £1.10 to 50p and you could park your car next door in the main car park for 10p for four hours or 20p all day! Coincidently 'Cinderella' was the first pantomime produced at the old Playhouse in 1943.

The production was, of course, a huge success and most performances were sold out. It also went without a hitch as the production team made full use of the larger stage and better facilities. There were also no live animals! which in the past had caused some pantomime problems as Reggie Salberg watching this production must certainly have remembered!

One December afternoon several years ago, during the run of 'Cinderella', the stage manager nervously knocked on Reggie's door:

'Excuse me Mr. Salberg' he said 'but I think the ponies have escaped!'
Let Reggie continue the story:

> Down the lane by the old theatre in Fisherton Street I glimpsed the
> Cinderella ponies who had escaped from their makeshift stabling in
> the workshops, heading towards the snowy car park.
>
> It was snowing heavily. By the time the stage manager and I caught
> them, they were heading up Castle Street where the bewildered
> motorists, thinking they had overdone their seasonal festivities, had
> stopped to view the spectacle. We got them back just in time for
> their stage entrance, no time to clean them and to calm them down.
> Never before or since has Cinderella's coach been drawn by such mud
> spattered and steaming ponies!

But in the far off Salisbury days of 1953, not any old ponies
would do – let's get a real live elephant from Chipperfield's circus!
They examined the stage at the Playhouse. They advertised for a
source that would provide £9 worth of hay a week. They searched
for a giant sleeping berth and decided that the paint shop would
be sufficiently large and comfortable enough and they sought out a
male companion in case she had first night nerves. This heralded the
arrival of Sally the elephant who was to play a starring role in that
year's pantomime – 'The Sleeping Beauty'. She was not just any old
elephant but one that would sit on a tub, stay calm in the face of bright
lights and an orchestra and be able to carry Prince Charming on his
important quest to find the beautiful princess!

Fortunately the regulations governing performing animals have
changed dramatically since those far off days and we are never likely
to see a performing elephant on the Playhouse stage again. Leave the
pantomime to the actors and to that special pantomime magic that
the backstage crew can conjure up!

The first straight play to be produced in the new Playhouse was
George Bernard Shaw's 'You Never Can Tell', starring Lionel Guyett,
Patience Tomlinson and Jane Quy. The Journal critic wrote:

> Whether attracted by the chance to see a fine play or the novelty of
> the new theatre, audiences are obviously pleased with the company's

performance as shown by the sustained applause which it thoroughly deserves. It is a good play with Shaw having a go at late Victorian society with typical shock tactics and incredible happenings at a seaside hotel.

Lionel was to have another starring role in 1980 as Nell Gwynne! The International Stores a few yards from the Playhouse had a gala opening when the cast of the current production, Terence Rattigan's 'While the Sun Shines' were in attendance, along with Lionel dressed as Nell Gwynne giving out oranges to the many people in the crowd waiting for early bargains! It was certainly worthwhile for the Playhouse to spend a few pennies on oranges because the International had decided to sponsor the next season to the tune of £3,000.

Lionel remembered with affection working with David Horlock but he nearly incurred his wrath on one occasion when he went riding and fell over and broke his collar bone. Actors were not allowed to go riding during a run so Lionel sheepishly went to David and explained that he had got drunk and fallen down the stairs. 'Oh, is that all?' dismissed David!

That first year proved to be a very successful one as there was not only the attraction of going to a new theatre but also the attraction of an excellently varied range of productions. This included two favourite musicals – 'Joseph and his Amazing Technicolor Dreamcoat', complete with the school choirs of Harnham Junior and Bishop Wordsworth schools and 'Godspell.' as well as Alan Ayckbourn's trilogy: 'The Norman Conquests'; Anthony Shaffer's 'Sleuth'; 'Jane', a play based on the life of Jane Austen and 'Close Secret' written by local playwright, Jennifer Curry which had the added attraction of the appearance of a real helicopter on the stage!

If you were walking backstage at the Playhouse, at the end of a corridor you may come across a large empty box room. Walk into it and you will see a small space with four walls and some seating. It could easily be a store room and you could simply walk on by. But this empty space does not stay empty for very long. It waits patiently for magicians to turn it into a myriad of wonderful places. For this is the

Salberg Studio and since it first opened in 1977 it has been used for an amazing variety of productions for all ages and for all tastes.

Part of Reggie Salberg's dream was to have a small studio theatre which as Roger Clissold described: 'would have a mixed programme of alternative viewing presented by our own and visiting companies.'

Reggie himself chose the opening play and on Wednesday 23rd February 1977 there was an informal ceremony to unveil a plaque that bore his name and *'Kennedy's Children'* by Robert Patrick officially opened the 'Reggie Salberg Studio'. All seats available at 80p. It starred Brian Ellis and Richard Clews and was appropriately directed by Reggie's wife, Noreen Craven.

Kennedy's Children: Richard Clews as Bartender; Brian Ellis as Sparger, February 1977 (Photographer Peter Brown)

Roger Clissold thought that eventually this studio would become known as 'The Reggie'. It is now known simply as 'The Salberg'. Initially it only seated about 100 but in 1996 thanks to a lottery grant, 40 balcony seats were added.

Not be outdone by its big brother, the main theatre, in that first year, the Salberg put on a wide variety of productions that included Joe

Orton's '*Entertaining Mr. Sloane*'; two plays by the Playhouse's resident playwright Derek Graham: '*Mutual Consent*' and '*Compliments of the Season*'; Chris Harris's brilliant one man show '*Kemp's Jig*', a Lute and Guitar Concert and a lecture series entitled: '*Doing Our Own Thing*'. Derek Graham also worked with Stage 65 and in July 1977 he wrote the play '*The Show Must Go On*' for them.

The Salberg area is quite small and intimate and sometimes the actors and the audience can be too close to each other. At the beginning of one performance a group of ladies came in and put their coats and bags on what they thought were spare seats. Unfortunately they were part of the set and some of the cast were supposed to sit on them! One actress at first perched on the edge of one of the seats but then when she had nothing to do in the scene she went around and placed all the coats and bags on the ladies' laps!

As well as a Resident Playwright, the Playhouse also had a Resident Musical Director, Chris Littlewood who arrived at the old Playhouse in 1971 and was very much involved in the production '*Welcome to the Playhouse*' and in all of the musical shows during the last few years of the old building and the early years of the new.

He was always involved in the pantomimes and the Old Time Music Hall shows. In one programme note in 1976 he was billed as: 'Melodious Music under the direction of Maestro Chris Littlewood who also performs on the pianoforte with digital dexterity!'

His musical play '*Miss Leading Lady*' earned excellent reviews such as the one in the *Salisbury Times*: 'It has just about everything – a good plot, lovely music, first class lyrics, colourful costumes, splendid acting, ear-taking piano accompaniment by Chris Littlewood and Alison Malcolm, some grand singing and plenty of action and humour. It really deserves to succeed and go places and is a show not to be missed.' He also was responsible for the Book, Music and Lyrics for '*Gilgamesh*' The *Sunday Times* critic, Frank Marcus wrote: 'I had to penetrate the regions to find a musical that possessed originality and imagination.'

Also working at the Playhouse at this time was Kevin Flynn and David Goodrich both of whom joined the new Playhouse when it opened. Kevin came from the Bristol Old Vic and designed the lighting for all the main house productions. He also went to London to re-light 'Under the Greenwood Tree', 'Old Herbaceous' and 'Make the Little Beggars Hop' when they transferred to the West End.

David arrived at the Playhouse as a stage technician but gradually worked his way through the ranks to become Company Manager. Perhaps David's most eye-catching effect was the rain for 'Pygmalion' which involved precision drilled conduit fed into a hosepipe. The most difficult part was catching the rain and making sure it didn't seep across the stage! Who would have thought at the time, that many years later, the Playhouse would be performing 'Singing in the Rain'! In January 1980 Kevin and David both left to start their own business, Stagecraft Promotions Ltd. This business, based in Salisbury would find them abroad lighting shows as well as conferences, exhibitions and business promotions.

Kevin's position was filled by the redoubtable and talented Peter Hunter who moved down in 1980 from the Redgrave Theatre in Farnham. Like Kevin Flynn, Peter would be responsible for lighting all the main house productions and he soon gained the reputation of being one of the finest lighting designers in regional theatre and beyond. Hampshire born, Peter attended Magdalen College School, Oxford prior to joining the stage management and technical course at LAMDA. One production that Peter always enjoyed was the annual pantomime. 'I enjoy the challenge of coming up with new ideas every year.' However, production week days would often run from 9am until 11pm 'that's if we're lucky, otherwise it can be until 3 or 4am!' he firmly stated.

David Goodrich's post was filled by Benjamin Sumner, becoming at 22 one of the youngest Company Stage Managers in the country.

For designers, the Playhouse could not have wished for a better partnership than Richard Marks and Stephen Howell. They tended to work in different ways. Richard would prefer to work from his beautifully painted sketches whereas Stephen preferred to work from scale model sets. Stephen once said: 'I'm not a painterly designer in the sense of creating a series of two dimensional pictures on stage. I always tend to think in terms of breaking up the stage space with solid forms and structures,' although to start with Stephen was also responsible for painting the scenery.

Having completed a very busy preparatory period leading up to the first performance he said that the first night was often an anti-climax as his work was then complete and the play is then taken over by the actors and the audience. At first he also found it difficult to realise his work is temporary and that eventually it would all be broken up and end up in a skip! Stephen eventually became Head of Design in 1983 under David Horlock.

Richard Marks, originally became Head Designer in January 1979, succeeding Neville Dewis who held the post since 1970. Amongst many other successes, he was responsible for the design for '*84 Charing Cross Road*' and '*Cider With Rosie*' in the Summer of 1981. '*Cider With Rosie*' was something Roger Clissold had wanted to do for some time but the rights had been withdrawn since its West End showing in the sixties. His approach to James Roose Evans, who had done the adaptation, led to a very happy and, as it transpired, a very lucky double because when he mentioned that a piece he himself would like to adapt was '*84 Charing Cross Road*', James Roose Evans replied : 'You can't – I've got the rights!' Roger came back with: 'OK, you do it at the Playhouse then!'

These were eventually to be Roger Clissold's last two productions and he commented: 'It's great to go out with two plays so close to my heart'.

It was the first time in 15 years that '*Cider With Rosie*' was to be performed on the stage and the credit goes to Roger Clissold, who in fact grew up in Uplands, near Stroud, the next village to Laurie Lee's home in Slad. Indeed, Roger remembers his mother pointing Laurie Lee out to him when they went shopping: 'That's Laurie Lee, the poet.' she would say.

Laurie Lee told the *Western Daily Press*: 'Roger has a special sympathy with Gloucestershire and I am sure he will present the play sensitively. I hope to be down there on the first night – August 27 – to see what he makes of it.' Although he did say: 'In a way I would have been happy to creep in wearing smoked glasses and a big hat and sit in the dark without anyone knowing I was there!' He had held on to the rights of the play since the sixties when it attracted only meagre audiences to the Garrick Theatre in the West End and it hadn't been staged since. Laurie Lee continued: ' I think it was not a success because the Motor Show was on at the time, and there were some popular revues in London. I think the circumstances that Salisbury offers are the most promising to date for a really excellent performance.'

Mr. Lee had no need to worry because the play was a great success. The *Western Daily Press* wrote: 'For quality and sheer entertainment there could not have been a better tribute to theatre boss Roger Clissold than this lovingly crafted gem of a play.... Excellence and authenticity are the key notes.' And the *Guardian* wrote: 'from its bustling beginning the audience was ensnared in its magic.' Among a cast of Salisbury stalwarts, was Roger Hume, recently returned from a successful tour of '*Old Herbaceous*' as the Narrator, Laurie Lee. Beth Ellis played the mother and Emlyn Harris was Lol, who one glorious Summer's day, found cider with Rosie.

84 Charing Cross Road: Rosemary Leach as Helene Hanff, David Swift as Frank Doel, July 1981 (Photographer Peter Brown)

Popular as this production was it is '*84 Charing Cross Road*' that holds a very special place in the story of the Playhouse. This simple tale of the correspondence between Helene Hanff, an American writer and Frank Doel, owner of an antiquarian bookshop in London's Charing Cross Road seemed to touch a special nerve amongst Salisbury theatregoers and critics as they warmed to this simple human story. Over 16,000 flocked to see it, with a 74% capacity. It was an unlikely love match between a feisty American woman and a fusty old London bookshop but it seemed to touch the hearts of so many theatregoers and critics.

B.A. Young of the *Financial Times* wrote:

During the evening, we watch it (the story) mature between 1949 and 1971. No one is murdered there. No one is seduced. No one is robbed. No one turns out unexpectedly to be someone else. The stock of books changes leisurely from year to year, the staff grow older. The only noticeable development is the gradually increasing postal intimacy between Frank Doel, buyer ands seller of books and Helene Hanff, who orders books by mail from her bed-sit in New York. This play is one of the most delightful I have seen for years.

Of course it was helped by having two famous actors, Rosemary Leach and David Swift in the leading roles as well as one of Salisbury's favourite actresses, Charmian May.

R.M.W of the *Salisbury Times* wrote: 'This unusual play deserves to go far.' And go far it certainly did. It transferred successfully to the West End, then to America and it was subsequently made into a film starring Anne Bancroft and Anthony Hopkins. All thanks to Roger Clissold wanting to produce *'Cider With Rosie'* at the Playhouse!

There is also a rather strange coincidence in this story because the address of the old Playhouse was 84 Fisherton Street!

The play was revived at the Playhouse in 2015 with Janie Dee as Helene Hanff and Clive Francis as Frank Doel and once again it captivated Salisbury audiences. Once again the lighting was designed by Peter Hunter.

Although Peter had kept all his designs from 34 years ago he deliberately didn't refer to them this time, preferring to start again from scratch. 'I do remember some of what we did before and it may well be that we have some of the same lights doing exactly the same job as they did back then. Many of our lights date back that far and still do a perfectly good job,' he recalled. Working on the revival of '84 Charing Cross Road' brought back many fond memories for him.

Peter Hunter (Photographer Robert Workman)

'It is a show I have particular affection for, especially as that was the first time I'd worked in the West End. I'd only come to the Playhouse the year before and suddenly we had this hit show. This revival is like rediscovering a long lost friend.'

During Roger Clissold's tenure as Artistic Director there were several other notable productions that one must mention. In August 1978, *'Under the Greenwood Tree'*, directed by Patrick Garland transferred to the Vaudeville in the West End. It had mixed reviews. Radio Two said: 'The whole production was smooth, swift and adventurous. Patrick Garland's obvious love of rustic life – vividly brought to life – absolutely real and three-dimensional. A joy to watch.' and J.C. Trewin of the *Birmingham Post* wrote: 'This is one of the most magical productions of the year and I would like to think it would run for longer than the Christmas season.' Although it was a great success in Salisbury, sadly the rustic charm of this Hardy novel did not give pleasure to the citizens of London for very long.

In November 1978, performances of Ben Travers *'Bed Before Yesterday'* were all sold out. The *Salisbury Journal* called the January 1979 production of *'Murder in the Cathedral'*: 'An impressive poetic drama. From the moment you take a seat and look towards the stage you get the feeling that you ought to talk in a hushed voice as you would in a church or cathedral, This is undoubtedly the result of the combined talents of Richard Marks, the new head of scenic design and Kevin Flynn who designed the lighting.' Brian Tully played Thomas Becket and the production was directed by Knight Mantell.

In October that year, 'Privates on Parade' whilst being very successful, created something of a furore amongst the theatregoers of a certain age. The local critic wrote: 'There is much to laugh at, a great deal to admire and certain episodes to touch the heart in 'Privates on Parade'. Some theatregoers though felt it necessary to vent their disgust at the nudity and the racy dialogue. E. Cowdrey from Hindon wrote: 'Being middle aged and ex service (Egypt and East Africa) I mistakenly thought 'Privates on Parade' would be just my cup of tea. Can I please raise my voice in protest at the antics supposed to be entertainment at the Salisbury Playhouse? There is I am sure, a demand for this kind of performance but surely not in a family theatre. Like Queen Victoria I was not amused, just saddened.' A sign of the times. If this play was produced now it would be accepted by most theatregoers. One is reminded of the time when in 1975 the Playhouse dared to put on Peter Shaffer's 'Equus' and there were many grumblings of disgust from the Shires about the nudity. However, in 2000 Joanna Read in her first season, produced 'Equus' and the only murmurs were ones of approval.

Another sign of the times was that in the 1980 pantomime 'Babes in the Wood' there appeared Troy Foster, a black actor, unusual for the times, playing Little John. He commented that he 'doesn't want to dwell on the fact that he may be the first black actor to penetrate Sherwood Forest or even to spend a season rather than a single production with the Playhouse.'

The wide range of productions continued with the likes of classics, modern drama, Shakespeare, comedy, Music Hall and Agatha Christie to please the patrons. Some things never change and in the programme notes for Agatha Christie's 'The Hollow', Roger wrote with tongue in cheek, about the behaviour of some theatregoers: "On the first night of 'The Hollow', the raising of the curtain was a cue for the striking up of a positive orchestra of throat clearers enlivened from time to time by bronchial soloists. Silently suffering members of the public complained that the audience strumming their catarrhs, rendered inaudible both vital parts of the plot and more, the answers to the International Stores Christmas Quiz!'

Reggie Salberg once said: 'A cough can ruin a theatrical moment and the rustling of sweet wrappings is a cardinal sin!'

The Salberg, again, not to be outdone by its big brother, put on an even wider range of shows. Some were considered more suitable for a smaller, perhaps more discerning audience such as '*Krapp's Last Tape*'; '*The Killing of Sister George*', '*Who's Afraid of Virginia Wolf*' and a very memorable production of '*Waiting For Godot*' starring Lionel Guyett, Alex Johnston and Roger Leach. Although one annoyed military gentleman was heard to mutter after seeing '*Waiting For Godot*': 'No wonder we lost the colonies if they put on drivel like that!' There were one man shows such as Roger Leach's '*Colonial Boy*'. Late night shows such as '*The English Venice*' which was a Salisbury anthology. Stage 65 used this special space for plays such as '*The Resistible Rise of Arturo Ui*'. There were talks; children's shows, demonstrations as well as visits from other theatre companies. Oxford Playhouse put on '*Trial Run*' with Art Malik, Nicholas Lyndhurst and Nigel Planer, a very talented trio who would be very difficult to cast today!

And what of Reggie Salberg, what has he been doing since retiring as Theatre Director after the opening of the new Playhouse? Reggie moved to Greenwich in London but could not break away from the Playhouse altogether, that would have been almost impossible. He became the theatre's consultant and came down to the Playhouse on a regular basis to assist Roger Clissold. In a programme note entitled: 'Not Exactly Goodbye' for the '*Welcome to the Playhouse*' show, he wrote:

> Although my wife and I will be moving to London shortly, I am not severing my connection with the Playhouse and will be helping Roger in many ways – for example, most of our casting is done by seeing actors working at other theatres or sometimes at drama schools and Roger will have little time to spare for such visits. He has therefore asked me if I will cover such shows for him when he is interested in someone and would like a report on his or her work. I shall also read

new plays for him (we get a great many) and pass on only those of sufficient merit for his consideration. Above all I will be concerned with the budgeting and accounts, and will be back in Salisbury a couple of days a week, so you see the break is far from being total, although I imagine my present average working week of about 60 to 70 hours will be halved.

Later in 1977 in a 'Letter From London' he wrote:

And so to myself. One of the main reasons we are able to keep our prices down to their remarkably low level is because the administrative staff is so small. Accordingly no one, other than myself, has the time to deal with the accounting and essential budgeting. When I retired as Theatre Director and became Consultant I hardly expected to have most of my time occupied in this way, but I enjoy doing the work. Above all, I am happy that Roger Clissold finds it useful to discuss casting and play choice with me. Thus the happy partnership we had in the old Playhouse continues although the last word is now his, rather than mine.

Roger Clissold must have valued enormously being able to continue working with Reggie and to call upon his great knowledge and expertise but perhaps there may have been times when he would have wanted to have made his own decisions, to succeed or fail on what he alone had decided. It is a little like a head teacher taking over a school and having the previous head suggesting how the new head should plan his time-table and how he should spend his money. It must have been a double-edged sword.

And of course the black clouds of financial problems would continue to float over the Playhouse even though the building stood there shiny and new. In 1977 the first electricity bill came as a shock as it was eight times higher than the corresponding months in the old building. Consequently seat prices were raised to £1.40. £1.10 and 85p with seats in the Salberg costing £1.

In 1979 it was revealed that the size of the Arts Council grant would depend on whether or not the local authorities could be persuaded to find another £16,000 between them. The link between the Arts Council's contribution and that of the local authorities was always going to be a constant sticking point. With no increase from the school's sub-committee of the £850 already pledged and only a £80 rise from the county council's education committee, the Playhouse had to look for other sources for the majority of that £16,000.

Also in 1979 the Southern Arts Association decided to cut the regional subsidy scheme that had allowed parties of ten or more to claim a refund on travel costs.

Then in 1980 the Playhouse found the grant of £850 given by Wiltshire County Council was to be cut altogether.

This prompted the following, in letters to the *Journal*. 'If other grant giving bodies were to follow the example set by Wiltshire Education Committee, not only would there be no further Playhouse schools' tours but there would soon be no Salisbury Playhouse.' wrote Roger Clissold. And Guy Jessop, the Chairman of the Playhouse Board, wrote:

> Our own earnings cover two-thirds of the enormous coast of maintaining this building and its equipment and paying for the work of the company and staff.
>
> The remainder comes from grants – mostly from central government through the Arts Council. We now therefore have the melancholy distinction of being one of this country's most successful theatres whilst receiving practically the lowest level of local authority support.

The local Finance Committee were asked to give another £4,000 but they decided that the theatre, one of the few in Britain which manages to break even, was not desperate for the money.

Guy Jessop also wrote in November that year: 'We will continue to project an image of confidence and success to the world but those who really know the workings of the theatre appreciate that this façade already conceals economies which could be dangerous. Without I hope of breaking my promise not to act the Oliver Twist, I would just say please do not penalise us for good housekeeping.'

The Arts Council's drama director told the district council that the Playhouse's running costs were rising faster than the general inflation rate. 'Salisbury has a valuable cultural and amenity asset in the Playhouse but the choice between continued health and a slow future decline now lies not only with the paying public. It also lies in the level of priority in expenditure which their elected representatives accord to it.'

At present the Arts Council contributed £112,500 of the annual subsidy of the Playhouse of £133,000 and the local authority £8,000.

Fortunately at the beginning of 1981, Salisbury District Council decided to increase their grants from £2,600 to £3,000 which meant more money for the Playhouse and then Wiltshire County Council agreed to give the Playhouse an increase of 11% on the previous year, to the tune of £4,440. Swings and Roundabouts continue.

In his annual report to the directors in November 1980, Roger Clissold referred to the past year in terms of 'non-complacent satisfaction.' He went on:

> Even though the audiences were slightly reduced since the early days of the new theatre, the Playhouse's attendance record, the number of its productions and the length of its season are the envy of most comparable regional theatres. Likewise the Playhouse succeeds in balancing its books by earning the high proportion of 65% of its total income while most theatres depend on grants to a much greater extent. Every production in 1980 would have the support of sponsorship and although there has been little progress in improved grants, the Playhouse had gratefully received news of 100% rate relief from Salisbury District Council as well as a contribution from the lottery towards a new van.

He drew attention to the unceasing work of the Theatregoers' Club.. and he was gratefully aware of the affectionate support given to the Playhouse by all who worked in and for it, but he hoped that this would never become passive and unquestioning.

As an anonymous theatregoer had written of Salisbury Playhouse: 'We love it, defend it, and – criticise it!'

For everyone in the theatre business there is a time when they know it is right to move on to their next position, usually to gain more experience and in the summer of 1981, it was announced that Roger Clissold was to leave the Playhouse at the end of August after 16 years association with this theatre, in order to become Artistic Director of the Thorndike Theatre in Leatherhead.

One of the attractions was that the Thorndike had an administrator and a fuller staff structure so he would be able to be free to direct more plays. He said: 'Since taking up my present post five years ago I've been increasingly aware that I've spent more time behind a desk than directing plays.' The Thorndike's nearness to London, which meant seeing more plays, having more actors easily available and making it easier to get critics and managers along to see work was another factor as well as 'a desire for change and stimulus.'

In one interview for the *Southern Evening Echo* before his departure, he recalled two amusing moments, Despite his acting and speech training, he recalled a painful comic debut in public speaking, something he realised reluctantly he would have to undertake in his early directing days. He asked someone if they could arrange a gentle introduction by way of an informal gathering but wires got crossed and he found to his horror, that he was committed to making two formal lectures to sixth formers on academic aspects of Shakespeare!

He revised like mad and jotted his notes down on cards and then faced what looked like 'rows of truculent adolescents.' Rattling through his cards at a nervy rate of knots, he soon realised that they would never last the time out, so in desperation he went straight on to the second lot of cards. 'I was twittering away when it suddenly hit me that even the second lot wouldn't last the time. In my alarm, I dug my shaking hand deeper into my pocket and must have jabbed my cigarette lighter for a jet of flame suddenly shot out and burned my leg!

I was so nervous I just yelped 'Ouch!' in mid-sentence and carried on with the lecture. They must have thought I was a lunatic!'

He also recalled a time in the old building when he was busy rehearsing Ibsen when two men suddenly strode down the aisle demanding to speak to him about the drains!

However, he saved his last correspondence for the theatregoers and in the programme notes for '*Cider With Rosie*' he wrote:

I have been in the hot seat here for five years and working for the Playhouse in one capacity or another for the majority of the past sixteen years so my decision to move can hardly be described as premature or impetuous as one member of our audience was kind enough to suggest. I am convinced that a change will be good for me and the Playhouse but inevitably I cannot leaved this much-loved and remarkable organisation, nor close what has been such a significant chapter in my life without a sense of conflict in my emotions.

Demolition of the old building, 1979 (Photographer Peter Brown)

He did not wish to mention his favourite shows for fear of upsetting anyone, so he wrote:

Let me therefore share with you a single memory of a show which appeared for my benefit alone. One Sunday I was walking past the ruins of the old Playhouse at a time when the rear wall had been demolished but the auditorium was still unchanged, and there in the wintry dusk was a bonfire in the middle of the stage. The glow from this lit the old theatre with a shifting orange light and then dimmed to blackness and like a speeded-up tape the theatre's past productions flashed through my minds. Perhaps that is the answer; to let the past go up in smoke – and sparks – and to admit that we cannot tell what the future holds.'

The future for the Playhouse however, came in the large shape and personality of David Horlock. As Roger Clissold moved to Leatherhead he could have passed David Horlock on the Surrey roads as David travelled to Salisbury from Farnham where he had been Artistic Director.

Another chapter in the story of the Playhouse was about to begin.

16

THERE ARE NO STARS AT THE PLAYHOUSE, ONLY A HAPPY, DEDICATED TEAM.'

David Horlock

I picked my way gingerly past the charming shaggy ponies in the yard. Though prettily effective in pulling Cinderella's coach, their hooves can pack hefty kicks. It was eleven o' clock on a January morning. Inside the Playhouse the Box Office was busy, the restaurant full. The last vestiges of the 'Meg and Mog' set were being dismantled in the Salberg Studio before a short tour of schools, and the cast of 'Lloyd George Knew My father' was rehearsing on the 'Cinderella' set in the main auditorium – without the ponies. In an upstairs room, the three resident designers are huddled over their respective drawing boards, furrowing their brows, worrying whether the six sets they had to design, erect and paint by the end of the month would be ready. In fact it was a Salisbury theatre day just like any other.

So wrote Derek Weeks in January 1990. However, two months later, tragedy was about to strike the Playhouse.

Before that though the Eighties had been a golden time for the Playhouse thanks mainly to one man, David Horlock, who was appointed as Theatre Director to replace Roger Clissold.

After Roger left, Graham Berown took over as Caretaker Manager. He was no stranger to the Playhouse and past credits included '*While the Sun Shines*', '*Babes in the Wood*' and '*Privates on Parade*,' so the Playhouse was in safe and talented hands. The post of Theatre Director was then advertised and 80 people applied, knowing it was a plum job for whoever was appointed.

That person was David Horlock from the Redgrave Theatre Farnham.

David had been at Farnham for five years and had already built up a reputation as a talented and innovative director. He will go down in Farnham's history as the man who fitted 300 people on stage for his revival of Noel Coward's '*Cavalcade*.' without misplacing the actors or losing his audience. Most of the cast were from local drama groups and many of them were schoolchildren. 'and don't forget the one dog!' David would remind people. His love of large casts and sprawling landscapes was to come to fruition during his years in Salisbury.

David was born in Shoreham in September 1942 and was an only child. His father was killed at Arnhem, a victim of war so sadly he never saw his son. David grew up being very close to Nellie his mother, a bond that was always very special to him.

He attended Chichester High School for Boys where he was a good rugby player. Whilst there he won the Sussex Classical Association's Schools Reading Competition and played with distinction, leading roles in a succession of House and School plays. He then gained a place at Hertford College Oxford where he studied English and Classics.

On his first day as a teacher at Lancing College someone told him that as he had an interest in Drama, he might like to direct the school play. 'I suppose that's where the rot set in!' he commented. He took to directing his pupils with enthusiasm and he went on to produce many other plays in the next four years. He began to feel though that he wanted to do the drama more than the teaching but at the same time he felt that he didn't really know that much about directing. So at the age of 27 he left teaching and returned to the family hotel business for a year to earn some money and to learn all he could about the theatre.

When he left, an article appeared in the Lancing College magazine of 1969 that said: 'David Horlock has left and with him go not only a magnificent pair of side whiskers, the envy of so many wispy, pubescent sproutings but also a certain theatricality of speech and gesture which made him a godsend to the school mimics. To extend an arm with elbow flexed and upturned palm, enunciating in orotund tones, 'The door!' could be guaranteed to have an audience rolling in the aisles.

He was a rigorous and demanding teacher who insisted on high standards and whose constant interpretive theories kept his English Literature classes in a state of perpetual alarm and apprehension.'

During his year of theatrical education, he was a quick learner and eventually he was offered several jobs in theatres and in just one week of looking for an entry into professional drama, he was offered four different jobs.

He accepted one as Assistant Stage manager at the Bristol Old Vic and stayed there for seven years. For a while this theatre had to close for re-development so the company went on tour nationally and to South America from a base at the Theatre Royal Bath. Rodney West who worked with David as a young theatre manager recalled: 'The mile-wide smile and deep chuckle were indicative of David's sense of fun – a pre-requisite for anyone on tour! That sense of fun (allied to a sharp wit and always tempered by infinite compassion) never deserted David, and of course communicated itself across the footlights in all that he did.'

David rose to become Deputy Assistant to the Theatre Director when he said: 'It was difficult, because suddenly I was no longer one of the lads and had to make decisions about them.'

This experience eventually led to him being appointed Artistic Director of the Redgrave Farnham. Maj. Grant, David's secretary at Farnham fondly remembers:

It usually happened that the only time we could spend together to discuss phone calls, messages, correspondence etc was at the end of the day. By then he was on a 'high' with the rehearsal behind him and he would gradually unwind as we went through the office happenings. Invariably, as he became more relaxed he would slip lower in his chair with his feet poised precariously on the edge of the waste paper basket until, when the work was completed he would end up with his feet right in the basket! Eventually it became a standing joke and I would bring out the waste paper basket as soon as he emerged from rehearsals and his feet would go straight in with much chuckling!'

When he left the Redgrave she bought him the biggest waste paper basket she could find and it went with him to the Playhouse.

It took him four months to hand over the reigns at Farnham and in a letter to the Salisbury Theatregoers he wrote: 'The last few weeks have been a flurry of packing and moving – one accumulates so much over the years (waste paper basket et al!) But now at last I am here, and I am so very glad to be here.' In the programme of his first production, he wrote:

There was a time when I thought that I would never actually be here in Salisbury. It seemed that I was getting to know the main road from Farnham far better than the Playhouse as I drove in for meetings and to see performances. However, when I finally did arrive in January, the snows immediately fell as if to assure that I would not drive off again. And now that the snows have cleared, I am delighted, at last, to write and introduce myself as your new Theatre Director.

David Horlock outside the theatre
(Photographer Peter Brown)

In the letter to the Theatregoers he set out his beliefs and plans.

I believe that a theatre should do everything it can to serve the community, offering the fullest range of culture and entertainment, with plays, concerts, exhibitions – it should be in every sense the centre of the area. I am particularly interested in theatre for young people. I aim to send theatre out to schools and colleges and to get young people into the theatre as much a possible for plays, for theatre workshops and for other activities.

He continued: 'I believe that a theatre should celebrate its local authors, and you may expect to see from me a good deal of work by the many writers who have lived and created in and around Salisbury.' He concluded by stating: 'Finally, I must say how much I look forward to meeting you, the Theatregoers. You are the very life- blood of our theatre, you give us so much.'

In 1983, having settled into his new role, he stated: 'A theatre should be as busy as a railway station with plenty for people to see, hear and enjoy both inside and outside of play-viewing hours.'

For his first play he chose Wycherley's 'The Country Wife'. In his programme notes he wrote: 'It is one of the most famous Restoration Comedies, vigorous, earthy, colourful and very honest. It attacks hypocrisy and it has a lot to say about love and marriage. On the whole it is the men who get the worst end of the bargain, and in this instance, they deserve what they get!'

The play was a great success. The *Salisbury Times* critic wrote: 'On merit it should be a sell out; first and foremost because it is so well done and secondly, it is such a treat to get something different, witty, colourful and bawdy, without being offensive and biting.'

Once again the hardworking and talented trio of Barbara Wilson for her costumes, Richard Marks for the set and Peter Hunter for the lighting were given considerable praise.

Sonia Woolley who appeared as Mrs. Dainty Fidget wrote: 'Working for the first time with any director is always a stimulating experience and being in the company for David's first production in Salisbury was no exception – his insight into the text was fascinating and his direction of the technical aspects of the production meticulous in its attention to every detail of the stage picture.'

The Country Wife: Granville Saxton as Harry Horner; Carolyn Moody as Lady Fidget, March 1982 (Photographer Peter Brown)

In his first year David fulfilled several of his aims and promises. 'Kes' was performed in the main house with over two hundred children from local schools taking part ; Stage 65 continued to flourish by producing an exciting production of 'Oklahoma' in the Salberg and the Theatre in Education Team took out two very successful tours to local schools – An Introduction to Theatre for Middle Schools and An Introduction to Shakespeare for Secondary Schools.

Harking back to the old theatre days, there were two highly successful tours of 'The Killing of Toad' and 'Gasmasks and Greasepaint' to venues in Wiltshire, Hampshire, Sussex Dorset, Berkshire and Oxfordshire. There was also an eclectic mixture of classic and modern drama in the main theatre from classics like 'A Christmas Carol' to modern works like 'Duet for One.'

Roger Leach who was in both of these productions, remembers that it was one of the few times in Salisbury that there was a 'black market' for tickets during the run of 'A Christmas Carol' as most performances were sell outs!

In 1983 David wrote:

A wide and varied range is stimulating for both company and audience. A slightly longer run of a popular play like 'The Ghost Train' will pay for a shorter run of a more costly classic like 'Richard III'. Having a Studio Theatre (The Salberg') means that the range can be extended still further without a

Bent: Kevin Moore as Max; Bernard Finch as Horst, February 1983 (Photographer Peter Brown)

significant loss of income. During February, we played 'Bent' in the Studio whilst 'The Reluctant Debutante' played upstairs in the main auditorium.

'*Bent*' caused quite a stir. It is the story of two homosexuals who were persecuted by the Nazis and sent to Dachau. There were grumbles and voices of complaints coming from a certain section of the Salisbury audience but the play went ahead to great critical acclaim. Not like in Ipswich where the voices of outrage almost caused the Wolsey Theatre to take the play off. 'Anger as homosexual sex play starts rehearsal' screamed the headline in the local paper!

Bob Kolbe in the local *Journal* wrote: '*Bent*' by Martin Sherman has drawn from David Horlock a simply brilliant directorial effort as well as a great deal of courage; and from Kevin Moore and all the other actors, performances that do enormous credit to their Art. Salisbury Playhouse has distinguished itself.'

Crocodiles in Cream: Kevin Moore as Lewis Carroll, April 1983
(Photographer Unknown)

Later on in the year, Kevin Moore again distinguished himself by portraying Lewis Carroll in David Horlock's '*Crocodiles in Cream*' in the Salberg . Bob Kolbe wrote: 'The fine actor at once performed the works and revealed their significance by some kind of unspoken magic-thought transferral. A masterful piece of work this.' Kevin Moore continued to perform this play for many years and he once said: 'I still use the same script that I used in rehearsals then and opposite every page of the text are the notes that David gave me. They are still valid and I still read them and use them every time I do a performance.'

Kevin Moore spoke of Salisbury as being a wonderful period in his life. 'I loved working with David' he once said. 'He liked actors, he trusted their instincts and he brought out the best in them. Rehearsals were informed by a sharp intellect, great kindness and a wonderful sense of humour.'

Another of David Horlock's aims was to celebrate the works of local writers and he kept his promise by producing eight adaptations of English novels for the Playhouse stage from 'The Woodlanders' in 1983 to 'Jamaica Inn' in 1990.

Criticism of these adaptations varied. Barry Fogden wrote of the 1985 production of 'Far from the Madding Crowd' : 'This is a genuinely theatrical experience, a work of dramatic imagination and craft.' Whereas Alison Fife wrote: 'I recognised very little from my reading of the book. The charm and the charisma were nowhere to be seen.'

The 1985 production of 'Emma' was, according to Chris Newman, 'the best adaptation done at the Playhouse since 'Under the Greenwood Tree' in 1978. That production went to the West End. This one would be a worthy follower. And I am sure Jane Austen would approve.' He also wrote: 'As Emma, Helen Gemmell gives the performance of her career. It is a tour-de force of a role – powerfully funny in Miss. Gemmell's hands.'

Mick Martin wrote about the 1987 production of 'Tess': David Horlock's achievement as director is to blend all the elements into a coherent mosaic of colour, sound, light and action. It is a broad undertaking and it works magnificently.'

But he was visibly hurt by Mick Martin's criticism of his 1988 adaptation of 'Brighton Rock.'; He wrote:

> The moments of stylised theatricality with which Horlock punctuates the proceedings never really succeed in elucidating the deepest themes of the novel, and serve instead to interrupt the dramatic flow of the play and dissipate the tension. Dominic Letts' Pinkie lacks the necessary charisma, and for too much of the time puts you in mind

of a strange cross between James Cagney and Frank Spencer, who you would suspect would be hard pushed to frighten anyone!

Roger Leach commented about David's adaptations: 'With David you get your full three hours. Now I can't bear that frankly. – if I'm in the theatre for longer than two and a quarter hours then I get a sore bum and I think I should be in the Bar. You shouldn't really direct your own adaptations. You need someone with a blue pencil who you would listen to.'

Sonia Woolley recalled: 'David was an enormous purist about language – it was one of his strengths. The other was that he was very good on the technical side. But sometimes you would have to say, 'Oh, David, this is a bit too long' but he would always say, 'Oh, no, no, they will enjoy it.' Some actors who hadn't worked very much with him would complain but he rarely took criticism on board. He was very sure of himself.

David Horlock and cast outside Jane Austen's House : "Emma", April 1985.
Cast: Helen Gemmell (Emma) in centre with David Horlock, Russell Kilminster,
Steven Elliot, Maria Heidler, Susan Stone, Robert Aldous, Alex Johnston, John R.
Moorhouse, Jeanne Downs (Photographer Peter Brown)

To help him create his adaptations he would often visit places on which the stories were based. He took the cast to Jane Austen's home, Chawton House for '*Emma*'. He went with Dominic Letts to Brighton for '*Brighton Rock*' and he went to Bodmin Moor for a holiday for '*Jamaica Inn*.' In the programme notes for this production he wrote: 'It's like going back in time up there. Those villages are tucked way, haunted and the cliffs on the North coast – terrifying.' He went on: 'It was Morwenstow which I found truly haunting – cliffs which turn your knees to jelly, spines of jagged rocks stretching out to sea and a graveyard full of shipwrecked mariners.'

He also co-authored with Jack Chissick on four pantomimes starting with '*Mother Goose*' in 1986, even dressing up as a penguin as part of the publicity! Together they would often write in the attic room of David's house in Lower Bemerton. David would forget he was a tall man and he would often leap up in excitement or amusement only to bang his head on the attic's low ceiling!

'He was a great big bear of a man, thoroughly genuine' wrote Jack of David. ' Very warm and affectionate, always enthusiastic and encouraging. The fun and joy I had working with him was wonderful.'

Jack Chissick became one of the best loved pantomime dames during his time at the Playhouse. In the programme notes for the 1987 production of '*Jack and the Beanstalk*' he wrote:

> I always knew I would play a pantomime dame and so be part of a tradition that will hopefully carry on for as long as people can be children. To anyone who says to me it's demeaning to women, I say, we must have the ability as human beings to laugh at ourselves. Of course, I've never met a woman like a pantomime dame, but I've never met a bloke who wears fishnet tights, slaps his thighs, climbs a beanstalk, or has a cat that talks to him!

Broken knicker elastic set Jack on his acting career at the tender age of three. He was a child in a dancing class when his small partner's knickers began their slow descent. He kept pointing at her and laughing and of course the audience responded. Their reaction struck a chord and he knew from then on that he wanted to be an actor.

During the eight years that David Horlock was at the Playhouse he directed over 50 plays. Although he directed the bulk of the productions each year, there were other notable directors such as Simon Whitfield who was appointed Associate Director, Hugh Waters, Graham Berown, Brian Ralph, Paul Tomlinson, Michael Stroud, Lynn Wyfe, who was responsible for many Stage 65 productions and Noreen Craven who everyone was pleased to see making a welcome return to the Playhouse boards.

Lynn Wyfe came to the Playhouse in 1983 and as well as being an actress and a director she was appointed as the young people's Theatre Director, and soon helped to boost the size and importance of youth projects. Stage 65 soared from around 50 members to 130 and increased its appearances in the Salberg threefold. Lynn was also responsible for the Theatre in Education project (TIE) which helped indirectly to secure funding for the Playhouse. This project continued to tour local schools to present plays that often had a social or historical theme which would make pupils think and question.

Coming from a teaching background Lynn was always at ease with children from five to secondary school age and they readily responded to her. Her chief pleasure was in seeing young people realise their potential as actors and back-stage helpers. 'Some people seem to think of children as small adults which is patronising,' she once said, 'or imagine there are barriers between them. I've never thought there were. It's surprising what children can do, especially when you let them know you are sure they can do it. However, sometimes workshops and rehearsals can get noisy and they're not all angels but they work hard, achieve a lot and best of all, they enjoy themselves.'

David Horlock must have occasionally said the same about his rehearsals. Actors though, responded well to David's direction but like all directors he had his very own personal idiosyncratic methods. When he was directing a scene, only the actors in that scene were allowed to be present – no one else at all. It was a private thing between the actors and himself. Actors not in that particular scene had to wait in the Green Room until called. Actors would say though, that it was a joyous experience to be directed by him. There were frequently gales of laughter. Sidney Vines wrote: 'His technique was to suggest...

'Perhaps if you did it this way...'. He never laid down the law although he could be firm if he judged that the actors needed it. He could show anger at anything unprofessional such as laziness in learning a part. He worked to the highest standards and expected the same of others.'

Kevin Moore commented: 'If he was impatient it was usually because you were wasting precious time, 'faffing about', probing the sub-text or even worse, not knowing your lines properly.'.

David felt that 80% of directing was man management. Actors who have been in the business know what they are doing and he would let actors get on with rehearsing and then tell them what he didn't like. He would watch the first night and then rarely see the play after that. Once he had created, he wanted to move on to the next project. 'They know what I think – once it's under way they can get on with it.' However, occasionally he did love to sit and watch the audiences' reactions and he would always pop in to see his favourite parts of the pantomime!

He would go to the Bar after the first night because that was expected but he would not want to stand around gossiping. Socially, he often seemed awkward and if not talking about his present project them he would rather be alone.

Tim Meats loved working with him and Michael Lunts knew how lucky he was to have worked with David having worked with many other directors who fell below David's high standards.

Mick Martin said of David: 'He inspired fierce loyalty and pride amongst those he worked with and young actors in particular benefited from the mixture of warmth, sincerity and confidence that characterised his approach in the rehearsal room.'

Roger Leach said that David was a good director, but he could also be rather 'schoolmasterish.' Also he could be rather petulant and sometimes he would cut you dead – and not acknowledge you. Tim Meats felt the same. He felt that David could sometimes be very distant, often in a cloud and not always the easiest man to have to deal with. One could imagine that this was often because David took so much out of himself whilst rehearsing and needed time and space for his own thoughts. He once said: 'I like to spend time alone. That is the time to sort things out.' There was a part of David that he kept jealously to himself. Much the greater part he shared unstintingly with others but there was a part of David that only perhaps his mother Nellie knew about and that is surely as it should be.

'The wide and varied range of productions' which David Horlock aspired to, continued throughout the eighties.

During 1984/85 the productions ranged from classics such as '*Hamlet*', '*An Inspector Calls*' and '*A Tale of Two Cities*' to modern comedies and thrillers such as '*Present Laughter*' and '*Double Cut.*'

A Tale of Two Cities: Maria Heidler as Therese Defarge, October 1984
(Photographer Peter Brown)

There was also a Mozart Festival which included a production of 'Amadeus' in the main theatre and a celebration of his life in the Salberg presented by a group of opera singers. As well as a revival of 'Salad Days'.

Keith Drinkel particularly remembers the production of 'Cyrano de Bergerac.' in February 1984:

> I had asked for a very long prosthetic nose which had been made by the creator of John Hurt's make-up for 'The Elephant Man'. It was slight but I worked with it in the final days of rehearsal. On the first night, I was sweating so profusely that it fell off! I had my back to them, so the audience didn't see this and it was one of the rare moments that Cyrano doesn't speak. I walked off stage, got some glue, stuck it back on and was back on stage for my next line. Poor David in the audience thought I had got frightened and gone home!

There must have been a mini-explosion in David Horlock's office in March 1985 when he heard that the BBC had planned to screen 'A Murder is Announced' as part of their Miss.Marple series a few weeks before he was about to produce it at the Playhouse, thus revealing 'whodunit.' However, a quick change of plan and 'And Then There Were None' started in rehearsals instead. 'A much better play, anyway!' said David with a twinkle in his eye!

In his report of the Year 1985/86 he also spoke with pride of the Playhouse's Theatre for Young People going from strength to strength and Theatrescope continuing to tour over a wide area.

'In addition,' he reported, 'we have managed to embrace an extensive programme of maintenance and refurbishment, including the recarpeting and redecoration of the Bar, Restaurant and Foyer.' He was also pleased to report : 'Theatregoing in the Salberg has been rendered considerably more enjoyable by the provision of new, comfortable seats, for which we are grateful to our Theatregoers Club.'

Other successful productions followed, such as 'The Duchess of Malfi' in 1986 that featured Penelope Beaumont as the Duchess and Graham Padden as the cruel cardinal. 'We were especially encouraged by the high attendance for 'The Duchess of Malfi', an ambitious work rarely mounted in a theatre of this scale.' David Horlock wrote in his review of the year; followed by 'Pravda' in 1987. This caused quite a stir amongst certain sections of the audience because of the language: Will Rogers wrote to the local paper in disgusted tones:- 'I must protest in the strongest possible terms my objections to the play 'Pravda' at the Playhouse. Its gutter language of such obscenity was repulsive and nauseating.' As is often the case, he was in the minority and theatregoers rushed to defend this fine play., For example Mrs. Lessor replied: 'The English language with all its richness, has been full of crudities as well as perfections since the days of Chaucer and before and it would be similar to 'doctoring' the Bible to cut out all foul language whether we enjoy it our not. Congratulations and thanks to the Playhouse for giving us such a stimulating and thought provoking and entertaining evening.'

Roger Leach who played the main character Lambert LeRoux often spoke of this part as being one of his favourite roles.

In 1988 the Playhouse proved they could do comedy as well as any other genre when they performed 'The Happiest Days of Your Life' directed by Lynn Wyfe and featuring an excellent cast that included Doreen Andrew and Donald Pelmear as the two head teachers, with the Playhouse stalwart Tim Meats as one of the long suffering teachers and Robert Kingswell as the school porter, forever carrying a netball post in the background! 'Side-Splitting School Farce' was the headline in the local *Journal* and Vanessa Coryndon wrote: 'Who could believe that such an unlikely piece could still bring more than nostalgic pleasure?' Then in 1989 the Playhouse produced a rare treat in the musical 'Cabaret.' Like all successfully written plays this again split opinion.

This time it was the *Journal* that on the whole, did not enjoy the production. . 'Ultimately this is a patchy *Cabaret* in both staging and performance.' wrote June Martin. This review was fortunately counter-acted by a letter in the *Journal* from Dennis MacLaren who said: 'I am writing to protest most vehemently against your publication of June Martin's review of 'Cabaret' at the Playhouse. Not only did it frequently miss the point; it was a totally inadequate review of any musical play. It also failed completely to reflect the outstanding quality of the entire production and the audience's acclamation of it.'

. Cabaret: Kalli Greenwood (Sally Bowles); Cazz Scattergood; Nicola Blackman; Samantha Hughes; Karen Chatwin as the Kit-Kat Club girls, May 1989 (Photographer Peter Brown)

Seeing and understanding other people's points of view was something that David Horlock was especially keen on, so perhaps this time the criticism did not hurt too much, although he would have taken it on board and made use of it. He once said: 'To have one's own opinions is not the prerogative of the super-brains, to put it forward in opposition to somebody else's may often lead to a fruitful issue and to think and talk is exciting and exhilarating. Often one of the strongest affirmations of being alive.'

Throughout this decade there were also several World Premieres including 'The Secret Garden' in 1983, 'The Wrong End of the World' in 1987 and 'Mary Stuart' in 1988. This last play came about in a very unusual way. Gertrude Smith, a fluent speaker of German and French, was in an audience at the cathedral a few years ago when she heard David Horlock speaking about his desire to stage the play based on the story of Mary Stuart, if only there was an English translation of Schiller's German play. Mrs. Smith was inspired and promptly bought a copy of Schiller's massive five act work when she next visited Germany and on her return she set about translating it. It took her

The Pied Piper, Stage 65: Mark Barlow as the Pied Piper; Directed by Lynn Wyfe with a cast of over 100, December 1990 (Photographer Peter Brown)

three to four months working on it at two to three hours stretches. With the task duly finished she popped the hand-written manuscript into a carrier bag and delivered it to the Playhouse. Claire Luckham gratefully then took over and produced the finished article!

The main auditorium's smaller companion, the Salberg, also continued to go from strength to strength. It was the ideal place to produce plays that would perhaps attract a minority audience such as '*The Birthday Party*' in 1985, '*Happy Days*' in 1986 (a virtuoso performance by Doreen Andrew) and '*Kiss of the Spider Woman*' in 1987. It was also the ideal arena for Stage 65 to exhibit their multitude of talents in such plays as '*The Boy Friend*' in 1984, '*Our Day Out*' in 1986 and '*Grease*' in 1989. There were plays of a local appeal such as '*Melchester*' an evocative collection of works about Salisbury and '*A Shepherd's Life*' an equally evocative story set in and around the Salisbury countryside. It was also the ideal place to try out new works such as '*Winter in Majorca*' the story of Chopin. Above all though, it was also the ideal space to produce an alternative to the annual pantomime, a cabaret show complete with dinner.

Roger Leach and Michael Lunts had often worked together, and they soon realised that they were on the same comedy wavelength and so they began working on material together. The first Salberg Christmas cabaret was '*Tom Foolery*' based on the works of Tom Lehrer, but it was '*Quirkish Delight*' in 1987 that truly brought Leach and Lunts to the attention of an appreciative Playhouse audience, who wanted to be entertained and to enjoy a night out away from the cries of 'He's behind you!' coming from the main auditorium!

The two of them had always planned to produce their own cabaret show using a mixture of tried and trusted material from such writers as Noel Coward, Tom Lehrer, Paddy Roberts and Flanders and

Quirkish Delight: Roger Leach and Michael Lunts, November 1987
(Photographer Peter Brown)

Swann, but regulations would limit them to the number of published songs they could use so they decided to collaborate and write their own material. In the first 'Quirkish Delight' show, 7 out of the 30 songs they used were their own.

Michael Lunts explained: 'They have been our inspiration. We haven't tried to emulate them, but rather show our respect for them by filling a gap and bringing this type of entertainment up to date.'

Roger Leach added: 'What we want to do is to bring back the notion of intimate revue through the wit of words and music. It's a fun way of spending an evening – for us and we hope for the audience.' The show certainly proved to be a great success as all shows were eventually sold out.

Vanessa Coryndon wrote after seeing the first 'Quirkish Delight': 'looking like two subversive choirboys, Michael Lunts and Roger Leach take a transformed Salberg theatre by subtle storm in their intimate review 'Quirkish Delight.'

The audience is welcomed to a glittering nightclub by Alan Corkill and a contingent from the theatre restaurant. A glance at the menu provides a taste of things to come. Each dish is described apparently by drama critics (alias Leach and Lunts) as 'whimsical', 'impertinent' or a 'magnum opus.' Unobtrusively looked after and extremely well fed we are then entertained superbly.

She continued:

These two are a polished team. I think of Lunts' sympathetic glances at Leach as a lonely warthog and his marvellous piano accompaniment to Leach as he makes his gently debauched way through 'I wanna be seduced.' Their own songs are clever successors to the masters. Can you guess what 'The Job that dares not speak its name' might be? Could you imagine that Chaucer's prologue to the Canterbury tales might lead itself to a song for a revue?

The show proved to be a huge success as four more Christmas 'Quirkish Delights' were to follow.

Many other dinner cabaret shows were also showcased in the

Salberg as an alternative to the pantomime. Many focused on the works of famous composers such as Frank Loesser and Stephen Sondheim. Sadly though, due to health and safety regulations, the dinner side of the evening eventually had to be abandoned but there was always a bar available. In 1998, Leach and Lunts made a welcome return to the Salberg with '*Three's Company*'. This time with the added attraction of the beautiful and very funny Sara Weymouth.

David Horlock always encouraged actors to stay for at least four or five plays. Apart from the economic viability, they stretched creatively, identified with the community and the work therefore gained immeasurably. So during his time at the Playhouse he gathered together several companies of very talented and versatile actors. Many have already been mentioned but to name just a few more there were also on show the talents of Alex Johnston, Christopher Robbie, Emlyn Harris, Rebekah Janes, Julia Chambers, Rosemary Williams, Dominic Letts, Colin Hurley, Richard Cordery, Carolyn Backhouse, Jill Mortimer and Tracey Halsey. Many of them were able to use the Playhouse as springboards to further their successful careers.

There was also Bill Deamer who acted in several plays such as '*Rebecca*', '*The Recruiting Officer*' and '*Jamaica Inn*', but more importantly he became the Playhouse's choreographer, working on such shows as '*Cabaret*', '*A Chorus of Disapproval*', '*Sweeney Todd*' and '*Grease*' for Stage 65. He was also responsible for the choreography for several Horlock and Chissick pantomimes. The three of them enjoyed an excellent working relationship based on mutual respect and complete empathy. 'It is ideal because we understand each other perfectly,' Bill Deamer said. 'We rarely make a move without consulting one another and that makes for a smooth running production. David really is a fantastic captain of the ship.' But he was also quick to pay tribute to the sound and lighting crews and the musical director, Millie Taylor. Without their talented contributions, he said, his job would be infinitely harder.

However, it wasn't long before Bill's multi-talents saw him moving on to wider more famous and more lucrative fields. He is now regarded as one of the leading West End choreographers and has worked on such musicals as '*Hello Dolly*', '*Evita*' and '*Top Hat*'. His name also regularly appears in the credits of many television shows

Bill Deamer in Perfectly Frank (Salberg), November 1985
(Photographer Peter Brown)

such as 'So you think you can dance' and 'Strictly Come Dancing.' Like so many other actors though, it is doubtful that he will ever forget his time at the Playhouse. He once said: 'Out of all the repertories I have been to, Salisbury is by far the best. It has such a high standard.'

Like Bill Deamer, most actors and theatregoers recognise the importance of those who work behind the scenes. It is these people that help to raise the high standard that he spoke about. They are not always mentioned in a critique of a play but without them there would be no play, certainly not a play of a 'high standard.' The ubiquitous Barbara Wilson and Peter Hunter deserved all the praise they were regular given but mention must also be made of people like the Stage managers such as Ellen Quinn and Sound Engineers such as Peter Higton. All aspects of lighting and sound would be dealt with by the Playhouse electricians headed by Peter Hunter. However, not only did the electricians design the lighting for the shows, but by tradition they were also responsible for the theatre's plumbing and all other electrical problems. 'Anything with a plug on it!' Peter once said.

Richard Marks was still the set designer when David Horlock arrived. Richard started his career as an actor – a time he describes as 'fairly disastrous' but he soon realised that his talents belonged backstage.

His design room was often littered with the designs from previous productions including one that he was extremely proud of – '*The Country Wife*', David Horlock's first Playhouse production. David must have known that the baroque period was Richard's favourite

Graham Turner and Stephen Howell (Photographer Peter Brown)

as he let Richard's imagination run wild with proscenium doors and backdrops that took a long time to paint but slid together in seconds. Pantomime though was Richard's favourite time. Although it was an excellent chance to let his imagination fly loose it was also the most difficult time of the year. As well as the sets to design and build there was an endless number of backcloths to paint. These were done in a hangar away from Salisbury because of lack of space in the workshop and there was never enough heating in mid-winter!

His assistant Stephen Howell eventually became Head of Design working with his colleagues, Bill Crutcher and Graham Leonard (Turner). They also had a talented group of carpenters such as Garth Reid and Richard Hunt to build the sets. 'In my time here,' said Garth, 'the sets have always been ready on the night, I'm quite proud of that!'

Stephen Howell was sure that the pressure of theatre work drew the best results from his team and he was always aware of the demands expected of a Salisbury audience. 'They are a sophisticated audience and expect to see something good and three dimensional. They don't want the two dimensional effect of painted flats any more.' The team approached each show as a puzzle and the trickier the demands the more pleasure they found in solving it. When 'Wild Honey' was produced in 1986 it called for a steam train to thunder across the stage complete with smoke and lights with terrifying reality. The back-stage team ensured that it did just that. Like so many stage effects it was a big cheat and although the audience knew that, it still lost none of its impact.

Bill Crutcher (Photographer Peter Brown)

Bill Crutcher eventually left towards the end of the decade and soon made a name for himself on television as a production designer on such programmes as 'Cracker' and 'Father Ted', eventually moving into films as supervising art director, in such films as 'Hysteria' and 'The Iron Lady'.

As well as his design work, Graham Turner also took over the running of 'Togs' the costume hire business based at the back of the Playhouse. It had come a long way since the early days in a cupboard in Chapel Place when Roger Clissold started it as a contribution for the then new Playhouse appeal.

1986 saw a big increase in turnover of costumes and Graham needed more space, more time and more staff alongside his group of regular helpers that included Betty Roberts and Graham's wife. Together their fancy stitchwork, applique, re-cutting and other trade tricks could transform plain or outdated garments into the magical splendour of a whole new personality.

There could be little that 'Togs' could not cater for with various uniforms, national costumes, period outfits and an array of novelty outfits including animals, harlequins and Halloween specials. They even once had an elephant costume until it went AWOL after a garrison party on Salisbury Plain! And a dainty pink fairy costume from Togs found fame one year in the London Marathon!

Sadly 'Togs' is no more, thanks to cost cutting but also because of an infestation of the enemy of all theatre wardrobes – moths! The name lives on though in the Playhouse as the corridor that leads out to the workshop is still known as the 'Togs' corridor.

So David Horlock was the 'fantastic captain of the ship' but during this decade like those before, the Playhouse ship had to face many a stormy sea as the dark clouds of financial problems often covered over this successful theatre. The Playhouse now had a reputation as one of the most important and successful regional theatres in England, but it was not always a decade of 'days of wine and roses' and once again the prospect of the Playhouse closing was very real.

17
'THERE IS ONLY ONE POT OF HONEY AND AN AWFUL LOT OF BREAD TO BE SPREAD WITH IT.'

David Horlock

In the *Sunday Times* of October 4th 1981, Elizabeth Grice wrote an article under the headline 'Arts Council puts 16 more theatres on the danger list.' According to a member of the panel, the eventual hit list - drawn up only after the government's annual grant-aid to the Council is revealed – could be even more devastating than last year. 'Its like a roulette wheel. The wheel stops at the point the government announces its grant and whoever is in the doldrums then will have to go.'

Amongst those 'in danger' were the Salisbury Playhouse and the Mercury Theatre in Colchester. These two were on the hit list because they were not raising enough money from their local authorities. This particular problem has dogged the Playhouse throughout the years – the disparity between the subsidy given by the Arts Council and that given by the local authorities.

This scare prompted Reggie Salberg to write to the theatregoers under the heading: 'Shadow of the Axe':

The hard fact is that we were notified by the Arts Council earlier this year that unless the grants from our local authorities came more in line with that of the Arts Council, we would probably have to face at least a cash standstill, which in these inflationary days is tantamount to a reduction. It must be emphasised that the Arts Council does not question our high standard of productions nor our exceptionally good management record.

The sole reason for the threat is the fact that our local authority grants were practically the lowest in the country. In the present financial year they total £22,830 against the Arts Council's £142,000.

In fairness to the local authorities it should be said that they gave extremely generously to the building of the new theatre and are still paying loan charges on that money. The Arts Council does not accept that this is in any way a revenue grant.

At the moment the Local District Council's contribution is the equivalent of a 0.069 penny rate. Not a bad bargain for what is arguably its greatest amenity.

Is it conceivable that a theatre playing to well over 80% capacity, earning 65% of its keep, whose work (which included a good proportion of new plays), has been praised by the national critics and which has balanced its book for the past 27 years, may possibly lose its grant?

I can not believe that the Arts Council, which on the whole has acted wisely and justly in the past, has suddenly been seized with a fit of insanity, but there lurks a fear that in this time of stringency it might be tempted to support only a few centres of excellence – if indeed these are definable. Such a feeling was mooted in the fifties but luckily it was rested and the regions were in a short time flourishing as never before – as they will surely flourish again unless too heavy an axe is wielded.

One wag suggested that the Playhouse's next pantomime should be 'Puss in Boot' in order to save some money or that the next drama should be 'The Two Sisters' by Chekhov rather than the usual three!

Fortunately though, the Local Council came up with an enhanced grant for both the Playhouse and the Arts Centre for the next year so the problem subsided, but it would not go away completely.

Then in September 1984 it was announced that seat prices at the Playhouse were set to rise as part of a lifeline arrangement to provide more local government funding. The Local Council pledged to increase backing for the theatre by £2,200 over the next four years a rise of about 11%. This would bring the Council's level of grant aid to the Playhouse to £22,500 by 1988.

In addition Wiltshire Council was proposing to raise its grant from £5,800 to £10,500 over the same period which, with help from other councils in its catchment area, would mean the theatre getting a total of £52,500 in local government assistance. However, the catch was that the theatre management would be expected to increase its seat prices by 40% over the four year spell.

Raising seat prices was something that Reggie Salberg was always vehemently against because he felt it would only lead to an inevitable downward spiral. Higher prices would lead to a drop in attendance, which would then lead to less money being available to put on the quality of plays to draw in the theatregoers. It was inevitable though, that seat prices had to be raised, slightly.

In March 1984, Jonathan Hyams, the Director of the Arts Centre, wrote an impassioned plea for more support for the Arts in an article entitled 'Must Salisbury become a cultural backwater?'

In it he sympathised with Reggie Salberg's fear. He wrote:

As to whether the Arts are really necessary, figures can only show so much but it is worth noting that last year (1983) there were over 236,000 attendances in Salisbury. Considering the population of Salisbury and the district which is only 70,000, this is a mammoth vote in favour.

The Arts always need subsidies to survive. They are by nature labour intensive and require costly buildings. If the Playhouse lost all of its subsidy and tried to make up the loss by charging higher ticket prices the initial increase would be at least 50%. But this would in return reduce the number of attendances as many theatregoers simply could not afford to go any longer. The costly spiral – higher prices, less attendances.

Each pound allocated by the Council can be worth many times its face value. The arts organisations are spending their money with local suppliers, they are generating further spending in hotels and restaurants and most importantly they are employing over 130 people and giving contracts to over 850 artists per year.

In 1985 Reggie Salberg concurred:

Even a small theatre like Salisbury which received a grant of £145,000 from the Arts Council gives back more than that amount in VAT, NHI contributions and tax paid by its employees and by the authors of its plays. If the Playhouse were to close, not only would this income cease, but the situation could generate claims on unemployment benefit of up to £73,000 per annum.

In 1985 the Arts Council issued a publication entitled 'The Glory of the Garden' in which it outlined a new strategy for subsidy: it declared its intention to feed more money into the regions at the expense of London. It optimistically assumed a considerable increase in its own subsidy from the government. However, the sum unfortunately fell far below expectation, but the Council decided to press on with its new policy.

Many theatres suffered, but the Playhouse was given an increase of 3.5% which was a recognition of the management's good housekeeping, the theatre's exceptional attendance figures and partly because of the increased generosity of the local funding authorities.

All was not well though in the theatre world and early in March that year, theatre directors from all over the country met at the National Theatre to voice their disquiet over the present policies of the Arts Council and it was generally felt that the theatre-going public should be made aware both of the realities of subsidy and the danger to the theatre in Britain. In an article entitled 'The Arts in Danger' Reggie Salberg concluded by saying: 'For it is about the state of the whole country's theatre that we should be concerned. Here we have few worries – at the moment!

More financial trouble though, was brewing just around the corner. Throughout this decade, as always, though there was the Theatregoers Club. Founded many years ago in the old Playhouse mainly to raise money to help save the theatre at a time of financial crisis, and originally led by such stalwarts as Francis Pullen and Daniel Pettiward, it was once again there to help the Playhouse.

Like a kind, benevolent, omnipresent relation it was always there to give a helping hand, mainly financial but also in organising activities for theatregoers and in publicising the theatre.

Under the Chairmanship of Keith Allner and Ray Smith, and with the support of so many excellent committee members, such as Pauline Richardson, Audrey Lovett, Sally Levinson, Sydney St, John, Ron Meek and the ubiquitous Simon Thornton, to name but a few, they organised a whole variety of events which would entertain but also raise money.

At their AGM in 1981 it was reported that since 1974 they had raised over £20,000 for the theatre. Then during this decade they raised money for such large items as new seats for the Salberg and a new van for TIE. Over the years cheques of £500 were constantly being presented to the theatre management.

Sponsoring plays continued to be an important part of their activities and as well as sponsoring David Horlock's first production *'The Country Wife'* for several years they sponsored the whole of the Salberg season.

Initially for a £1 a year, subscriptions, rising slightly during the decade, theatregoers could enjoy such events as Theatre Balls, Celebrity Dinners, talks by famous theatrical people as well as by Playhouse staff, treasure hunts around the city, jumble sales, auctions, coffee mornings, Sunday lunches at the Richardsons, stage parties, open rehearsals and garden parties.

There were also many theatre visits to such places as Bath, Chichester, Southampton and London organised by Jane (Dalton) Ware and Cliff Ware. Cliff eventually became Chairman and represented the Theatregoers on the Board of the Theatre.

Special mention must be made of the annual garden party which was such an important feature of the Theatregoers calendar. This was usually opened by a celebrity. In 1982 Ruth Madoc, who had appeared at the old Playhouse, but now more importantly was from television's 'Hi-de-hi!' was a great attraction. The following year a heavy storm prohibited any outside event so the 'Garden Party' was held in the Playhouse. It was opened by Michael Aspel with other celebrities such as Raymond Baxter and Gayle Hunnicutt in attendance.

Some older members may have had memories of past garden parties opened by such celebrities of the day as Brian Reece (PC 49) and Ben Lyon and Bebe Daniels and perhaps some people could remember Ollie Gordon's infamous 'Fishing for Champagne' stall!

Ollie wanted to run this stall and he managed to convince Reggie Salberg that is was unlikely that any bottles of champagne would be won and that it would make a great deal of money. The stall opened at 3.15 and by 3.30 four bottles had been won. The stall promptly closed at 3.45!

So the Theatregoers Club made a huge contribution to the life of the Playhouse and it was often said, 'how could we possibly exist without it?'

How vital it was to have the support of the Theatregoers Club became evident again in 1986 when news came that the Arts Council had frozen their grant to the Playhouse. The *Southern Evening Echo* reported:

> Angry Artistic Director David Horlock believes that the theatre is being penalised because of its success. The big freeze means that there will be virtually no increase in the £147,000 grant to the theatre and taking account of inflation, that means a cut of some £5,000.
>
> The Arts Council says that the reason is that the cash from local authorities for the theatre is low compared with their grant and gave the chilling warning that they may have to reconsider the whole grant position in the following year. Current grants from Salisbury District, Wiltshire County Council and Hampshire totalled £50,000.

So the old problem had raised its ugly head again. Apparently the agreement negotiated with the local authorities in 1983 whereby they would increase their grants quite considerably over a period of four years, provided the Playhouse increased their prices by an average of 10% per annum over the same period was not enough to satisfy the Arts Council.

This time it needed prompt action and David Horlock wasted no time in gathering support from the patrons, from the media and from the general public. In a letter to the *Journal* he wrote:

> The Playhouse will be turned into a supermarket within two years unless more financial support is found. We are not 'crying wolf' – the wolf is already at the door!
>
> The theatre will go into a spiral of decline. First things to be

axed would be the pantomime and TIE. Ticket prices would have to be increased substantially and would be out of the reach of many patrons. The range of plays would have to be reduced and the emphasis on 'safe' plays with low production costs. This in turn would reduce the theatre's ability to attract first class actors and possibly lead to a total withdrawal of the Arts Council's grant.

David Horlock rehearsing for 'The Wrong End of the World', May 1987 (Photographer Peter Brown)

In further letters and articles both David Horlock and Reggie Salberg bombarded the patrons and the general public with information to support the theatre's cause:

We earn a very high proportion of our own income. Over £428,000 was earned during 1984/85 giving the theatre an earned income level of 72% against a national average of 50%. Grants from the Arts Council and the local authorities contribute a significant 28% towards our annual income.'

During 1984/85 over 146,000 people attended some 460 performance at the Playhouse. We have balanced our books every year since 1955. This is an unequalled record. We are a non-profit making organisation and subsidy is primarily used to maintain ticket prices at a level which we consider within the range of our audience's pocket.

We need increased subsidy not only to beat inflation but to develop areas of our work which have so much potential, especially our Education programme, our studio programme and the need for new and bigger work to be seen on the main stage.

We play to a higher percentage of capacity than any of the other 42 subsidised regional theatres. Last year we achieved very nearly 90%.

Without subsidy there would be a dramatic reduction in the service we give now and in 2 years we would close.

In a programme note Reggie Salberg concluded by saying: 'How can you help? I would not suggest a hunger strike like the one staged at Worthing by two brothers when subsidy was withdrawn and their theatre closed! But you can make your voice heard in the press and by letters to your MP, to Local Authorities and to the Arts Council. After all as one patron wrote to us recently, 'life in Salisbury without its theatre is unthinkable.'

As David Horlock once put it: 'There is only one pot of honey and an awful lot of bread to be spread with it.'

Coming to the aid of the Playhouse was the Theatregoers Club of Great Britain. In a letter to the *Journal* they wrote:

Our organisation is just one of many that brings groups into Salisbury for Playhouse matinee performances. Our members support local restaurants and spend their afternoons sightseeing and exploring the shops and market. On April 26 we had one coach at the matinee but there were seven other coaches outside loading up when the performance ended. A lot of people were clutching shopping bags full of local purchases.

Strong support also came from Wiltshire County Council. Their leader Jack Ainslie said that the Council 'would fight tooth and nail, and shoulder to shoulder with Salisbury Playhouse if the theatre's future was threatened. 'It is ironic that the Government via the Arts Council is pressing local authorities to spend more on the arts,' he declared, 'But at the same time it is screwing them by reducing their rate support grant and forcing them to reduce services. Then it complains bitterly if county councils increase rates.' The county leader said that Wiltshire had honoured a commitment to increase its grant every year. 'We shall continue to do so.' he pledged. 'I am not looking for a confrontation but I don't think we can be put over a barrel on this.'

Of course there will always be voices of dissent, such as Duncan Grove who in a letter to the *Journal* wrote:

Let the people of Salisbury decide for themselves whether they want a Playhouse. If the productions are good and the advertising effective, we the locals and our tourist visitors will pay the price for tickets which will enable the Playhouse to make a profit. Should this not be the case then the Playhouse should close.

In either case it should be of no concern to local councillors. They should be more concerned with ensuring that the ratepayers money is more wisely and frugally spent.

A very simplistic and narrow minded view of the situation. Fortunately he was in the minority as most of Salisbury rallied round and supported the theatre. Many wrote to David Horlock offering financial support and a willingness to start fund-raising again.

Fortunately as Churchill would have put it: 'Jaw, jaw, not war, war!' was the answer to this seemingly unanswerable problem as all those involved, the Arts Council, the Local Authorities and the Playhouse management put aside their differences and talked, and talked and eventually came up with a £100,000 four year development plan. It was becoming obvious to both the Arts Council and the Local Authorities the importance of the Playhouse in its community and the threat of the Playhouse closing was becoming very real unless the problem of parity of subsidies was finally solved.

It was an example of what could happen when all parties approached the problem with a willingness to pursue a solution without rushing to see each other as enemies.

However, the Local Authorities were not willing to give the extra money unconditionally. In particular before concluding the agreement they wished to make sure that the Playhouse would not 'trundle along in the same old way.' There was a strong feeling in some quarters that the Playhouse had become bogged down in an unexciting policy of 'safety first.' Of course, with extra funding, David Horlock would have been only too happy to move away from that image.

So in exchange for the extra funding the Playhouse was to continue to provide a TIE service which would be free to Wiltshire schools and also available without payment to the neighbouring

Alan Corkill inside the foyer (Photographer Peter Brown)

counties of Hampshire and Dorset; to broaden the scope of the main house productions; to the development of the Salberg programme; to a programme of refurbishment of the building to be partially funded by an increase in ticket prices and to the establishment of a full time Financial and Administrative Director.

There was scarcely much in this package of conditions to cause the theatre management sleepless nights. On the contrary the Playhouse emerged from the crisis as party to a remarkable bargain –

extra funding against the undertaking to do a number of things it had wanted to do anyway.

The only possible cloud on the horizon was the theatregoers' reaction to a change in the policy of productions. Perhaps the majority of the Salisbury audience might have been only too happy to see the theatre 'trundle along' as it has done in the past. Was the Playhouse really about to cast off its 'safe image' and if so, how would this new direction, hoped for by the minority, be received by the majority?

It was a balancing act that David Horlock would be facing certainly with excitement, but also with great care, understanding and also with a certain degree of trepidation.

Appointed as the new Financial and Administrative Director was Patric Gilchrist from the Mold theatre in Clwyd. Much of this area of Playhouse management was still being covered by Reggie Salberg but as Guy Jessop, the Chairman of the Board in a letter sent to board members pointed out:

> Their (The Arts Council and Local Authorities) recommendation is in no way a criticism of Reggie, and all that he has done for the Playhouse. Indeed the Arts Council holds up the Salisbury Playhouse, with its long-standing financial record, as a model to other regional theatres. Our major funding authorities are, however, like us, deeply concerned with the question of continuity and development, and they are suggesting that, especially with a view to the long term, the financial running of the theatre as a large and expanding business operation, warrants the appointment of an officer who is based at the theatre all the time.

Before this appointment, the change in management was discussed in full with Reggie, who could see that his involvement in the theatre that he had devoted so much of his life to, was beginning to loosen, but also he could understand the need for progress. Some might have said, 'why doesn't he just retire and leave the theatre management to younger people?', but surely, someone with Reggie's incredible theatrical knowledge and insight should always be welcomed and not be dismissed.

He wasn't finished yet, and in a letter to Guy Jessop he pointed out some financial figures and how he could continue to help in the future:

> When the new theatre opened I was given a yearly amount as Theatre Consultant and also a pension. It was not visualised that I would act as finance officer as well as consultant and I am not quite sure how it happened! As a result, although my pay has been increased over the past 18 months quite considerably, the fact is that over the period I have been working anything between 20 and 50 hours a week at an average of about £1.50 per hour. No complaints, because I have enjoyed doing so!
>
> As to the future I would like to make it clear that on consideration, I welcome the extra leisure time the appointment of a Finance Officer will give me although I would feel completely lost if I were not to play some part in Playhouse affairs.

He then suggested ways in which he could continue to help David Horlock, such as reading and advising him about new plays; visiting regional theatres so he could advise him about actors who he might be interested in; continuing to act as the Salisbury representative at meetings of the Theatre Managers Association and to attend Board Meetings.

He then suggested how his pension may be increased and finished with:

> Whilst considering my request I think the Board might like to take into account that my acting as Financial Officer has saved at least £30,000 in wages since the new theatre opened and that my salary in the old Playhouse was considerably below that of most other Theatre Directors at the time – in fact it was probably the lowest in the country.

So Reggie had no intentions of going into complete retirement yet!

For some time during the late 80s the City Hall, which is adjacent to the Playhouse, had been suffering many problems both financially and in its management.

In 1988 the Playhouse Board, seeing a ready-made opportunity to expand the Playhouse's empire and to boost its finances, decided to make a bid to operate the City Hall. At present the Hall was let out on an occasional basis to outside organisations and the council's only profit came from letting charges. Profits from events went to the organisers. Under the proposed scheme the Playhouse, in consultation with the Arts Centre, would handle the programming of events at the City Hall maximising its use as a top venue for a wide variety of events.

Patric Gilchrist said: 'There is considerable potential in running the two buildings in such a way that they would compliment each other.' He added that the staging of any event was a risky business but if it succeeded it could make money. 'As it is us taking the risk, there could be something in it financially for the Playhouse.'

Rosemary Roe in the *Journal* commented: 'The two are side by side and under joint control, would create a unique conference centre and leisure venue to take the city into the 21st century'.

Unfortunately, like the plan in 1975 to 'create a new civic centre uniting the Playhouse with the City Hall, the new Library and the proposed new museum' it did not materialise and now in the 21st century the City hall stands proudly and independently beside the Playhouse, creating its own programmes and its own successes.

~~~

In March 1989 David Horlock was looking forward to the opening of his adaptation of '*Jamaica Inn*' and further ahead to his production of '*Sweeney Todd*', advertised as 'the most ambitious and spectacular musical ever seen on the Salisbury stage.' Sunday 25th March was Mothers Day and he decided not to go to a memorial service in London in honour of Reggie Salberg's wife Noreen Craven but to visit his mother, Nellie in Pagham. He stayed to watch a film on television so left half an hour later than he normally would have done. He stopped at the gate to pick a bunch of primroses before waving goodbye.

Nellie vividly remembers the policeman and policewoman knocking on the door at about 10 o'clock that night to report to her of David's death in a car crash. She said that she found it remarkable that she was able to describe David. Tears came later; she had a sloe gin and slept well. She felt no anger against the other driver involved in the crash, only sorry and pity for him. She said: 'I cannot be an unforgiving person. When God calls, there is nothing you can do about it.'

On his way home from Pagham, David's Renault estate had collided with a camper van outside a garage on a notorious A36 black spot at Landford. The car in front of the camper van had slowed down in order to turn into the garage forecourt forcing the driver behind to slow down. He tried to brake but found that the rear brakes did not respond as the van had run out of brake fluid.. Witnesses saw a huge plume of blue smoke engulf the back of the van as the driver tried to steer it around the car in front but he came face to face with David Horlock's car coming in the opposite direction. David could not slow down in time and the collision catapulted the Renault estate into the forecourt of the carpet showroom next to the garage.

Four other cars collided in the mayhem and another in the garage forecourt was extensively damaged. David died instantly of multiple injuries. None of the other drivers suffered any serious injury.

The shock to the Playhouse and indeed to the whole of Salisbury was immeasurable. There was not only a feeling of deep sadness but one of disbelief that this man who was such a vibrant and important part of the life of the Playhouse and of the life of Salisbury was no longer there.

There were the immediate heart-felt tributes such as the one from the Bishop of Salisbury, John Baker who said: 'There seems to be an enormous empty space where he used to be. He will be remembered for a very long time' and the tribute from Reggie Salberg who simply said: 'He was a splendid man of the theatre and a splendid individual.'

As with any death, there is always a flurry of activity as events have to be arranged and many people become involved, even more so, when the death is sudden and the deceased is involved in the running of a theatre. 'The show must go on' is an old cliché but this had to be the case at the Playhouse. The shows in both the main auditorium and in the Salberg continued to be performed and behind the scenes,

Patric Gilchrist and Alan Corkill picked up the pieces and held the Playhouse together.

A day of celebration of the life of David Horlock was held on Good Friday 13th April. The Playhouse was open at midday when patrons could see an exhibition of photographs and other material from David's productions.

At 4pm there was a special performance of 'Winter in Majorca' written and performed by Michael Lunts and produced by David.

At 7pm 'The People's Passion' would be performed around the streets of Salisbury. This was written by David and was going to be directed by him.

At 9.30 there was a special performance of the current sell-out production of 'Jamaica Inn' which had been adapted by David and directed by him.

At midnight the Playhouse closed and the theatre community continued with a private celebration of his life.

All proceeds from the day's activities went towards a special fund in memory of David which would provide a bursary or training to assist young theatre professionals at an early stage of their careers.

This bursary was eventually closed in 2016 and the remaining funds were donated to the Playhouse and to the Bristol Old Vic, the two theatres that meant so much to David.

Then there were the official arrangements to be made.. First a Requiem Communion service was arranged at the Cathedral for Friday 30th March and then David's funeral was to take place at the Parish Church in Pagham on 2nd April. A memorial Service was then arranged for the Cathedral on Saturday 5th May and later in June, a Memorial Service was held at the Actors' Church, St. Paul's in Covent Garden.

David was finally laid to rest behind a seat at the edge of the pathway leading up to the entrance to the Parish Church of St. Thomas a Becket in Pagham, in a church, in a town that meant so much to him.

The Service of Thanksgiving for his life which was held at the Cathedral on Saturday 5th May, was a production that David himself would have been proud of. Not only did it contain pieces by the Cathedral choir and organist but readings by Sonia Woolley and Toyah Willcox, piano music by Michael Lunts as well as part of 'Noyes Fludde', which David had directed as part of the 1989 Salisbury Festival with Richard Cordery speaking the voice of God.

Bishop John Baker's address was a masterpiece, as it summed up perfectly David's personality and his life. His opening paragraphs immediately brought an image of David:

> The memory of that magical smile of David's with his head on one side, reminds me of the scene in 'Through the Looking Glass' when Alice is shaking hands with Humpty Dumpty. 'If he smiled much more,' she thought, 'the ends of his mouth might meet behind and then I don't know what would happen to his head! I'm afraid it would come off!'
>
> The first thing so many of us seem to remember about David was that intensely living physical presence... He was just alive with a force and a warmth meant to be found in all of us, but which so few achieve.

He spoke of David's strong Christian faith: 'He was convinced that the heart of the meaning of life was to be found in Jesus. Someone once said of him that 'he was ideal disciple material, Christ would have chosen him' and I for one believe that is bang on target.'

And he spoke of the busy life David led. 'He crammed the suitcase of each day full to bulging.' Not only did he have his busy life at the Playhouse but he was also a Steward at the Cathedral, Chairman of the Salisbury Dyslexia Association; President of the Sarum Chamber Orchestra, worked with the St. John Singers and readily chaired meetings when such local topics as Stonehenge and the By-Pass were discussed.

David also enjoyed producing plays with children such as his towering production of '*Noyes Fludde*' in the Cathedral.. In an article David described the problems he encountered when rehearsing '*School for Scandal*' at the Playhouse simultaneously with '*Emil and the Detectives*' at the Cathedral School. He wrote:

> At first it was very strange going straight from my own theatre rehearsals to the school. I remember particularly one afternoon, a concentrated rehearsal on the Screen Scene of '*School for Scandal*'

David Horlock rehearsing Noyes Flodde, September 1989
(Photographer Peter Brown)

followed immediately by a session of the '*Emil*' gang songs. Very bracing! And there have been days when I have found myself addressing my actors like prep school boys!

During those first few weeks after his death, memories and tributes tumbled over themselves to be read. Many were sprinkled with the humour that David so much loved. Richard Shephard wrote:

For a time while his New Street house was being renovated, David stayed in my house in the Close. One day he returned home, tired after rehearsal and decided to rest. He went to his room, only to find the cat lying on the bed. He thought that there was enough room on the bed for them both to lay down, whereupon the cat bit him! He used to tell this story with that great guffaw which I, and many others will miss so much.

Alison Jensen reminisced about working with him:

He was not afraid of returning to the drawing board to re-assess where necessary, even at the eleventh hour, and had a way of doing so without causing offence. I well remember taking him my designs for the sets of a Cathedral School musical. He was full of enthusiasm and I went away brimming with pride. It was only when I got home that I realised he had replaced every one of my ideas with something better! You learn so much, so painlessly from David!.

But perhaps the most poignant piece though, was from Alan Richardson who wrote:

The day he died was Mothering Sunday and the bond between mother and son drew him home to spend the last day with her. Indeed fate was to write a tragedy. On his way back to Salisbury his life ended and he embraced the father he had never seen.

Alison Jensen also wrote: 'But undoubtedly the greatest emptiness he leaves is that of his unfinished work. He had so many irons in the fire and was constantly occupied with numerous projects, always heading towards another venture. In fact Nellie Horlock always said that one day David would stop directing and concentrate solely on his writing.

In her article, Alison Jensen also asked the question: 'Who can replace him? we all ask. No one, is the answer.'

But although there would never be another David Horlock, there definitely had to be another Artistic Director of the Playhouse. 'The Show must go on!'

The Board now had the incredibly difficult task of replacing David Horlock. It needed very delicate and tactful handling if they were to replace a much loved and very talented person successfully. The new person had to be someone who could keep the Salisbury theatregoers happy and who could continue and then further the success of the Playhouse as it moved towards the millennium. There was also the problem of a rather large financial deficit to cope with.

18
'WHAT ON EARTH IS GOING ON AT THE PLAYHOUSE?'

From a letter in the Salisbury Journal.

'The standard was gratifyingly high.' Nicholas Bourne, the Chairman reported to the Board concerning the applications for the position of Artistic Director at the Playhouse. Many aspiring theatre people saw this as a plumb position and once again there were many who were eager to move to Salisbury and to stamp their mark on this very popular and respected regional theatre.

Thirteen candidates were short listed and these were eventually whittled down to five: - Graham Berown, Ivan Cutting, John Durnin, Robin Herford and Deborah Paige.

Deborah Paige (Salisbury Journal)

'Anyone of whom would be likely to make a success of the post. But we were particularly impressed by Deborah Paige.' reported the Chairman. So she was invited back for a second interview and was offered the post. The appointment surprised many people, not least the fact that the Playhouse was to have its first female Artistic Director. However though, the climate of the time spoke very much of 'the new generation of women theatre directors.' Once again the safe, familiar figure of Graham Berown was overlooked. It was as if it was a case of, 'If we can't get another David Horlock, then let's get someone completely different.'

At the time Deborah Paige was working with the Soho Theatre Company having had experience with other major regional theatres: Bristol, Ipswich and Leicester.

In her CV she wrote:

> I have a deep respect for regional theatre, which I believe is an invaluable resource and which has a vital role to play both locally and nationally. I am particularly interested in the importance attached to extending Theatre in Education, Young Peoples' Theatre and Youth Theatre Work in Salisbury Playhouse's three year plan and would see this as a vital part of the process of developing new, younger audiences.

The Board stressed that this was an important requirement of her appointment: To find and encourage 'a new, younger audience.' She was congratulated by many people in the theatre but there was also a word of warning from the Gulbenkian Foundation: 'The programme at Salisbury has lacked something for years. I am delighted that you are going to inject new spirit into it.'

However, immediately following David Horlock's death the first task though, was to complete the programme he had planned and there were some noticeable successes, the most popular being the production of Sondheim's 'Sweeney Todd'. This was directed by Graham Berown with Bill Deamer as assistant director and Rob Mitchell as musical director. It was said by those who worked on the show, that it was the most ambitious and technically biggest the Playhouse had ever seen. David Horlock himself was due to direct it.

Sweeney Todd, May 1990: Michael Heath
as Sweeney Todd
(Photographer Peter Brown)

Vanessa Coryndon in the *Journal* wrote: 'Obsession, revenge, madness and murder – and yet here is a show of immense comic charm. Paradoxical, stunning entertainment from the first flourish of the rolling pin to the last flash of the razor!'

The Salberg continued with a packed programme with several Stage 65 productions including '*Stags and Hens*' and '*The Life and Adventures of Nicholas Nickleby.*'

However, all was not well down the administration corridor. Following David Horlock's death, Patric Gilchrist was appointed Acting Director and the management of the theatre was entrusted to five key personnel of which Alan Corkill was one. This group was entrusted to meet on a weekly basis, but in fact only met on five occasions in the six months leading up to Deborah Paige's appointment. In effect Patric Gilchrist assumed complete control of the management and artistic side of the theatre which led to several problems, the main one being the gradual erosion of Alan Corkill's position. This was exacerbated later by the appointment of Danny Moar as Marketing and Development Officer who would be taking over some of Alan Corkill's responsibilities. This was a veritable 'kick in the teeth' (Alan Corkill's words) to someone who at the opening of the new building in 1976 was responsible for running the theatre alongside Roger Clissold with assistance from Reggie Salberg.

Once she had arrived at the Playhouse it was naturally an exciting time for Deborah Paige and in the programme notes for her first production: she wrote: 'It is a tribute to the theatre, its audience and indeed to David Horlock himself, that since his tragic death in March, the Playhouse has survived, thrived and maintained excellent standards throughout an enormously difficult time. We have a lot to

The Second Mrs. Tanquerary, March 1991: Helen Schlesinger as Paula; Richard Howard as Cayley Drummle; Ruth Gemmell as Eillean (Photographer Peter Brown)

be proud of, not just in the past, but right under our noses! I'm sure the future will be equally brave and exciting and that together we'll continue all the best Playhouse traditions as well as inventing some new ones. I'm looking forward to it!'

For her first production she chose Pinero's 'The Second Mrs. Tanqueray' which was mainly greeted with praise. Mick Martin called it: 'Deborah Paige's minutely thought out and exquisitely realised revival.' and Vanessa Coryndon wrote: 'This was an unconventional choice for a director's debut at Salisbury but the result is an absorbing, rewarding evening.' Her assistant director was Joanna Read who went on to become Artistic Director of the Playhouse in 2000.

Deborah Paige was eager to start putting her marker down and to show the theatregoers that a new era, a new dawn was about to take place but already she was very much aware of the huge effect David Horlock was still having on the Playhouse and in no way wished to tread on his memory. However, the spectre of David Horlock was to haunt her all the time she was artistic director of the Playhouse, both artistically and financially.

The financial problem she had inherited was huge; it was a little matter of an operating deficit of £125,000. For years the Playhouse management had boasted that they had always kept their budget in the black, but hard times were beginning to catch up with them. In her book *Bringing Down the Curtain*, Olivia Turnbull wrote:

> Long before Paige's arrival, attendance figures had begun to show signs of decline. The older end of the loyal audience, who had been committed theatregoers since the 1950s, was literally dying off, while others were becoming increasingly unhappy with the standards of production under Paige's predecessor, David Horlock. [Although it must be said, that many theatregoers had been very happy with David Horlock's productions!] And an inefficient system of administration that had been organised manually, lacked the involvement of a fully qualified accountant and employed only a part-time bookkeeper.

In a local newspaper report it was stated:

> The theatre did a brilliant job in surviving six months without an artistic director but inevitably costs were incurred. There was a sharp drop in ticket sales and extra administrative expenses. Money was also needed for a long overdue refurbishment of the building, inside and out.

The Playhouse for many years had also been the victim of problems arising from the Arts Council's emphasis on parity funding. Financial threats had dogged the Playhouse throughout the 1980s when on three occasions the Arts Council froze its grant and on one occasion threatened to withdraw funding altogether unless local authorities brought their funding up to matching levels.

Then in the early 1990s, partly in response to the recession, Wiltshire County Council's grant to the Playhouse was frozen for two years and actually decreased in real terms.

The situation was further complicated by the delegation of responsibility for the theatre from the Arts Council to the Southern Arts Board in 1992. Then later, compounding the situation even further was the fact that devolution coincided with a freeze on government spending on the Arts. This inevitably meant that Arts Council's grants to regional arts boards were frozen and so, in turn, were the grants made through these regional boards to the theatres.

It was often said that the Playhouse suffered financially because of its early successes. High attendances in the past had meant lower subsidies compared with other theatres. Something had to be done to address the financial problem and fast.

In June 1991, Stage 65 under the direction of Lynn Wyfe performed 'West Side Story' on the main stage. It was a sell out and it received great critical acclaim. It also generated over £6,000 for the Playhouse. In a letter to the *Journal*, Julie Wilds wrote: 'Lynn Wyfe and everyone involved are to be congratulated on the hard work and commitment which such a production requires. The whole show was a thrilling entertainment and I quickly warmed to the sheer exuberance of such a dedicated cast.'

Amongst all this euphoria it was unfortunate that this was the time when the Playhouse decided to announce that it was about to launch an appeal for money to save the theatre.

A Press release was put out that stated:

Rising production costs, the tragic death last year of the much-loved artistic director, David Horlock, and the recession which has seriously affected theatre audiences throughout the country, means that the Playhouse is currently facing intense financial difficulties.

The problems are compounded by the fact that although the theatre enjoys excellent relationships with local and national funding bodies, it is seriously under-funded compared with other organisations of a similar size, particularly if it is to continue with its existing wide range of theatre provisions.

The Playhouse is doing all it can to help itself, unprecedently stringent financial controls are in place, new market initiatives have been undertaken to retain existing customers and develop new audiences; bar and restaurant facilities are being improved and all staff salaries have been frozen.

The fund raising appeal had two main aims; the first was to generate one-off gifts to help stave off the immediate financial crisis; the second was to generate ongoing public funds via a 'Friends and Members Scheme' which would entitle contributors to special perks when visiting the Playhouse. 'The whole community rallied round to help build this theatre and I hope our public will support us again.' said Deborah Paige.

One option to effect economies was that the Salberg Studio should be closed. Fortunately this was saved by a legacy of £50,000 given by the late Mary Moore. A letter to all board members by the Chairman stated: 'Deborah and I recently called upon Mary Moore's sister to discuss with her how best Mary's magnificent bequest might be used. We wished to establish what Mary really wanted. Miss Moore expressed herself in agreement with the proposal that the legacy be used over the next two seasons to fund Studio productions which otherwise would not be possible and to that extent, thanks to Mary's generosity, the short-term future of the Studio is much more assured.'

Robert Hawkings, who was the Chairman of the fund raising appeal and who was mainly responsible for raising the extra money from the public which enabled the new Playhouse to be built, wrote a letter to Alan Richardson in which he explained his misgivings about the idea of another fund-raising appeal:

> I can see little chance of completing a successful capital appeal in the immediate future. The problem is not just the current recession, indeed the Building Appeal took place at the time of the disruptive three-day working week. Then however, we had, enormous good-will and all the excitement of watching the new building take shape. And it is much easier to obtain money for a new building than to fund raise for its maintenance.
>
> Regarding 'The Friends of the Playhouse' scheme. The Theatregoers Club has recently circulated a letter to all its members expressing dismay at the new proposals. The Theatregoers were apparently informed that 'The Friends' scheme would certainly go ahead, but that the theatre could not carry two supporters' organisations. This inevitably means the phasing out of the Theatregoers Club and an end to all the devoted support it has given over the past forty-five years. As a compromise, following discussions, the Playhouse has now offered that existing members of the Theatregoers Club should be allowed to join the Friends organisation at reduced rates and this offer is to be considered at the annual general meeting, next month, of the Theatregoers Club. There can be no doubt, however,

that many Theatregoers will be unable or unwilling to pay even the reduced subscription on offer. This insensitive proposal has already caused deep resentment. I can see no possible objection to the two organisations working side by side.

After much acrimony, the two organisations merged into one to be known as the 'Friends and Patrons Scheme.'

.An emergency plea was put to Salisbury District Council for £50,000. However, the request was denied. It was thrown out after some members said it would be unfair to give the theatre more cash after a concessionary fares scheme for the elderly and the handicapped had already been abandoned because the council was operating a 'no-growth' budget strategy.

Cllr. David Parker commented: 'The Playhouse got itself into this mess, they should pass the cost on to their customers. It is not about to close. If it were, there would be 50,000 patrons ready to give £1 each to save it.'

One of the first areas to be hit by the cuts was the Playhouse's youth organisations. In June 91 the *Journal* wrote:

Local youngsters are set to become the chief victim of sweeping cuts planned by Salisbury's cash-starved Playhouse theatre. Six of the Playhouse's eight strong Theatre In Education (TIE) company, which also runs the youth theatre group Stage 65 have been made redundant.

The cuts to TIE and Stage 65 were very badly received and letters started to flood in to the *Journal*.

Hugo Stewart wrote: 'Why do the children of Salisbury and district, who are tomorrow's audiences, have to bear such a large part of the cuts? The theatre is being short sighted and is shooting itself in the foot.'

'We appreciate that it is a very bad financial situation but it does seem very short-sighted to cut an area of the theatre that has been so successful.' wrote Tim Meats. 'It was almost presented as a fait accompli, there was no lobbying of local authorities by the theatre to increase any funding for young people's theatre.'.

Gavin Stride wrote:

The youth theatre gives young people not only the chance to engage with the broad skills of stagecraft, but also a sense of ownership of the building. That the theatre is a part of all our lives. Where will the next generation prepared to commit themselves to promoting theatre come from?

More than one child drifting directionless, dissipating creative energy, has discovered motivation teamwork, social and work skills and the purpose of meaningful education as well as making friendships through belonging to Stage 65.

Tim Treslove, who went on to become a very popular and versatile actor both at the Playhouse and at the Mercury, Colchester once said: 'I joined up in 1976 as a 13 year old. I was there for five years and it turned my life around. I had been getting into lots of trouble and hanging around with the wrong crowd.'

Derek Jones had an interesting suggestion on how the Playhouse could save money:

That sort of talent, enthusiasm and dedication must not be abandoned by short-sighted management policies. If they are seeking to save money, perhaps they should heed the advice of the recent executive of Saatchi and Saatchi: 'You don't get anywhere by sacking ten secretaries. You've got to go for the big salaries. A glance at the lengthy list of administrators, financial and management directors of the Playhouse, not to mention their assistants, would seem to offer plenty of scope for savings.

Mrs. Gladys Brown offered another suggestion:

During this current financial difficulty, seek the support of families and friends of the young people to promote fund-raising efforts. This has to be achieved by all amateur groups and societies. If the public is to be asked to support and save our theatre, it should primarily be to enable actors who earn their living by theatre. They are also facing redundancies and this is surely more serious than having Stage 65 suspended for a while.

The members of Stage 65 and their families had already decided that this was the way forward and 'The Stage 65 Association' was formed, initially to set a target of raising £6,000 to subsidise the assistant youth organiser, Kevin Shaw's salary for the next 12 months.

The traditional practice of taking productions out to schools was also abandoned in favour of a reduced, more economical in-house programme providing workshops at the Playhouse based around the current production in the main auditorium. There was a huge outcry in the local community partly because the changes put the onus on bringing children to the theatre on to schools, something the 1988 Education Reform Act had made increasingly difficult.

A meeting was organised by the Stage 65 Association so Deborah Paige could explain why these cuts were necessary.

Paul Gahan wrote:

As it was pointed out to Ms. Paige at the Stage 65 meeting, the parents and teachers of Salisbury are a powerful lobby and had they been given some months warning of the cuts something might have been salvaged.

Ms. Paige presented with this possibility confessed that the decision to withhold the information until such a late stage was a mistake. What she failed to explain was how and why she had reached such a decision. Rumours had abounded for months and some must have reached her ears; deliberately to wait until the cuts could be presented as a fait accompli with no recourse for the parents, children or teachers seems inexplicable, unless the powers that be actually wanted TIE and Stage 65 cut back so drastically that it could barely survive in its old form.

The Playhouse underestimating the popularity of the youth programmes, was an example of poor public relations between the theatre and the public. The result of all this was a mass boycott of the theatre by those previously involved with the Playhouse programme including friends and relations who represented a substantial part of the regular audience in the main house, so whilst the initial cuts cleared £80,000 of the Playhouse deficit, falling revenue from the box office meant that it began to mount up again.

It is not surprising that Kevin Shaw and then Lynn Wyfe left soon after and it fell to Sarah Bradnock to pick up the pieces. Lynn left after a performance of the musical '*Whale*' in the Salberg to take up the position of TIE director at the Royal Theatre in Nottingham. She had spent eight very successful years at the Playhouse and had been involved in 26 productions.

In 1992 a 'rolling membership' to Stage 65 was introduced in which young people were to belong on a 'one year in, one year out basis.'

However, Peter Docherty wrote: 'It has been a clumsy, cosmetic exercise which has fooled no-one and irritated everyone, particularly the children. There should have been a discussion by all concerned but sadly this is not the current Playhouse style.'

~~~

Deborah Paige said that one of the reasons for her appointment was that the board was aware that 'they wanted to be more adventurous', but she also emphasized that her own plan had been 'to continue more or less the same sort of programming policy but to work on improving standards of direction, design and casting.'

In August 1991 she wrote: 'I'm not doing a radically different programme but choosing a different style. People come not knowing what to expect, which is healthy I feel. You have to keep being brave. There's no time to sit still and be 'bunkerist'. You have to excite people about the things you care about.'

In a letter in 1993, she wrote:

When I started at Salisbury Playhouse in 1990 it was very much a traditional regional rep, with (unusually) all its parts still up and running: a TIE team, a Studio, a main house which played to a consistently solid, if elderly audience. But it quickly became apparent that none of this would be sustained in its existing form.

So I had to ask some questions. 'What's the job of theatre like this? How does it relate to the wide and wonderful range of theatre that's grown up in this country over the past 20 years? Not I think, by continuing to exist as a kind of play factory, endlessly turning round the same type of play; doing the same thing better isn't enough. Our own work should be informed and inspired by other influences, people who work from different starting points. Audiences need to know that there are lots of different types of theatre, not just the kind that three weekly rep can produce.

In an article in 1993, she wrote: 'If you want to find a future for a building like this, you can't go on like a corner picture-house. We've built a national profile and changed the quality of direction and design so we can attract better people here.'

Deborah Paige clearly knew what she wanted to do, but would the Salisbury theatregoers allow her to carry out her plans? Reggie Salberg, Roger Clissold and David Horlock gave the Salisbury public what they wanted and had earned the Playhouse a reputation, as one critic at the time said: for 'Strip, strip, Hurray' and proscenium curtains and box sets and a staple diet of 'Ben Travers, Agatha Christie, Kenneth Horne, Alan Ayckbourn *et al.*' To win over the Salisbury theatregoers was going to be a very hard journey.

In her tenure as Artistic Director of Salisbury Playhouse Deborah Paige directed 15 plays (11 in the main house and 4 in the Salberg.) Having produced Shakespeare's 'The Winter's Tale' in the Salberg in 1991 she turned to the main stage to produce one of her earlier successes 'A Midsummer Night's Dream. in 1992. This was the first Shakespeare at the Playhouse for seven years and it was enhanced by a grant from the Arts Council under the 'Be Bold' scheme designed to encourage innovative large scale work in regional theatre..

The critics loved it. *Wiltshire Gazette* wrote: 'If you are studying Shakespeare go to see this. If you think your children might study him in the future take them. If you want a good evening's entertainment, go to the Playhouse.' Wiltshire Sound reported: Deborah Paige's production of 'A Midsummer Night's Dream' is one of the best performances of this play that I have ever seen.'

She followed this up in 1993 with a production of 'The Tempest' which again won considerable approval, even though Christopher Ravenscroft tore a ligament in his leg and had to play the part of Prospero on crutches!

Her final Shakespeare production was 'Twelfth Night'. As well as in Salisbury, it was performed at the Royal Lyceum in Edinburgh and it toured China, funded by the British Council.

The British Ambassador in Peking, Sir. Leonard Appleyard, wrote:

Twelfth Night performing in China programme cover, October 1994

It was a great pleasure to see the Salisbury Playhouse and Royal Lyceum, Edinburgh's new production of 'Twelfth Night' performed in China. It was a superb performance which will have brought home to the Chinese people the immediacy and wit of Shakespeare. The acting was excellent throughout and the audience appreciated the enjoyable and inventive staging not only at the Shanghai International Shakespeare Festival but also in Peking and Canton.'

It was equally enjoyed locally. Peter Blacklock wrote in the *Journal*: 'Deborah Paige can only enhance her artistic reputation with her *'Twelfth Night'*. In a word it is brilliant. Brilliant in the direction; brilliant in the design; brilliant in the acting; brilliant in the choreography; brilliant…well I could go on!'

For all three productions Deborah Paige used the designer Isabella Bywater and the lighting designer, Peter Hunter, both of whom received much well deserved praise.

In 1993 her production of Somerset Maugham's *'For Services Rendered'* achieved critical acclaim. Peter Blacklock wrote: 'Director, Deborah Paige's decision to follow the turn of the year's fun season by dusting off this Maugham neglect, is vindicated triumphantly. In a sentence: It is a knockout.' It transferred to the Old Vic with Sylvia Syms taking the lead role. This was the 6th transfer of Playhouse plays to the West End in 14 years. Unfortunately though, the run was only very short.

Her director's skills were often praised: Two of her Salberg productions *'States of Shock'* and *'Wild Things'* received much praise: Barbara Christie-Miller wrote: *'States of Shock'* was quite, quite brilliant – your direction was superb.' and the playwright Anne Reynolds wrote of *'Wild Things'* : 'Deborah Paige has been an inspiration, wonderful, brilliant. Everybody in the theatre is talking about her and says I'm lucky to work with her and I agree.'

In January 1993 she was also responsible for introducing a young Ewan McGregor to Salisbury audiences in Joe Orton's *'What the Butler Saw'*. This was his first play, having just left the Guildhall School of Music and Drama. It was an excellent cast that included Jeremy Child and Isla Blair and it was brilliantly directed by Penny Ciniewicz.

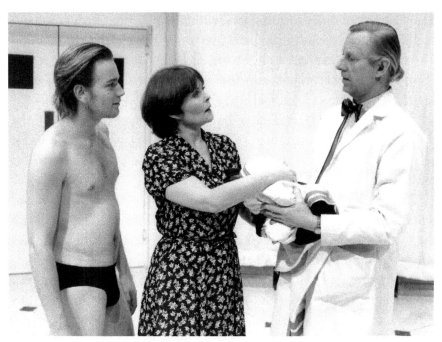

What the Butler Saw, January 1993: Ewan McGregor (Nicholas Beckett); Isla Blair
(Mrs. Prentice); Jeremy Child (Dr. Prentice) (Photographer Peter Brown)

There were gasps from the usually staid Salisbury audience when Ewan ran on stage naked! But the nudity did not stop the play from attracting packed houses. Peter Blacklock wrote: 'It can't be easy making your stage debut without clothes on, but Ewan McGregor does it like a future star. And his clothed acting confirms his quality. Nor can it be easy to make your stage debut in a bra and panties but Jacqueline Defferay does it to the manner born. She too confirms her quality when fully clothed. Let's keep an eye on Ewan and Jacqueline. We could have seen the birth of two fine actors.' – Perhaps a role in a 'Star Wars' film?!

Ewan loved prancing around the stage stark naked. He said that it was great and you couldn't even be arrested! But that he wouldn't do it as Ewan McGregor!' Mick Martin in the *Guardian* wrote: 'There has been a discernable move by the management of Salisbury Playhouse to broaden the horizons of the theatre's large and loyal audience, and offer them more in the way of challenge, than they have been used to. And it is good to see that they are now far enough down the road, not only to risk Orton but also to fill the auditorium with a play like '*What the Butler Saw.*'

However, older theatregoers will remember that Reggie Salberg had no qualms about putting the play on at the old theatre in 1971! The nudity and explicit scenes were accepted in this play but it was in 1993 that the grumbles and the complaints about choice of plays really hit the fan.

Deborah Paige was at a huge disadvantage because of the popularity and circumstances of the death of her predecessor and it seemed that there was little hope that she could ever live up to his reputation.

In 1991 a large scale production of George Orwell's '*Down and Out In Paris and London*' in collaboration with P:aines Plough was not the success that had been envisaged and there were already grumbles about the choice of plays .'What was essentially a social documentary has been tampered with and turned into rather a disappointing plot for the stage. I preferred the book.' wrote Helen Scott in the *Avon Advertiser*.

Then in 1993 a poor selection of plays meant that the noise of dissatisfaction was beginning to reach a considerable crescendo .

The play chosen for April that year, John Godber's '*The Office Party*' however, proved to be a huge popular success. It broke box office records and brought in the younger audiences that Deborah Paige was asked to bring in. But as she commented in hindsight, 'It was possibly a little too contemporary and there was not enough for the conservative, older audience.' What the 'conservative, older audience' found to complain about was that it was full of four letter words and as Derek Jones put it: ' it was an embarrassment to those with female or younger

The Office Party, Directed by and starred Gareth Tudor Price as Gavin Chapman, April 1993 (Photograph from publicity still)

The Europeans, April 1993: Julian Forsyth as McNoy
(Photographer Leslie Black)

company.' It gave more cause to criticise the management.

Following this was Howard Barker's '*The Europeans*'. This playwright is never the easiest to cope with. He once said: 'My expectations of an audience are that they will come out of the theatre with their lives more complicated than when they went in.' One critic wrote: 'Mr. Barker is shunned by both the theatrical establishment and television. I think the people who make up Deborah Paige's audiences, and who have undergone a series of surprises lately, will agree with them.' And Dee Adcock in the *Journal* wrote: 'There are no niceties in Howard Barker's '*The Europeans*', People walked out of its first Playhouse performance – others melted away in the interval. You couldn't blame them.' However, she praised the play and it also had a sterling cast that included Nicholas Le Provost and Philip Franks but the Salisbury theatregoers, with a few exceptions, did not approve.

Later that year there were two more plays that gave more fuel to the disgruntled Salisbury theatregoers. In October '*Celestina*' was performed. This was a little known Spanish Renaissance play that was considered to be experimental because it was performed in modern dress against a contemporary set and used non-realist acting styles. The subject of the play was also highly sexual and called for some scenes of nudity. The use of Renaissance English was also unacceptable to many in the audience, variously described in letters to the *Journal* as 'complete gibberish' and 'gobbledy gook.'

Jim Souter wrote:

What on earth is happening to the Salisbury Playhouse? I went to the Saturday performance of the last production of '*Celestina*' to find an audience of about 20% and soon found out why! The play was advertised as being bawdy and it was certainly that. It was also extremely boring to the extent that one of our party fell so soundly asleep that he snored and provided the only light relief of the evening! In common with a considerable number of the audience, my wife and I did not bother to go back for more punishment after the interval!

Unfortunately this play was followed by 'Escape at Sea' which again left many theatregoers 'all at sea.' Mrs. Templeman wrote: 'I have just seen 'Escape at Sea' at the Playhouse. I came away wondering what it was all about. How many in the audience understood it I wonder? A lot of movement, a lot of scenery dragged around by the actors. Why do directors and producers think we all want this avant-garde stuff?'

The Sunday Times critic wrote: 'Escape at Sea falls victim to a long proven pitfall of the mixed media format, that it is impossible for an audience to concentrate on dance and a spoken or sung text, if they are going on simultaneously. In this work, that matters. I came out feeling in need, not so much of more programme notes, as a poultice.' Once again Dee Adcock approved, and her message was : 'Don't escape, see it again and again!'

Most Salisbury theatregoers though, were only too happy to look forward to the Christmas feast of Ayckbourn's 'Absurd Person Singular' and the fun of the pantomime, 'Aladdin!'

'Celestina' 'The Europeans' and 'Escape at Sea' were all touring productions and not 'in house' but by the time the mistake was realised by theatregoers, any attempts to explain this, simply added fuel to the fire as they still assumed that they were part of the Playhouse's artistic policy.

During the early days of the Playhouse when it was weekly or two weekly rep, it was easy for Reggie to slip in a controversial play in between two popular crowd pullers. And he always had Pauline Astin at the box office who would guide patrons to the next week's play if she felt that they wouldn't enjoy the present one. Not so easy to do if your season consisted of plays that ran for three weeks!

The departure from traditional styles of production to more experimental theatre gave credence to the suspicion that Deborah Paige was imposing an experimental educational programme that was not 'what regular theatregoers wanted to see, but what the producers think is good for them.' wrote Marie Stride. This theatregoer was quite vociferous in her criticism of the present artistic policy and like many critics she would harp back to 'the good old days' of her predecessors.

There was also the feeling of 'ownership' of the theatre amongst many theatregoers and that the present management was 'treading on their memories.' That there was a feeling of hurt and indignation that someone was tampering with 'their theatre' against their wishes.

'I say 'our Playhouse' because it was built with subscriptions from many local theatre lovers and businesses, coupled with efforts from a number of dedicated people. The average age of theatregoers is well over 40 and they remember the excellent performances of the likes of Nancy Herrod, Sonia Woolley, Lionel Guyett and many others.' wrote Jim Souter.

'Our theatre' rooted for generations in the community boasts a long line of competent, creative managers who shrewdly interwove classical drama, experimental theatre and new plays into community choice. Each in their own unique style built a working partnership with the public, which enabled them to tap into a rich vein of goodwill, energy and effort. This proved rewarding for all.' wrote Marie Stride.

Betty Anderson wrote: 'When we had a resident company, if the play was a doubtful draw, a lot of people would go to see what Roger Hume, Robert Scott, Christine Edmunds, or whoever their favourite was, might be doing that week/month/production. In fact a couple of people said to me recently, 'nice to see Stephanie Cole is coming back.' meaning not Stephanie Cole the famous TV actor, but our 'Steph. Cole.'

Sidney Vines was very direct: 'The Playhouse exists for the people of Salisbury and the surrounding area.'

It seemed that Deborah Paige's attempts to vary the type of plays and to introduce new and innovative productions was not working, as the theatregoers wanted to stick to the tried and trusted programmes of the past.

Reggie Salberg was always willing to experiment and to try something new. In 1967 he wrote: 'New ideas are the life blood of our theatre. I have watched too many managers let their companies decline because they have become bored or have stuck too firmly to outworn policies.' In the 80s he also wrote: 'It does seem as if the secret of success lies in the presentation of only familiar favourites. However, I think that a theatre which adheres to such a formula is doomed and that it is necessary to be adventurous from time to time otherwise the audience finds itself getting bored.'

These ideas were obviously acceptable from Reggie Salberg but not apparently from Deborah Paige! In 1994, Deborah Paige returned to a more traditional programme that included 'Shirley Valentine', 'Private Lives', 'The Importance of Being Earnest', 'Sleuth', 'Wait Until Dark' and 'Great Expectations' – a programme that any regional theatre would have been happy to put on.

'I went to see 'Sleuth' a day or two before it finished its run and was absolutely, totally and completely knocked out by it. The work itself was quite brilliant, the standard of acting peerless. It was the best of many enjoyable productions I have seen at the Playhouse. The place was packed and the quality far in excess of anything I have ever witnessed in the West End.' wrote an anonymous theatregoer.

After seeing 'Wait Until Dark', Peter Blacklock wrote in the Journal:

> This is the one that the malcontents have been waiting for. The play is from the sixties with echoes of weekly rep; there's not a naughty word in it; there's no social comment, no call for brain power and even a curtain rising and falling. The result is the greatest audience participation I've seen at the Playhouse, some of the warmest applause and the most animation among the departing audience, the Panto excepted.

During this season however, there were a few blips. The production of 'Tyger Two' was cancelled because Paines Plough had difficulty in finding funding and 'Biloxi Blues' did very badly at the box office because 'it was American and was on in the Summer' explained the management. The Salisbury theatregoers were again demonstrating what they liked and what they wanted the Playhouse to produce.

Terry Sullivan put forward a very contentious point in a letter to the Journal:

Your critics of Salisbury Playhouse are pointing in the wrong direction. Its most intractable problem isn't the plays but the audience. I remember 'the good old days' of weekly rep but am grateful that television killed it. Actors had no time to understand the plays, so that you often saw the same characters in different weeks with the same words. And what dreadful plays most of them were!

However, it would perhaps have been wiser for him to have listened to some of these actors from the old theatre: Roger Leach said: 'Audiences will have one disappointment, perhaps two, but not three – if it takes three months for an audience to leave, it will take eighteen months to get them back.'

Sonia Woolley said: 'She didn't just put on some plays which people didn't like – some of the productions were bizarre.'

And Stephanie Cole wrote: 'Of course you want to make your mark but you jolly well make sure that you don't lose the audience that you've already got.'

Meanwhile the Salberg managed to survive despite the problems surrounding the theatre. Stage 65 had their fair share of the programmes with such delights as 'The Demon Headmaster', 'Wizard of Oz', and 'Rumpelstiltskin'. There were the usual very popular Christmas cabarets slots such as 'Quirkish Delight' and several notable small scale productions such 'The Choice' which starred Toyah Willcox and Mick Martin's 'The Handicap Race.'

There was also a rather strange play called 'The Danube' with an even stranger poster. It was of two nude people with fish heads! Melanie Hibberd, Head of Marketing said: 'I'm not sure what it means. It's a visiting company so we have no control over their print.

A spokesman for Shared Theatre Company said: 'The design represents two very vulnerable people in a world of ecological decay.' She added that the poster wasn't meant to be taken literally, there is no nudity in the play and no fish!

Theatregoers have the right to criticise but they were also doing damage to the profile and reputation of the Playhouse. As Olivia Turnbull wrote: 'Many of the aggrieved public considered their protests were made in the interests of saving the theatre. While ignorant of many of the administrative challenges faced by senior management, the vocal members of the community were perhaps equally unaware of the damage they were doing through their vociferous criticism.

Of the voluble public outcry, Paige commented 'I regret that people feel able to criticise in the way they have done, which I think has ultimately been very destructive to the Playhouse.' This sentiment was echoed by the arts editor of the *Salisbury Journal* where most such complaints were published.

'If the Playhouse closes, I will blame those 'friends' whose strident criticism, the point of which I could never grasp, created a climate to turn off potential audiences.'

In 1993 Deborah Paige signed another three year contract and spoke of the Playhouse winning 'a national reputation for herself and for the theatre.' In a *Journal* article she wrote:

> We've allowed ourselves to listen too much to the people who've said we are going to the dogs – I believe a relatively contained bunch of people. We're known in the theatre as a company that produces extraordinarily high quality work on low production budgets. Actors and designers say we do the kind of work that attracts them to come. The range of opinion shows we must be doing something very vital, vibrant and extraordinary Against all odds, I feel enormously optimistic and enthusiastic about what we are doing and we really are doing it for Salisbury.

This was a strong and brave front to put on, to show the people of Salisbury that the Playhouse was in good hands. She must however, have been very aware of the loud feeling of discontent bubbling throughout the Salisbury community.

There was also criticism that for some considerable time Deborah Paige stayed living in London and was therefore not heavily involved in local activities. As Marie Stride put it: 'Reggie Salberg, Roger Clissold and David Horlock promised and delivered commitment to the community ... dwelling in the city they identified with local issues. Recognised, greeted in the street, they responded and respected people as individuals.' Deborah Paige became aware that she needed a higher local profile so she eventually moved to Love

Lane in Salisbury and started to wear a name badge in the theatre because many people did not know who she was. She conceded that she did not put herself about 'in certain parts of society here. I am more of a back-room person.'

Was she using the Playhouse as a stepping stone to further her career? Artistic directors often move on to gain more experience, that is a natural progression in any job, but many theatregoers were suspicious that her ambitions overweighed the needs of the Playhouse. Olivia Turnbull wrote: 'Through the perceived alterations to artistic policy and the new administrative positions that were created on her arrival including the introduction of a marketing director and an administrative and development director, a suspicion grew that she largely saw the Playhouse in terms of personal ambition.' However, these changes had the full backing of the Board, particularly because of the burgeoning deficit left over from the previous regime and the theatre's failure to develop a new, younger audience. More appointments though, meant more salaries and less money to spend on productions.

The Board continued to support their artistic director, which is natural, after all they appointed her in the first place! However, ill feelings and suspicions of the Board's actions were also seeping into the theatregoers' minds. There was also division amongst some Board members and there could be resignations on the horizon.

Financial and Artistic problems and poor public relations were affecting both Deborah Paige and the Board and there was no way these problems were going to go away.. There was trouble brewing at Salisbury Playhouse and there was the distinct possibility that once again, it was faced with the possibility of closure.

19
'EVERYTHING THAT COULD GO WRONG, WENT WRONG.'

Hilary Keenlyside

In the *Salisbury Journal* of 8th December 1994, there appeared a notice from the Salisbury Playhouse that stated: 'Notice of Public Meeting. Sunday 11 December in the Main Theatre…at which the Board of Directors and consultants Bonnar Keenlyside will present a review of the Playhouse's activities and an outline plan concerning its future.'

The last few years of discontent concerning the running of the Playhouse had led to this. The London consultants, Bonnar Keenlyside had been called in by the Board to look into the Playhouse affairs and point a way out of the present impasse.

At the beginning of the year, due to a more populist programme of plays, box office takings had begun to improve and sales of subscription tickets had risen. It was announced by the theatre that 'The Playhouse was out of the slump.' Sales for '*Private Lives*' had reached 76%. Apart from pre-Christmas Ayckbourn, this figure had not been reached for two years and '*Wait Until Dark*' was often playing to full houses.' Stage 65 was also nearly always drawing in capacity audiences.

But many Salisbury theatregoers were still disillusioned with the choice of plays. In November, Timothy Stroud wrote: 'Playhouse-goers want productions which will fill their spirits, provide enjoyment and be fun. They do not want to be forced to understand the angst and despair of kitchen sink artists who belong well – in the kitchen sink or down the plug hole.'

And in the same month, John Pinder wrote:

The Wizard of Oz Stage 65, April 1993: Lion   Joe Bosano; Tin Man   Richard Morley; Dorothy Lucy Elcock/Louise Rolt; Scarecrow David Partridge (Photographer Peter Brown)

I'm willing to agree that there is a small minority of pseudo intellectuals in this country who go to abstract plays by little known authors, not because they understand them any more than you or I, because who knows, they may be clever and one must not be thought stupid. One sees these people in art galleries gazing hopefully at blank canvasses and piles of bricks. These same people seem to feel that if Shakespeare is performed in a pin-stripe suit or a pair of old jeans it will, if one listens very carefully, enhance the beauty of the words.

Surely though, this is not just true of those times, many theatregoers still suffer from 'The Emperor's New Clothes Syndrome!' – believing in something because they don't want to look ignorant!

Of '*Rookery Nook*' which was performed at the Playhouse in November, Betty Anderson wrote: 'The 'Kulture Vultures' will no doubt look down their noses at the play and it will certainly not tour China, but here and now it drew in a willing and enthusiastic audience.' (It played to 80% capacity compared to '*Biloxi Blues*' which only played to 25% capacity.)

However, in March of that year, Robert Vincent wrote:

What do the critics want? There has to be a mix for it to be called theatre in the full sense of the word. Are Shakespeare and Sheridan too out of date? Are Beckett and Berkoff too modern? I suggest therefore, that its critics should not walk away if they disagree because that sounds like righteous pique. Let us know their alternative programme for the next season.

Support continued to come from the *Journal*'s art critic, Peter Blacklock: 'The Playhouse, compared with the amateurish productions at many professional theatres outside London with their 'end of the-pier plays pandering to the crumblies' clock-turning, is a beacon of culture.'

Early in that year, there was even talk of a million pound planned revamp of the theatre. The theatre's Administrative and Development Director, Allanah Lucas announced: 'The curtain will drop down on the auditorium between 3 and 7 months. The money will come from sponsorship, funding bodies, trusts and foundations.' This would be the first major refurbishment since the theatre opened in 1976. There was talk of replacing large sections of the leaking roof, re-upholstering the theatre seats, work backstage, extending the restaurant and revamping the foyer. One reporter suggested that the revamp might include 'the notoriously awkward toilets!'

However, to consider such a plan which involved closing the theatre at a time of uncertainty and criticism was very surprising and it simply added to the complaints.

Derek Jones wrote: 'How much of the reported million pound revamp is really essential? Does it make any sense in the present economic climate to close the theatre for a whole season? Not only will this result in a huge loss of revenue but some theatregoing public could well lose the habit.'

While Alan Richardson wrote: "How many of the 500 seats actually need renewal? In most theatres and cinemas when re-seating is required they block off sections and do it in stages.' He also asked: 'Why cannot the Salberg continue? This would at least keep the theatre alive in patron's minds.'

This proposed closure was soon scuppered however, by Wiltshire County Council. They agreed to give the theatre an £84,000 injection but imposed strict conditions which included dropping this closure plan and demanding that the Playhouse needed 'to submit a balanced budget and coherent plan with monthly reports of income and expenditure.' When the conditions for the loan had been met the council would then hand over the remaining £56,000 of that year's grant.

There was also discontent appearing amongst members of the Board and in the summer of 1994 Veronica Stewart, a member of the Playhouse Board for seven years proposed a vote of no confidence in Deborah Paige as artistic director. Her motion was marginally defeated so she resigned along with Richard Leutchford who was Head of Drama at Godolphin School. She commented: 'I do not think that this theatre is in a real financial mess, but looking at the empty seats I think it is verging on one. The problem is that people have lost confidence now and are not prepared to take the risk. She added: 'The theatre was built by the community and has been supported by the community and the community wants to see it survive into the next century.'

The Board also began to feel the public's dissatisfaction with how the Playhouse was being managed.

Olivia Turnbull wrote: 'Perhaps the public would have been more inclined to listen had the Playhouse presented a united front. Unfortunately, the Board themselves never adequately communicated that the theatre's problems should by no means be attributed to Paige. Worse, they allowed internal tensions to be played out in the public eye and encouraged by the local media.'

The public also wanted information about the state of the Playhouse but it was not forthcoming. Derek Jones wrote: 'The act of actually listening to the people who care about live theatre in Salisbury might not only be good for their souls but maybe also lead to adjustments. It should also remove the rumours, distortions and inaccuracies.' Theatregoers felt that the only platform offered for debating theatre issues was the *Journal* which only at times added to the adverse publicity.

Alan Corkill commented that the Board were letting Deborah Paige do what she wanted instead of 'clipping her wings'. They didn't have the courage to say no to her and so many of her plays were over-ambitious and not the plays that the Salisbury theatregoers wanted to see. Alan knew what the coach parties in particular wanted to see and they were beginning to dwindle.

In her book, Olivia Turnbull wrote:

> At the time of Paige's arrival, the existing Board operated under the auspices of a system that imposed no time limit on the length of service. The inevitable result was a 'self perpetuating oligarchy' dominated by a significant number of members who had served over ten years, including former artistic director Salberg. This element shared a nostalgic idea of the past and the sympathy of the Playhouse's loyal audience and consequently carried strong ideas about what the theatre's priorities should be and how it should be run.. Many of these ran contrary to those presented by the new chief executive, Deborah Paige.

In March 1994, in defence of the Board and the management, the Chairman, Anthony Fanshawe wrote in the *Journal*:

> There have been problems, the recession, arts funding under pressure, health and safety requirements and additional tax burdens. As public funding becomes more scarce, the national distributors of that funding (Southern Arts) will focus on fewer but better quality organisations. The Board intends the Playhouse to be one of those centres of excellence.

He wrote about 'The wonderful stimulating work being produced at the Playhouse and that it was receiving national recognition.'

Criticism of the Playhouse management though, was also rife, mainly because of the increasingly large number of administrators. Olivia Turnbull wrote:

> Combined with the hostility in the community and rumours of a mounting deficit, increasingly costly administrators ensure that any efforts by the Playhouse to explain the reasons behind the new system failed to make an impact.

So while the Board's chairman told the local paper that 'comparisons (regarding the size and budget of the administration) were being made with twenty years ago', his comments were drowned out by the much louder complaints about 'the seemingly endless list of administrators'.

Working under these conditions, the staff often found it difficult and unpleasant. In a letter, Allanah Lucas wrote:

It was almost as if anything one did that was different, was seen as a desecration of his (David Horlock's) work. So whoever followed was going to encounter much more resistance than would normally be the case when one artistic director succeeds another. At times the resistance felt like a witch hunt of Deborah Paige and this was unfair and unpleasant.

I came in to the middle of all that and it was quite frankly a nightmare at first. I have to say though, that I think the staff at the Playhouse were very good to me, seeing I was a newcomer and so my memory of the latter part of my working there and leading the company through a gruelling time, with continuous financial problems, became rewarding because the staff did rally around and keep things going.

She eventually became Chief Executive Officer of the Playhouse.

This letter was followed by one from her husband, Graham Waine who wrote:

She and I had many heated discussions about the Playhouse management not responding to the vast amount of malicious misinformation that was being circulated about (some repeated without checking by the media) and I retain an admiration for how Allanah, her colleagues and their team continued to be objective and at least outwardly unruffled in what sometimes became a very unfriendly environment.

He continued: 'What Allanah and her colleagues inherited was both good and bad, but these influences made it hard to capitalise on the good and near impossible to remove the bad.'

When asked about the constant criticism, Brum Gardner, who was deputy stage manager, said: 'Sometimes you get angry. 'How dare you say that, you don't know what it is like to run a theatre. Give us a break.' Sometimes you try to ignore it. sometimes you simply have had enough.'

One of the big problems was the relationship between Alan Corkill and the rest of the senior management. Alan had been working at the Playhouse for 28 years and knew every nut and bolt of the theatre's workings. Some of the new appointments though were jealous of Alan because of his incredible knowledge of the Playhouse and the affection the theatregoers had for him but his role in the theatre was gradually eroded until he ended up by simply being box office manager. Patrons and staff would still go to Alan if there was a problem or if they wanted advice. He felt that there was not a great deal of loyalty to the present staff but as always he kept his head down and simply got on with his job of doing what was best for the theatre and for the theatregoers. He bided his time because he knew that there was bound to be change on the horizon.

Poor communication between the management and the theatregoers was again a problem. In March 1994 Mick Martin wrote:

> The management should make a far greater effort to get to know the community it serves and should take the needs of that community, rather than of some hypothetical metropolitan community into account. This does not mean doing what the audience wants. Pandering to an audience is as sterile as ignoring it, and it certainly does not mean returning to the past. What it does mean is regaining the confidence of the community, and earning the trust that will enable the management to take the audience with it in the development of a theatre that attracts national recognition for the excellence of its service to the region.

A point echoed by Marie Stride: 'The Playhouse is not an esoteric satellite spin-off from home base in London, its crew on a secret mission to civilise and educate uncultured natives.'

There were also two more factors around this time that did not help the situation. Deborah Paige decided in 1994, to take a three month sabbatical. During this time she spent six weeks directing 'A Midsummer Night's Dream' in Regent's Park as well as visiting Romania and America. Artistic directors often do this to further their experience; Peter Potter did it back in the 50s when he was artistic director of the Playhouse but on this occasion the timing didn't go down very well with many people.

Alan Richardson commented: 'I find it odd (almost bizarre) that the theatre can afford to let her be absent on three months sabbatical leave on full pay I imagine, at this critical time in our theatre's life.'

In a letter to the *Journal*, Christina Maude wrote: 'The theatre is going through a bad patch yet this is the time that its artistic director has chosen to absent herself on sabbatical leave. We need a director who is seen to be at the heart of things.'

The other factor that added to the melting pot was the tragic death of the actor Tim Sabel. It was reported in November of that year that after his romantic liaison with Deborah Paige he carried out his suicide threats.

'Sadness at the parting of the ways was certainly an element but was not the only matter operating on his psyche,' Deputy Wilts Coroner Bill Bache reported. He said that the 36 year old actor, who had a tendency to become very depressed especially when he was not working, was suffering an illness.

He was found in his car on a track at Petersfinger Farm on September 2nd and had died from carbon monoxide poisoning. He had written letters contemplating suicide and had talked of the method he intended. He had bought items needed and had made very determined efforts to prepare and seal his car.

He was found after Deborah Paige became alarmed and called the police when he delivered a letter to her home in Love Lane. She said that the envelope contained a watch which she had given him and a ring, which although was not from her she felt it 'was a sign that he was going to kill himself.'

A successful and talented actor, he had appeared in several of Deborah Paige's productions including 'For Services Rendered' for which he was awarded a Best Supporting Actor Award as well as 'Hound of the Baskervilles' and 'Jack and the Beanstalk.'

This was a very tragic event but one can imagine that it didn't go down terribly well with certain sections of the theatregoing public.

Matters eventually came to a head when Wiltshire County Council insisted that all the senior management should resign before it released the £59,000 balance of an £84,000 loan. They also wanted consultation and power of veto over artistic policy and all appointments of senior management in the future. However, calls for Deborah Paige's dismissal were contractually illegal; the Board members were legally bound to make their own decisions on such matters.

So many criticisms, so many questions, so many problems. It was considered time to bring in the consultants Bonnar Keenlyside to see if their recommendations could save the Playhouse from this crisis.

The Board and the senior management came in for considerable criticism. So a public meeting was held on 11th December when Hilary Keenlyside presented her review to a crowd of over 300 theatregoers. This meeting was announced at very short notice but that wasn't going to stop those theatregoers with strong points of view, from going to listen and to take part.

Ms. Keenlyside said that the theatre's funding bodies agreed that the Board was weak and there had been poor financial management. Public relations were deemed to have been a disaster. The theatre's artistic policy was unfocussed and was not communicated well, particularly to the audience, and there was no external or internal confidence in the Board.

Attendance at the Playhouse had dropped over the period going back to 1986 from just over 150,000 attendances to the present level of about 120,000 and box office income had fallen between 1989 and 1994. She identified the moment when things went wrong for the Playhouse as the Summer when 'The Office Party' and 'The Europeans' were put on.

'Everything that could go wrong, went wrong.' she said. She also stressed though: 'I am determined to be fair. The issue is very complex and everybody has some right things to say, though no one is as right as they think.'

At the public meeting, a member of the Board and a local

playwright, Brian Phelan though, issued a word of warning about choice of plays: He warned: 'Most major playwrights – from Shakespeare to Pinter – had outraged people in their time. Putting on a 'safe season' had become the Holy Grail but it was a self- deluding policy. Where would the new writers come from if there were no theatres to stage their work? New plays were always risky -They can only be judged by those who put them on, and that judgement can only be subjective.'

However, Hilary Keenlyside did praise the management, when they reported that production costs had gone down and she said: 'What you get for your money on this stage is value for money and something the staff here could be proud of.' She then identified the Playhouse's strengths and its artistic ambition, production values and the support from funders.

She set out five options for the Playhouse's financial future, including the possibility of total closure. Her recommendation though, was 'to stay the same but make fundamental improvements to activities and operations.' In their report Bonnar Keenlyside stated : 'If the Salisbury Playhouse is committed to continuing with current policy and operations, it must make significant improvements on all fronts: artistic, financial and management in order to survive': The points were:-

1. It must refocus its artistic policy and reinterpret that policy for its audience.

2. It must secure its financial position primarily through improved trading at the box office and in other commercial areas.

3. It must restructure its management in terms of board governance and executive responsibilities.

It also stated: 'There will have to be a considerable change in management and board, in terms of both structure and systems.

These recommendations would inevitably lead to the resignations of the current artistic director and the entire board. It was obvious that many 'new brooms' were needed. When the consultants condemned the Board for failing to retain either 'external or internal confidence' and called for their complete replacement, the public overwhelmingly concurred. 'We are told that the Board is to be replaced, many think it has been weak, secretive and largely to blame for the current situation.' the Friends Committee informed the Chairman.

Feelings ran high over the fact that it took over two years of media pressure to extract publicly the financial position of the theatre which prevented the local community and particularly the Friends of the Playhouse from taking the opportunity to actively help through fund-raising activities.

Olivia Turnbull wrote: 'The Board's internal divisions and failure to anticipate the extent of the animosity that changes to the theatre would generate meant that Paige was never properly briefed, but was still squarely blamed for a series of situations in which they were equally culpable.'

In a letter to Olivia Turnbull, Deborah Paige wrote: 'I wasn't prepared to work for a Board which didn't have confidence in me but weren't forthcoming about what I had done.'

This, plus pressure from the funders, made Deborah Paige realise that it was time for her to resign. She said: 'The decision to leave is mine. The Board has not been trying to get rid of me. I had made it quite clear to the Board that I did not want to stand between them and any funding agreement with Wiltshire County Council.' She continued: 'I think there's no way, but out.'

Initially she resigned as chief executive but then decided to resign as artistic director as well. This she announced at the public meeting in December. When she left she said that she would be leaving with many positive memories. 'The Playhouse has been my life for four years so I shall feel very sad but I think there have been really wonderful magical moments while I have been here. It's the work we should be talking about, not the people.'

Anthony Fanshawe concurred: 'I think we may look back on this period with regret but remember with admiration the many superb productions we have seen at the Playhouse during Deborah Paige's tenure as artistic director.'

The consultants report also stated: 'The Board wishes to proceed with a modified refurbishment of the theatre building.' and 'The Board recommends that the Playhouse continue its current season of operations until the end of the pantomime in January 1995. Following this there will be a period of closure to allow the Playhouse to relaunch itself refocused on art and its audience.'

Matters had certainly come to a very big head. Resignations and closures were now very much on the horizon..

The Playhouse issued a press release: 'The purpose of the closure is to enable the Playhouse to:

Make short term savings to ensure the long term viability of the Playhouse.

Actively seek additional sources of funding.

Improve the fabric and facilities of the building.

Review and re-present the artistic policy.

Re-launch a stronger and better Playhouse for the benefit of Salisbury and its surrounding district.

During this period of closure, the following will happen:

A new board will be appointed as quickly as possible by public process in which the three principal funders will participate.

The criteria for board membership are set as standard by the Arts Council. They underline interest, expertise and ability to serve the Playhouse rather than any special interest group and to avoid making biased judgements on the basis of information received from individuals.

In the short term, the board would be assisted by the theatre consultants, Bonnar Keenlyside, to manage the implementation of the Playhouse Business Plan and the development of its policy.

A fundraising appeal will be launched to assist in financing refurbishment and building works.

There will also be an open forum with the public to enable public input to the planning process to take place.

The Playhouse restaurant will stay open.

An education and youth theatre programme will continue.

Would the Salisbury theatregoers support another fundraising appeal though? Perhaps when there definitely was some money on the table to start the refurbishment they would.. Certainly the Friends of the Playhouse would make a huge effort to help but many theatregoers were still disillusioned, like Sidney Vines who wrote: 'They seem to assume that they only have to launch an appeal and the people of Salisbury will flock to hand over their cash. On the contrary, they may decline to throw good money after bad.'

The press release concluded with a note from the Chairman: 'We view the closure as a tremendous opportunity for reviewing the operations of the Playhouse and developing a blueprint for the future.'

Allanah Lucas sent a similar note to the Friends of the Playhouse, finishing with 'Your continued support through a closure period will be greatly appreciated. We do hope you'll feel able to continue your support of the Playhouse and participate in the grand re-opening of the theatre in its Fiftieth Anniversary Year.'

Notice was also given that other regional theatres were also in difficulties. The Redgrave at Farnham was also about to close in January and the Everyman at Cheltenham had to cut its planned programme and would share its productions with the Bristol Old Vic.

In a letter to the *Journal*, the staff of the Playhouse wanted the public to know that they supported the planned closure 'as the best means of re-opening a revitalised and better funded theatre in September 1995.' They wrote: 'For every criticism, we hear countless voices of praise, locally and nationally, regarding the high standard of work and service produced by Salisbury Playhouse. We are proud of the artistic achievements of recent years.'

In another letter to the *Journal* signed by the likes of Reggie Salberg, Robert Hawkings, Guy Jessop and Francis Pullen they stressed the need for Alan Corkill to stay on during the closure period and to be reinstated as Theatre Manager: 'Mr. Corkill's experience would be invaluable in planning and supervising the work. His organising ability will be vital when the box office re-opens and we need to regain the audiences which have been dwindling for the past four years and which will have been totally lost during the closure.'

At one point it seemed that his position was in jeopardy but the Board realised his importance to the future of the Playhouse and he was indeed reinstated as Theatre Manager.

Also fortunately, Peter Hunter was to stay on as the theatre's technical manager overseeing the refurbishments during the closure.

Alan Corkill knew everything about front of house and Peter Hunter knew everything about backstage!

Deborah Paige was to move on, initially to direct five short plays by women writers at the Hampstead Theatre in London and then on to become artistic director of The Crucible theatre in Sheffield.

Allanah Lucas eventually left to become the new administrator of the Cricklade theatre in Andover and then to become director of Arts in Western Australia.

Deborah Paige left with the following comment in the *Yorkshire Post* after taking up her appointment at The Crucible: 'One of the difficulties of working in Salisbury is that it is a very complacent small town. It is a beautiful place but without particularly wide horizons.'

Looking back many people will say that she was the wrong appointment – the wrong person at the wrong time. Perhaps at another time she may have been the right appointment and it certainly is true to say that whoever took over from David Horlock was going to have a very difficult time. Many mistakes were made and many people perhaps said and did things that they may later have regretted. But no one person is bigger than the Playhouse and it was a combination of factors that caused the crisis. The important fact to be salvaged from this dark and difficult period, though was the future of the Playhouse. The phoenix must rise again.

The Playhouse then was due to close for eight months after '*The Sleeping Beauty*' for refurbishment and with an entirely new Board and a new artistic director. All through its long history the Playhouse had survived a number of financial crises without having to close – 'To go dark'. It would be a momentous time in the history of the Playhouse. Certainly a huge amount of money was needed through, grants, loans, subsidies, gifts, sponsorship, fundraising, whatever, not only to cover the refurbishment but also to counteract the ever rising deficit, one figure given at the time was £300,000. An indefinable quality though, was also needed – a simple love of the theatre and in particular a love of this Playhouse to be shown not only by those who had always loved it but also by those who had critized it and shunned it in the past. Now was the time to rally round and to give it the 'TLC' that it desperately needed to make sure that it did not die like so many other regional theatre had done.

Sleeping Beauty, December 1994: Cast with Deborah Paige including John Halstead (Nanny Fanny Annie); Emma Sutcliffe (Princess Briar Rose) (Photographer Peter Brown)

Before the closure though, there was the pantomime to enjoy! This was written by the very talented team of Colin Wakefield and Kate Edgar who were also responsible for the very successful '*Aladdin*' the previous year.

For a while during all the trauma concerning the closure it was thought that the pantomime would never happen and that the Playhouse would be going to sleep even before the beautiful princess. Thank goodness for Salisbury adults and children that it did appear as it proved to be a such a smash hit. It was exactly what Salisbury wanted as they said a temporary farewell to the Playhouse.

It starred Emma Cuncliffe, who was later to achieve great success on television, in her professional debut as Princess Briar Rose, pitting her wits against the splendid John Halstead as 'Nanny Fanny Annie', who had already starred in over 25 pantomimes across the country.

In the *Wiltshire Times*, Sally Hendry wrote: 'This was pantomime as it should be – traditional, rhyming, not a strobe in sight – and all the more magical because of that. Just a glance at the face of my transfixed four year old was enough to spell out the success of this production, which had all the right ingredients. In all it was a delightful pantomime.'

In the *Stage and Television Today* Dee Adcock wrote: 'It is a splendid, stylish, extravaganza of high drama and simple charm. Part of its success lies in what it does not have – no soap stars, no sports personalities, no blue jokes. '*The Sleeping Beauty*' offers all that a proper panto should have, complete with an adorable dame, masses of hissing and booing and plenty of excuses for the audience to shout and cheer themselves hoarse. – yes, Salisbury knows how to concoct classic pantomime!.'

In a further article for the *Journal* she wrote: 'There has been a special rapport between the cast and audience at Salisbury's pantomime for years. Each loves the other. The last night will break hearts at the Playhouse. But only a sentimentalist would want Christmas to last for ever – and there will be another pantomime next year. Oh, yes, there will!'

Alan Richardson, who was now the President of the Friends and Patrons, wrote a personal letter to all Friends and once again his eloquent way with words summed up so well how many people were feeling:

> It will be with mixed feelings for those attending the last night of the pantomime on January 14th. They will have enjoyed a good laugh from the antics on stage but then maybe some of us will feel close to shedding a tear as the curtain comes down on 'The Sleeping Beauty' for as we all know by now, our theatre is having to take an enforce rest but hopefully a Prince will awaken her to new life in September next year. Thankfully, however, the Playhouse will not be completely dark, various ancillary facilities will continue and the restaurant will remain open. Let us support it and meet from time to time and keep the breath of life pulsing through the building that has become such a part of the artistic life of our city, then come September, we can bring the kiss of life to the sleeping 'beauty' that is our Playhouse.

Salisbury now waited patiently and with some trepidation for that magic to happen and for the 'kiss of life' to restore the Playhouse to its former glories again, but where was it going to come from?

20

THE ONLY WAY IS UP

The shouting and the laughter from the pantomime audience have stopped and the cast have packed their bags and moved on to their next engagements. The scenery has been taken down and the lights have been switched off. There is an eerie silence now in Salisbury Playhouse. There is now an eight month gap on the calendar, a hole that needs to be filled. When will the Playhouse open again? Will it open again? When we will see another production? When will we hear the voices of actors and the murmur of audiences once again?

Now more than at any time did the Playhouse need the Time Fairy from the pantomime to stay behind and sprinkle some magic dust to make it stay alive. It had the time, but would someone come up with the magic?

Unfortunately there was no magic available but there was a very strong belief amongst those that worked at the Playhouse and the thousands of theatregoers who supported it, that supported 'their theatre' that the Playhouse would definitely rise again and find its rightful place once again amongst the best of British regional theatres. No magic, but a very strong belief and determination and this sometimes can be as strong as magic. But where do you start?

First things first. The future of the Playhouse could not get very far without money but fortunately funding was soon secured. As a result of the new artistic policy and business plan, the three principal funding bodies gave strong financial commitments.

Southern Arts increased its annual commitment to the theatre by £50,000 – approximately a 21% increase. Salisbury District Council made a one-off grant of £300,000 towards the cost of the internal refurbishment and its revenue grant was increased by 2.5% to

£86,200. Wiltshire County Council reaffirmed its annual commitment of £84,000 to the theatre. In addition the Foundation for Sports and the Arts allocated a one-off grant of £100,000

All this was set to reduce the theatre's accumulated deficit to £230,000.

As part of the refurbishment plan was to replace the main house seats, it was also decided to resurrect the 'Seat Sponsorship' scheme.

Mary Bordass, Treasurer of the Friends and Patrons wrote: 'We have already raised £40,000 in seat sponsorship, mainly from individuals, theatre groups and businesses. Now we would like others to follow the lead set by Belle Vue Road and St. Thomas' Church (whose residents and congregation had combined to sponsor their own seats)so we can raise a further £40,000.'

Previous seat sponsors would have their plaques removed from the old seats and then mounted on a special board which would then be hung in the foyer so that there would still be public recognition of their support.

A new Board of Directors was also appointed following a process of public nomination and selection according to recognised equal opportunities criteria of expertise, interest, age and gender. From a field of 41 candidates, eight were selected, six were new. Peter Chalke who had represented Wiltshire County Council was re-elected and Cliff Ware continued to represent the Friends and Patrons.

The new Chairman was Simon Richards the general manager of New Hall Hospital in Bodenham, a private hospital just outside the city. He was a young, dynamic businessman, guaranteed to breathe new life into the Board. He was a regular theatregoer and his company, in the past had sponsored several productions including the pantomime.

He announced that the Board wanted the Playhouse to become a more community-based theatre, expanding its educational role and encouraging amateur companies. He also stated that the business of 'no comment' would change. He did not want the public to think any longer that the Playhouse Board and its Chairman were 'hiding' from the people.

Following a detailed evaluation of the existing structure of the Playhouse, the consultants, Bonnar Keenlyside recommended that a team of two directors – artistic director and executive director – be appointed to lead the Playhouse, acting as joint executive. Hilary Keenlyside would act as administrator until the post of executive director had been filled.

This was quite a dramatic move away from previous Playhouse management set ups when the likes of David Horlock and Roger Clissold combined both roles. Even Deborah Paige when she started took on both roles but later had the considerable support from Allanah Lucas.

There were 73 applications for the role of artistic director and 38 for executive director. Once again the Board took a risk when appointing the new artistic director as Jonathan Church was only 28 when he was appointed, thus becoming the youngest artistic director of a regional theatre in the country.

Jonathan Church (Photographer Hanya Chlala)

Jonathan Church was born in Nottingham in 1967, the son of theatrical parents who met at Nottingham Playhouse. His mother was an actress, Marielaine Douglas and his father a light and sound man at the Nottingham Playhouse before becoming head of arts features at Radio Nottingham.

As a youngster, Jonathan trod the boards at Nottingham and played a pit boy in Trevor Griffith's BBC TV adaptation of 'Sons and Lovers.' He was educated at Nottingham and Clarendon College of Further Education. He began his adult career as a lighting designer, but blossomed under Clare Venables at the Sheffield Crucible. Taken on there as an assistant stage manager, he was also encouraged to direct late-night shows.

He was spotted by Hull Truck where he became a stage manager. He then returned to his roots at Nottingham Playhouse where Pip Broughton further nurtured his directing. He eventually set up his own company, called Triptych and then became associate director at Derby Playhouse.

On his appointment to Salisbury, he said:

I am thrilled to be here and I do hope that you find many things to intrigue and delight you. It's a brilliant opportunity. Here is a city that genuinely wants its theatre back- and wants it to grow and flourish. I took the job because there is a strong and loyal community who want to be involved. If they understand what we're doing and why, I'm sure they will respond.

We must bring the audience back in and we must make them feel comfortable and that we are accountable to them. I am also committed to new writing and to see the re-opening of the Salberg as a showcase for new work.

On his views he stated:

I believe in theatre that touches people. When I go to the theatre I want to be moved, whether that's with laughter or tears. I want a theatre that is human that touches on fundamental conditions of the human spirit.'

I have no desire to shock people. My aim is to illuminate. I like to work with intelligent actors who contribute ideas and developments.

I don't want to just tell them what to do. I see directing as enabling, not imposing a design or a concept on anyone. I'm a believer in collaboration. As a director you are a filter and guide. I don't think that either the artistic or the practical can exist alone. I want to mine the middle ground and make theatre that's inspiring and accessible.

I'm passionate about existing plays and the classics but I'm also excited about new work. I do feel we have to speak to the audience of today.

A producing theatre is very dear to my heart and it is the only type of theatre I'd want to run.

A little while after his appointment, he also commented: 'I didn't imagine this post happening so soon but having started I do feel ready. I don't feel 28 any more!'

The other major appointment was Rebecca Morland as Executive Director. Rebecca was born in Somerset and was educated at Durham University. She began her career in the West End in a variety of posts from usherette to Front of House Manager. From 1987 to 1989 she was Front of House Manager at the Mercury in Colchester before moving to the new writing company, the Soho Theatre Company as Administrator. In 1991 she became Director of Marketing and Administration of the Worcester Swan Theatre.

On her appointment she said: 'The Playhouse is a theatre I have always admired. The theatre world is a small one and people have always been full of praise for the Playhouse and its good work. It has a very fine reputation.'

One of the first things these newly appointed people had to do was to meet the people of Salisbury so a Public Meeting was held on 24th May 1995 in which the Playhouse's new Artistic Policy was announced:

'To provide for the people of Salisbury, Wiltshire, Hants and Dorset, a high quality and well balanced programme of local, national and international theatre. Through presenting theatre which is exciting, stimulating and entertaining to its audience, Salisbury Playhouse will continue to be a significant force in regional theatre.' A rather bland statement but one which satisfied those present. It would be up to Jonathan Church now to put 'flesh on the bone.'

Jonathan Church and Rebecca Morland on re-opening the theatre in 1995
(Photograph Salisbury Journal)

Sitting in the audience was that wise man, Reggie Salberg who commented afterwards: 'I think the meeting went very well. Everybody made all the right noises and I think they meant them.' So that was OK then!

Before any date for the opening of the theatre was considered much feverish activity was starting to take place during Phase One of the refurbishment. Under the watchful eyes of Alan Corkill and Peter Hunter this involved focusing on developing the main auditorium. It was redesigned and new wheel chair positions were built in the boxes to the side and new production walkways above.

Architectural lighting was installed, the seating replaced and the interior redecorated. Panels holding lighting slots and counter-weighted flying systems were installed in the stage area and the entire stage floor was renewed. And to the delight of many patrons, the toilets were given a much needed face-lift!

The public was invited into the theatre during the closure to view the refurbishment and particularly to try out the new seats!

The theatre was then sufficiently ready to invite people to an Open Day on Saturday 30th September. 'Admission Entirely Free!' as

Timothy West re-opening the theatre, September 1995: Rebecca Morland; Timothy West; Simon Richards; Jonathan Church (Photographer Salisbury Journal)

the flyer proclaimed. Events included backstage tours, costume and archive exhibitions, open rehearsals of '*The Visit*' by Stage 65 and a balloon race.

The main event was a 'Grand Re-opening Ceremony at 11.30' with the Playhouse's old friend, Timothy West cutting the ribbon. Over 2,500 people attended throughout the day..

There was also a flurry of notes sent out to theatregoers from Alan Corkill to group organisers, from Cliff Ware to the Friends and Patrons and from Jonathan Church advertising the new season and also ways in which theatregoers could save money when booking such as special 'saver' performances and a subscription scheme.

A new season – so is the Playhouse ready to re-open? In the words of the pantomime – 'Oh, yes it is!'

The press release announcing the new season advertised:

This is a season which genuinely includes something for everyone – great drama, high comedy, new writing and of course the traditional Salisbury pantomime. The theatre benefits from newly established co-producing arrangements with other regional theatres which means, for example, that for the first time for several years, a play with a cast of no less than 19 can be presented in Salisbury.

To launch the season Oscar Wilde's '*An Ideal Husband*' was chosen. Jonathan Church was not available to direct this so the honour went to the comedy and drama actor, Nicholas Le Provost. It proved to be a box office hit with average attendances of 80% and several performance were sold out.

There was even a 'Gala performance on Saturday 7th October followed by a champagne reception at the Guildhall 'To celebrate the re-opening of the Playhouse.'

One can imagine the excitement and the anticipation when the curtain went up on a new production, at last, on the Playhouse stage. Dee Adcock wrote about the 'Joy, relief and anticipation which gave an extra buzz after months of enforced darkness.' The set and the costumes were very lavish and deservedly received much praise but the 100 year old play itself was an ideal choice.

An ideal Husband, October 1995: Gillian Hanna (Mrs. Markby)
(Photographer Peter Brown)

Dee Adcock wrote: It's Oscar Wilde at his best – surprising, funny yet shocking too with the deception under the surface of life. There's plenty of meat in it.'

The reporter from the *Western Gazette* wrote: 'It's a good night out in the traditional style, a well made play, plenty to look at, a few laughs and nothing to frighten maiden aunts.'

Unfortunately the performance on 20th October had to be cancelled because Liz May Brice, who played Miss Mabel Chiltern, which was a large part, was stuck on the M25 due to Friday rush hour traffic. Her estimated time of arrival was 8.45 which would mean a curtain up time of 9.00. This was considered to be too long to hold an audience so Alan Corkill had to make an announcement to the audience and a complimentary drink at the theatre bar, refunds and transfers were offered.

I wonder if Alan Corkill's mind went back to that episode with Robert Powell when he was in 'The Royal Hunt of the Sun', who ended up having to charter a plane, plus a lift in Reggie Salberg's car in order to get to the theatre just in time for the second act!

The stage manager's report stated that: 'The audience seems to take this very well.' However one would imagine that theatregoers at this time were probably only too pleased to see the Playhouse open again and were ready to forgive the management for anything!

This was followed by a production on the main stage of 'The Visit' by Stage 65 who were celebrating their 30th anniversary. The play was directed by the Playhouse's youth officer, Sarah Bradnock. For two nights it was presented as a double bill with a production by Romanian students who were in Britain on a return visit. Under their director, Grigore Gonta they performed a version of a Romanian folk tale.

Jonathan Church said that he wanted to integrate the theatre's education department into the Playhouse's overall artistic policy. He felt that Stag 65 and the education department had been out on a limb recently.

The Playhouse theatregoers though, were waiting eagerly for the next production as it would be Jonathan Church's first. It was a co-production with the Birmingham Stage Company of Arthur Miller's classic 'The Crucible.' It had a cast of 17 including some actors familiar to Salisbury audiences: Roger Leach, Carolyn Backhouse and Tony Bonza. The play proved to be a roaring success.

'This is the play that Salisbury has been waiting for – a production that will crush any doubts about the Playhouse and its artistic director, Jonathan Church. This 'Crucible' blazes like a beacon of excellence. Intelligent interpretation and towering performances with the force of raw emotions. It is bewitching in its stark beauty and bruising yet incisive in impact.' wrote Dee Adcock.

Elvira Romans of the *Wiltshire Gazette and Herald* enthused: 'I have seen many versions of this modern classic, but this is the one I am

The Crucible, November 1995: Martin Turner (John Proctor); Helen Franklin (Mary Warren) (Photographer Robert Day)

tempted to call definitive. As it ended, the first night audience sat in silence for a few seconds before breaking into applause which went on long after the cast had left the stage.'

And this fine accolade came from Bob Kolbe: 'A few years ago I sat directly behind Arthur Miller and his wife at one of his plays at London's National Theatre. During the performance he cupped his hand and whispered in her ear about one of the actresses: 'She hasn't got it right!' he hissed. I don't think anyone would dare say that about Jonathan Church and this fine production.' It was a powerful start and Salisbury audiences sat up and cautiously celebrated. Jonathan Church was off on his Salisbury 'yellow brick road.'

The perfect traditional family pantomime and probably the best loved of them all, 'Cinderella' brought to an end 1995, a year that started so sadly with the closure of the Playhouse. It was the perfect antidote to all the doom and gloom that had started the year. Once again the pantomime was written by Colin Wakefield and Kate Edgar, the wonderfully talented team that produced the last two pantomimes: 'Sleeping Beauty' and 'Aladdin'. And this time there was no need for the kind fairy to stay behind with her magic. The Playhouse was beginning to produce its own form of magic.

Not to be outdone again by its big brother, the Salberg also had a wide range of productions. There was the world premiere of Jack Shepherd's 'Comic Cuts' directed by Jonathan Church; Michael Mear's one-man play about homelessness 'Soup' which came to the Salberg direct from Edinburgh; there was a variety of performances for children including an adaptation of 'The Happy Prince'; several junior workshops; the older members of Stage 65 performed their own 'Christmas Cabaret' and there was a return of the incredibly popular 'Quirkish Delight'. The management was certainly making sure that the Salberg was not forgotten.

An innovation with which Jonathan enjoyed challenging his audiences was putting plays and casts into short repertory seasons.

He first did this in March 1996 when he directed Willy Russell's 'Educating Rita' and David Mamet's 'Oleanna' in the Salberg starring Nicholas Lumley and Carolyn Backhouse

The critic of the Daily Telegraph wrote: 'Seeing them together was one of the most rewarding and continually enjoyable theatrical experiences I've had for ages. Church directs both plays with tremendous assurance and a satisfying attention to detail. He has a spectacular double hit on his hands.'

And the critic from the Blackmore Vale Magazine also forecasted success: 'This brilliant young artistic director who is putting Salisbury theatre high on the national scene.'

Nicholas Lumley recalls the rehearsals: 'Jonathan was rather a shy man. He was very gentle with actors, allowing them to show him what they could do. He would often laugh and simply say: No, we don't want that thank you!' Nicholas also remembered the only time when he saw Jonathan angry. It was when he brought his dog, Capt. Blunt to rehearsals. Capt. Blunt used to sit on Jonathan's chair with his head on the table looking at the text!

That was fine, but at the technical rehearsal Nicholas couldn't leave Capt. Blunt in the dressing room because he kept barking so he brought him downstairs to the Salberg and tied him to a stage weight. The play started with Rita knocking on the door so Capt. Blunt started barking again but he also started to drag the stage weight around on a chain. 'Take that dog to your dressing room!' shouted Jonathan. 'I'm terribly sorry,' replied Nicholas, 'If I put him back in there he will eat it!' Fortunately a lady in reception looked after him for the day. 'I cost two wages that day!' remarked Nicholas!

Capt. Blunt though became quite the thespian dog having roles in 'The Cherry Orchard' and 'Rough Crossing'!

In April 1996 Jonathan directed 'The Banished Cavaliers' and

'*The Rover*' in repertory. Two Restoration comedies by Aphra Behn, known as Britain's first female playwright. He retrieved a copy of '*The Banished Cavaliers*' from a fragile seventeenth century script which had been preserved in the British Library. He breathed life into it and gave Salisbury what may have been its first production for more than three hundred years. Research by assistant director Kate Matthews suggested that it was banned by the shocked Edwardians!

They were huge productions involving removing four front rows and the side flanks of seats, extending the stage forward and setting seats on the revamped stage.

To produce two plays in repertory, that not many Salisbury theatregoers had heard of, was a huge risk but it paid off and the critics enthused about it.

The Sunday Times critic write: 'Hats off to artistic director Jonathan Church. It takes commitment and sheer guts, not only to put on Aphra Behn's raunchy 1677 play of love, lust and bad manners but also to follow it with its 1681 sequel.'

Dee Adcock wrote: 'The Rover' grabs Salisbury Playhouse by the scruff of the neck and takes it on an adventure that leaves its audience breathless. It is a big production with sprawling great fights, feasts of fabric in costumes, distinctive touches in lighting and a gloriously crazy carnival atmosphere. It is undeniably a special play.'

In the autumn of 1997 he also put Chekhov's '*The Cherry Orchard*' and David Hare's '*Racing Demon*' in repertory and Salisbury theatregoers were no doubt pleased to see several familiar local actors taking part: Tony Boncza from Blandford, Michael Stroud from Shaftesbury, Tim Meats from Salisbury and Nicholas Lumley from Hungerford.

It was also noticeable that Jonathan Church was now beginning to gather a familiar team around him in the designer: Ruari Murchison and the lighting designer Nick Beadle.

Of '*The Cherry Orchard*', David Humphrey of the *Western Daily Press* wrote: '*The Cherry Orchard*' has always presented audiences with a dilemma – not knowing whether to laugh or cry at it – but humour is to the fore in this version directed by Jonathan Church with the originality we have come to expect from him.'

Elvira Romans of the *Wiltshire Gazette and Herald* wrote: 'Chekhov is one of those writers you either love or hate. If you don't know which camp you are in, let this production convince you that you love Chekhov.'

'*Racing Demon*', a controversial play about modern beliefs and doubts about the Church caused considerable local interest when the Bishop and Dean of the Cathedral attended the Talk-Out with members of the cast. It is remembered that they both behaved themselves with great dignity! Not like one member of the audience who snorted: 'I think I've just been watching a bunch of buffoons!'

Richard Kane recalls the rehearsals: 'Jonathan Church is a calm centre, an almost invisible presence in rehearsal, but always receptive; encouraging an actor to dare, grateful for any morsels brought to the table. For me, it was a happy collaboration.'

No director can ignore Shakespeare for too long and Jonathan Church made two excursions into his work. In October 1996 he directed '*The Merchant of Venice*' which was memorable for a towering performance by Gareth Armstrong.

'Its ethereal air will give it the lasting image of a play with something rare and special. Magic shines through this hauntingly beautiful production where fairy tale blends with the realism of human nature.' wrote Dee Adcock.

Fiona Weaver was somewhat more direct: 'It is an extremely accessible, impressive and energetic production, well worth its weight whether in gold or flesh.'

In January 1997 Jonathan directed '*Romeo and Juliet*' with Dudley Sutton as the Friar and Josephine Tewson as the Nurse. This had a mixed reception. Dee Adcock liked it: 'Here too is an undefined olden day look with sensual fabrics and costumes evoking some time between Shakespeare and old black and white movies.' This time it was Josephine Tewson who was very direct: 'The set looked like a gentleman's loo. One leading actor didn't know his part very well and it was not a very successful tour!'

It takes courage to present a new play to a loyal and traditional audience but Jonathan Church gave the Salisbury theatregoers several world premieres, two of which he directed himself: '*Disappearances*' by Terry Eagleton in the Salberg in June 1997 and Stephen Lowe's '*The Alchemical Wedding*' in the main theatre in April 1998. Whereas the former earned considerable praise, particularly for Rudolph Walker's powerful performance, the latter however, received a mixed reception from the critics.

Stephen Lowe was commissioned to write this play after the Playhouse won the first Southern Arts regional new writing award worth £9,000.

It had the most amazing set designed by prize winning young designer David Stuart Nunn. Sean Street described it as 'a cross between a Greek amphitheatre and a Spielberg spaceship.'

Toby O'Connor Morse of The Independent wrote: 'The Alchemical Wedding' promises much but the play is an unhappy conjunction of 'The Crucible' and a second hand drawing room drama about the consequences of wife swapping!'

However, this play remained a production with which Jonathan Church was particularly proud to have been associated.

Another unusual play Jonathan directed in the Salberg was Caryl Churchill's 'Top Girls', a co-production with the Theatre Royal Plymouth..

'At Mariene's celebration dinner to mark her promotion to Managing Director of the 'Top Girls Employment Agency', she has five guests – a Pope, a Warrior, a nineteenth century Traveller, a Japanese Emperor's Courtesan and a Chaucerian Obedient Wife, all from centuries past.'

Several prominent people wrote in the programme their own choices of five women from history who they would like to invite to dinner! The actress Toyah Willcox chose: Joan of Arc, Trudi Styler, Virginia Wolf, Sylvia Plath and Princess Diana with Marilyn Monroe as reserve! I wonder who would you choose?!

In the play Catriona Hinds, who played Dull Gret, had to eat 19 big greedy dinners including two on matinee days by the time the last plate was cleared away! She said that after a while she didn't even taste it and that she warned Jonathan that he'd have to pay her bill at a health farm if she put on too much weight! Of the play Dee Adcock wrote: 'Top Girls' is coarse and sharp, funny and tricky. Smart girls <u>and</u> boys should see it!'

It was obvious that Jonathan Church was not afraid to take risks. One local critic described him as ' a little like the stunt rider. Every leap onto the stage, we are all waiting for him to come unstuck as the last bus passes beneath him. With unerring accuracy though, he always makes it safely to the ramp, and we all gasp in amazement at his brave achievement!'

There were of course other talented directors during this time and Richard Kane recalls the style of Robin Herford who directed him in Ayckbourn's '*Time and Time Again*':

> Robin Herford, a golf and cricketing enthusiast, punctuates his direction with a range of sporting gestures. A personal note is signalled by the slow approach, coming to rest three feet away, followed by a sideways turn. Then he bends, settles his feet and dispatches a short-putt into the waiting ear. Notes of a general and more rousing nature are accompanied by a fierce drive to the boundary!

Throughout his tenure as artistic director Jonathan Church made sure that the Salberg continued to shine by also showing a whole range of productions including Junior Theatre Workshops, plays for children, one man shows, performances by local authors and local companies such as Bootleg and Forest Forge, drama such as '*Speed the Plow*' and '*Krapps Last Case*' and of course performances by Stage 65.

Those who remembered the Michael Caine and Sean Connery film: '*The Man Who Would be King*' will be surprised that this play was also performed in the confines of the Salberg and looking through the list of plays for children during the late 90s, just what was '*A Wheelie Bin Ate My Sister*' really all about?!

Since the re-opening of the Playhouse there have been many plays where the costumes have been praised. This was often down to the very impressive talents of the Wardrobe Supervisor, Henrietta Worrall Thompson (known affectionately as 'Hen'.) Trained at Wimbledon, Birmingham and the Croydon School of Arts, Hen first came to the Playhouse in 1994 to finish off a show and then to work on the pantomime. When the Playhouse re-opened she was made permanent wardrobe supervisor. Working in what she considered to be the best room in the Playhouse, as it was at the top of the building and was light and spacious and with a deputy and assistants,, her days would often be very long, particularly during the run up to the pantomime. 'We sew until the last minute and it has been known for us to be finishing the walk-down costumes as the show starts and rushing downstairs to hand over to the cast in the interval!' she once confessed!

Hen never wanted to 'tread the boards' and she remarked that the part she particularly enjoyed was the process of taking the designer's idea and putting it on stage and doing it with everyone being happy and feeling comfortable about it. Sometimes that does not always work!

Hen is always beautifully organised, and looking through the 'bibles' of each of her productions you would see a kaleidoscope of wonderfully imaginative and colourful designs Theatregoers always love looking through them during backstage tours!

In September 1996 the Playhouse produced its first musical since 'Sweeney Todd'. This was 'Maddie' written by Shaun McKenna and Steven Dexter with a sterling cast that included Mark McGann, Summer Rognlie and Kevin Colson. It also included a previous member of Stage 65, Hattie Ladbury making her full-time stage debut.

An actress in the cast had dropped out after one day's rehearsal and the director Martin Connor found himself in a fix. Fortunately he remembered a student he had been very impressed by when he directed at the Guildhall School of Drama earlier that year. Without hesitation he called Hattie, even though it was almost midnight and she neede to start work on 'Maddie' the next morning! Hattie aged 22 from Britford, had graduated with first class honours and a gold medal. As a member of Stage 65 she had played in 'Grease', 'Nicholas Nickleby' and she played Maria in 'West Side Story.'

Salisbury theatregoers had waited a long time for another musical and this feel-good show, advertised as 'a ghostly romantic comedy', was a box office and critical success. The *Bournemouth Evening Echo* wrote: 'This is a musical with a big warm heart, a great story line, memorable tunes and it's very funny!'

There was a strong recommendation from Bob Kolbe: 'People who like musicals will love this show -people who don't like musicals will love it too. It's as simple as that!'

The *Telegraph's* Charles Spencer thought it had a great future: 'I don't want to start a frenzy of hype and inflated expectations but this show could be just what we've been waiting for. A new British musical by unknown hands which is blessed with wit, charm and a terrific star performance.'

Its immediate future was a transfer to the Lyric Theatre in the West End where unfortunately the fickle West End audience did not give it a very long run.

Around this time, Phase Two of the refurbishment was taking place. This was thanks to a grant of nearly £1,500,000 from the National Lottery. One of the reasons the Playhouse had achieved this award was that it had gathered most of the partnership funding necessary for such an award including the £300,000 from Salisbury City Council and also through the on-going Seat Sponsorship Appeal.

Phase Two would concentrate on improving the Front of House area, including changes to the foyer, the bar, the box office and the restaurant. The Salberg would also see the installation of new, more comfortable seating, an increase in audience capacity from 100 to 140 by way of an audience gallery and the improvement of technical facilities.

Phase Two would also increase accessibility for those with disabilities. A new larger lift would replace the existing small lift providing wheelchair access to the main auditorium. The administrative offices and dressing rooms would be re-organised to reflect the changing needs of the theatre.

The architect in charge of the planning and construction was Tim Foster who was responsible for the Phase One refurbishment.

Simon Richards was excited: 'Having begun the process over a year ago we are delighted this award has been realised. It's a tremendous vote of confidence for the Playhouse.'

In the copy of the July 1996 Playhouse Gazette in which the details of Phase Two were announced, there were also three more important notices. There was an advertisement for The Gallery. This was an exhibition of paintings by both local and national artists in the upper corridors that had been very popular for several years. Not only was it a regularly changing and attractive exhibition for theatregoers to enjoy before a performance and during the interval but it was also a very good fund raiser as well. This was organised by a 'hanging committee' and presided over by the Playhouse's Exhibition Officer Nancy Strike.

This particular notice advertised the return of Bill Toop's popular biennial Christmas exhibition. Bill Toop was probably Salisbury's most popular and prolific artist. In 1976 he opened his first gallery in New Street and in that year he had his first exhibition at the new Playhouse. However, he was involved with the Playhouse well before that. He painted watercolours of the old Playhouse including one of the production of 'What Maisie Knew'. These were used as fund raisers for the new Playhouse building. He also painted his vision of how the new Playhouse would look, which was used on many of the publicity materials including the cover of many of the early Playhouse programmes.

With Ken Lailey he also constructed the model of the new Playhouse which was taken around to many fundraising events.

Sadly though, at the end of 2016, fate dealt a cruel hand and he died in a car crash not far from where he was born. It robbed Salisbury and the art world of a man of remarkable talents. Fortunately though, his paintings will be his legacy so he will not be forgotten. The Playhouse would always be grateful to him not only for his wonderful exhibitions but also for his huge fundraising efforts to raise money to enable the new Playhouse to be built.

In this magazine there was also an announcement that Alan Richardson was going to retire from his role as Playhouse Archivist. Asked by David Horlock to start the Archives and to put some order into the huge collection of programmes and photographs of previous productions that were found in cupboards and drawers throughout the building. It took him over a year to organise it but it is thanks to his hard work and exceptional organisational skills that we now have a splendid record of the Playhouse's history. The Archives were then taken over by Arthur Millie and Jane Ware.

The third important notice was a small paragraph on the back pages welcoming two new faces to the Playhouse. One was Trevelyan Wright, who was to become the new Head of Education, and the other was Rupert Goold who joined the Playhouse as part of the Regional Theatre Young Directors Scheme, after assisting at the DonmarWarehouse for a year. This scheme was founded by Howard Thomas, the managing director of ABC television and at the time was sponsored by Channel 4. It allowed young directors the opportunity to gain valuable professional experience within the supportive environment of regional theatre.

Rupert Goold was born in 1972 and grew up in Highgate with his mother who wrote children's books and his father who was a management consultant. As a child, he loved playing with his soldiers but instead of fighting with them, he enjoyed re-arranging them and putting them into groups. Good training for a theatre director?! He described himself as a geek at

Rupert Goold

school but his love of order and the English language led him to study English at Trinity College where he gained a First and then to achieve his ambition of working in the theatre.

The play chosen as his directional debut in Salisbury was 'Bouncers' by John Godber, the author of 'The Office Party' which caused such a furore during Deborah Paige's time. The advert for 'Bouncers' read: 'Bored with the same old office party? Come to 'Bouncers' and have a night out with a difference. With a special price of only £6.50 per person for groups of 10 or more, let 'Bouncers' provide you with muscle, music and a great night out!'- rather ironic?! The critics liked what they saw and the *Journal* said that it was: 'pointing to a brilliant future.':

After working with Stage 65 he then directed Graham Greene's 'Travels With My Aunt' This was a very unusual interpretation with four actors all playing the same character, Henry Pulling and Ruari Murchison's set was certainly not a box set but more a set of boxes joined together with entrances and exits – but it worked and the critics were beginning to talk about this new, young director.

The *Western Gazette* wrote: 'If this is how he's beginning his career, we should watch out for a famous future.'

Dee Adcock enthused: 'Rupert Goold springs surprises from first to last in a play that has moments of pathos and reflection but is above all, wonderfully fresh and funny.' Nicholas Lumley, who was one of the Henry Pullings remembers the play as being very difficult but that Rupert Goold was 'a brilliant director' and he also added; 'He also always had some very pretty girls backstage which was very pleasant!',

Success followed success: In October 1997 he directed Graham Greene's '*The End of the Affair*' in the Salberg: Sean Street wrote: 'Rupert Goold's greatest gift, among many as a director, is that he is dangerous in what he does, yet his judgment does not desert him.'

Travels With My Aunt, March 1997: John Forsyth: Peter Holdway; Nicholas Lumley; Simon Jermond (all playing Henry Pulling) (Photographer Robert Workman)

In March 1998 he directed '*Dancing at Lughnasa*' Sean Street also wrote: 'Brian Friel's wonderful poem of a play positively glows in director Rupert Goold's reading.' and the *Avon Advertiser* spoke about the soon to be released film with Meryl Streep: 'It will do well to improve Rupert Goold's evocative production.'

In November 1999 he then directed Arthur Miller's '*Broken Glass*' The *Sunday Times* critic wrote: 'This production pulsates with intelligence and feeling. I'm totally star struck. He is one of the best of Britain's young crop of new directors.'

Working alongside the talented Jonathan Church was the perfect start for Rupert Goold. The sorcerer's apprentice was showing that he could certainly weave his own magic

This was Rupert's last play before moving on although he did return a couple of times to the Playhouse and in 2002 directed a memorable performance of Tom Stoppard's '*Arcadia*.'

'I'm interested in plays,' he once said 'that aren't afraid of ideas, arguments. I want people to leave my theatre with plenty to talk about for better or worse. Shows that are self consciously theatrical and embrace all the things that theatre can do.' He also once commented: 'Directing a play is like running towards a wall and hoping it becomes a door just before the curtain opens.'!

Certainly doors soon began to open for him and not just metaphorically. After his training at the Playhouse, where he directed 6 plays in the main house and 2 in the Salberg, he became Director of the Royal and Derngate theatres in Northampton; Director of Headlong Theatre; Associate Director of the Royal Shakespeare Company and eventually the Director of the Almeida Theatre. He also became a film director and recently directed the film 'Judy' starring Renee Zellweger.

He was made a CBE in 2017. Certainly a meteoric rise to fame! However, Jonathan Church beat him to it in the award stakes as he was made a CBE in 2015!

It must have given the Salisbury theatregoers a great sense of pride to know that these two brilliant young directors had 'cut their theatrical teeth' at the Playhouse.

It was soon obvious that Jonathan Church was also heading for greater challenges and in April 1999 he directed his last play in Salisbury, Moliere's '*Colombe*.' with another sterling cast led by the powerful presence of Kate O'Mara.

She definitely impressed Dee Adcock but then so did several others in the cast:

Colombe, April 1999: Michael Stroud (Du Bartas); Kate O'Mara (Mdme Alexandra)
(Photographer Robert Workman)

There are several reasons why this play is worth seeing – and Kate O'Mara is most of them. Her portrait of Moliere's great tragic actress is spot on with a ruthless pragmatism driving a colossal ego. But she does not hog all the limelight in this biting comedy, Richard Kane for one will not let her. His hugely comic image of Madame's secretary starts with his ludicrous appearance and build into a tremulous vision of tantrum and trouble.

And if you think he's a hoot you should see Michael Stroud. He is the leading actor and makes sure every one knows it with flamboyance and awfulness in equal measure.

'But above all it is Church's poetic direction, ' wrote Sean Street, 'emphasising the play's symmetry and self-conscious theatricality, that makes this a memorable night. Over the years he has given the Salisbury audiences many spectacular evenings and in this farewell production he has reached new heights.'

Toby O'Connor Morse of the *Independent* wrote:

Few productions achieve the cordon bleu standard. However, Jonathan Church's production of '*Colombe*' which marks the end of his plaudit laden spell as artistic director of Salisbury Playhouse, wins him his third Michelin star. This finely crafted piece of intelligent, entertaining theatre is a worthy parting performance by Jonathan Church and one for which the good burghers of Salisbury should be duly thankful.

Nicholas Lumley who appeared in the play said that it was brilliant and could have gone straight to the West End. The *Audience Magazine* wrote: 'Along with the excellent team that surround him, he has stretched and educated his audiences. He has brought us productions that have shocked, stunned, made us laugh, made us cry and left us speechless. But most of all he has entertained us. His skill has also drawn some excellent actors, directors, writers and designers to our stage.'

Anthony Thorncroft, the critic of the *Financial Times* wrote: 'Salisbury does not come quickly to mind as a cultural juggernaut – a huddled cathedral city surrounded by sheep. But in the last few years Salisbury has enjoyed an artistic jolt, thanks to Jonathan Church.'

On leaving Salisbury, Jonathan Church said:

It's only because the Hampstead post came up at the time it did, that I'm leaving. It was a hard decision and ideally it would have come a year or so later. But this theatre is now in a secure position, with funding increased, audiences up and the deficit more stable. It's the right time to hand over to someone else.

I'm very grateful to Salisbury. The board took a calculated risk by taking me on at a young age. They have given me a huge amount of experience and the audiences gave me support and I'm very grateful. There's no way that what we've done will vanish overnight.

He and his team have taken the Playhouse from the anxiety of 1996 when the theatre 'went dark' to the stability of a theatre that

The Winter's Tale, January 2000: John Flitcroft (The Clown); Katharine Barker
(Dorcas); Debra Penny (Mopsa); Fergus McLarnon (Autolyeus)
(Photographer Robert Workman)

once again is back on its rightful pedestal as a theatre respected and
admired throughout the theatrical world.

Jonathan recollected:

> When I arrived in Salisbury there were only five staff. But the
> closure period provided the energy to reinvent the Playhouse. The
> audience really cared about their theatre and what it should be doing
> – they cared about the relationship with it and I found that really
> stimulating. After four years in which the deficit was greatly reduced
> and the audience greatly increased I felt that it was either time 'to dig
> in or to hand over the baton.

He chose the latter and became associate director at Hampstead.

His successful climb continued and he became artistic director
at Birmingham Repertory and then the Chichester Festival Theatre.
There was a short period directing in Australia and he now runs
'Jonathan Church Productions'.

The *Sunday Times* wrote: 'I hope that the Playhouse picks a strong successor to Church as he ran the place with taste and courage and will be a hard act to follow.'

That mantle fell upon Joanna Read a young freelance director whose first play was to be Shakespeare's '*The Winters Tale*.' in January 2000.

A new millennium, a new artistic director, another new start. The Playhouse's journey has not been smooth. It has had many highs and had many lows but at the turn of the century it was in a strong position both financially and artistically. Over the years many talented people have passed through its doors and many talented leaders have guided it through its many traumas and successes. But above all it has had an audience of devoted theatregoers who loved their theatre and who are now able to face the new century with optimism, enthusiasm, excitement and above all with considerable pride.

EPILOGUE

And this is where my story ends. A new century, a new artistic director, another new start.

It is a good place to finish. I know that there are another twenty years of Playhouse history to tell but that is for another time, perhaps for someone else to write.

Apart from 2000 being a good place to finish, another 20 plus years would simply make the book far too large! But also having lived through those years as a volunteer at the Playhouse ,there are far too many people involved that I know so well and I would not want to write about them and tell their stories in any shape or form.

The Playhouse moved into another century and it continued to grow from strength to strength After the successful tenure of Jonathan Church and the rise of Rupert Goold, Joanna Read became artistic director but left after 8 years to become Principal of LAMDA (The London Academy of Music and Dramatic Art). She was followed by Phillip Wilson who left in 2011 to become a freelance director. Gareth Machin then became artistic director and is so to this day. This is a very successful partnership, working with Sebastian Warrack as executive director.

Joanna Read

During the last twenty years the Playhouse has been in very capable and talented hands. Of course there were a few bumps in the road but there were also many successes and the Playhouse has continued to be one of the most respected and popular regional theatres in Britain. Then in 2018 the Playhouse amalgamated with the Arts Centre and the International Arts Festival to become Wiltshire Creative. Together, they form a strong force delivering a whole range of arts throughout the region..

When Mr. Yates of the Wilton Carpet factory laid the foundation stone of the Primitive Methodist Church in Fisherton Street on that

SALISBURY

Saturday in May 1869, all those years ago, he could not have imagined that it was the opening chapter of an incredible story. A story not just of Methodists, but of soldiers and cinema audiences, of actors and directors, of backstage and office workers, of committees and councils, of theatregoers and critics, of fundraisers and theatrical giants., of success and failure, of laughter and tears but above all, a story of a theatre that would grow and flourish from the tiny acorn that was the little building in Fisherton Street to the mighty oak that is now the Playhouse which stands proud in Malthouse Lane – 'Our Playhouse.'

One day, walk down Fisherton Street and turn down into Chapel Place where the story of the Playhouse started. Listen carefully, and you may just hear the sound of actors' voices, the murmur of an appreciative audience and feel the presence of those theatrical giants that shaped the Playhouse .The guardians of the past will always be there. The Playhouse's past has created its future and it has given us an amazing story.

It is a story as dramatic as any play. Although for this story, there is no final act, and we haven't even reached the interval.

As we look back, we also look forward and thank the Playhouse for so many incredible memories.

The sketch of the old building and the photo of the extension (July 2007)

INDEX OF PLAYS

Note: Plays beginning 'The' are indexed under the next word of the title.

GENERAL INDEX

PLAYHOUSE TIMELINE

Opening of the Garrison Theatre	1943	
	1943	First Play: *Night Must Fall.*
Opening of the Arts Theatre	1945	
	1945	First Play: *Day of Glory.*
Barbara Burnham appointed Manager	1945	
	1948	First Pantomime: *Aladdin.*
Michael Wide appointed Manager	1948	
	1949	Theatregoers' Inaugural Meeting.
Our Lady's Tumbler performed in the Cathedral.	1951	
	1952	Prunella Scales first play: *Figure of Fun.*
Junior Theatregoers formed.	1953	
	1953	Midnight Matinee to celebrate the Coronation.
Arts Theatre Company performing in Carlisle.	1953	
	1953	Arts Theatre renamed the Playhouse.
Knights of the Round Table: World Premiere.	1954	
	1955	Reggie Salberg appointed Manager.
Leonard Rossiter in *The Bespoke Overcoat.*	1955	
	1957	Timothy West first play: *Mrs. Dane's Defence.*
Meet Me By Moonlight transfers to Adelphi Theatre London.	1957	
	1958	*Gwendoline* renamed *Caught Napping* and transfers to London.
Purchase of the theatre by the "Theatregoers of Salisbury."	1960	
	1964	Stephanie Cole first play: *Where Angels Fear To Tread.*
Company opened the Nuffield Theatre with *Twelfth Night.*	1964	
	1965	*Betzi* : World Premiere.
Stage 65 established	1965	
	1965	Roger Clissold appointed Associate Director.
Christopher Biggins working as student ASM.	1965	
	1966	*Lock Up Your Daughters*: 21st Anniversary Production. (Telegram received from Lord Olivier.)
Alan Corkill appointed as Trainee Manager	1966	
	1967	Theatrescope and T.I.E. established.

Appeal for the new theatre was launched.	1974	
	1974	Derek Nimmo "Turned the first sod."
Laying the Foundation Stone by Peter Hall	1975	
	1976	Last Night at the old Playhouse: *Old Time Musical Hall.*
Official Opening of the new Playhouse By Alec Guinness.	1976	
	1976	*Welcome to the Playhouse:* first play in the new Playhouse.
Kennedy's Children: first play in the Salberg	1977	
	1978	*Under the Greenwood Tree:* World Premiere transferred to London.
Make the Little Beggars Hop: World Premiere transferred to London as *Beecham.*	1979	
	1979	*Old Herbaceous:* World Premiere transferred to London. Also a Royal Command Performance.
84 Charing Cross Road: World Premiere later transferred to London and America.	1981	
	1982	David Horlock appointed Artistic Director.
The Secret Garden: World Premiere.	1983	
	1986	*A Midsummer Nights' Dream* performed in the gardens of Wilton House.
Wrong End of the World: World Premiere. (First Day Cover received from the TUC.)	1987	
	1987	First *Quirkish Delight* cabaret in the Salberg
Biggles Saves the Spire: For the Spire Appeal	1988	
	1990	Death of David Horlock in a car crash.
West Side Story: first Stage 65 production on the main stage.	1991	
	1991	Deborah Paige appointed Artistic Director.
For Services Rendered: transferred to London	1993	
	1993	Ewan McGregor appeared in *What the Butler Saw.*
Twelfth Night toured China.	1994	
	1995	Playhouse "goes dark."
Re-opening of the Playhouse by Timothy West.	1995	
	1995	Jonathan Church appointed Artistic Director and Rebecca Morland appointed Executive Director.
An Ideal Husband: re-opens the Playhouse.	1995	
	1996	*Maddie:* World Premiere.
Cherry Orchard and *Racing Demon* produced in repertory.	1997	
	1997	*Banished Cavaliers* and *The Rover* in repertory and partly in the Round.
Disappearances World Premiere in the Salberg.	1997	
	1998	*The Alchemical Wedding:* World Premiere.

The Birthday Party with Timothy West and 1999
Prunella Scales appearing together for the
first time at the Playhouse.

2000 Joanna Read appointed Artistic
Director

Fen and *Sharp Relief* – Springboard   2001
Project in the Salberg (Young Writers).

2002 *The Hired Man* by Melvyn Bragg and
Howard Goodall.

Going to the Chapel : World Premiere in the 2003
Salberg (Local Writer's Scheme.)

2004 *Home* and *Garden* Ayckbourn plays
Performed in both auditoria.

Launch of Original Drama   2004

2005 *To Kill a Mockingbird:* performed in
the Round.

Two Cities: World Premiere   2006

2007 Extension opened by Prunella Scales.

Philip Wilson appointed Artistic Director   2008

2010 *The Boys and the Girls* : celebrated
Stage 65 Anniversary.

Way Upstream : performed on a boat.   2011

2011 Gareth Machin appointed Artistic
Director.

Sebastian Warrack appointed Executive   2012
Director

2012 The first Theatre Fest West (now in its
seventh year.)

Up Down Boy: in the Salberg   2012

2012 *The Spire* : World Premiere.

Playhouse celebrates 70ᵗʰ Anniversary.   2013

2014 *Separate Tables* and *Bedroom Farce* in
repertory and in the Round.

Worst Wedding Ever: World Premiere.   2014

2015 Revival of *84 Charing Cross Road*
(prior to national tour).

The Magna Carta Plays : World Premiere.   2015

2015 *Clause 39* : performed by Stage 65 in
the Cathedral.

Little Shop of Horrors : Co-production.   2015

2016 *We're here Because We're Here* : to
commemorate the Battle of the

Somme.
Playhouse voted UK Theatre's "Most   2016
Welcoming Theatre" (South West).

2016 Playhouse celebrate 40 years in the
new building.

Echo's End : World Premiere.   2017

2018 *Moonfleet* : World Premiere.

Merger with the Salisbury Arts Centre   2018
and the Salisbury Festival announced.

Lightning Source UK Ltd.
Milton Keynes UK
UKHW022026080123
414983UK00007B/71